ModSecurity Handbook

Ivan Ristić

Feisty
Duck
LONDON

ModSecurity Handbook

by Ivan Ristić

Copyright © 2010 Feisty Duck Limited. All rights reserved.

ISBN: 978-1-907117-02-2

May 2010 revision. First published in March 2010.

Feisty Duck Limited
www.feistyduck.com
contact@feistyduck.com

Address:
6 Acantha Court
Montpelier Road
London W5 2QP
United Kingdom

Production editor: Jelena Girić-Ristić

Copyeditor: Nancy Kotary

Cover designer: Peter Jovanović

Cover illustration: Maja Veselinović

Interior designer: Ivan Ristić

Technical reviewer: Brian Rectanus

Table of Contents

Preface

I didn't mean to write this book, I really didn't. Several months ago I started to work on the second edition of *Apache Security*, deciding to rewrite the ModSecurity chapter first. A funny thing happened: the ModSecurity chapter kept growing and growing. It hit 40 pages. It hit 80 pages. And then I realized that I was nowhere near the end. That was all the excuse I needed to put *Apache Security* aside—for the time being—and focus on a ModSecurity book instead.

I admit that I couldn't be happier, although it was an entirely emotional decision. After spending years working on ModSecurity, I knew it had so much more to offer, yet the documentation wasn't there to show the way. But it is now, I am thrilled to say. The package is complete: you have an open source tool that is able to compete with the best commercial products out there, *and* you have the documentation to match.

With this book I am also trying something completely new—*continuous writing and publishing*. You see, I had published my first book with a major publisher, but I never quite liked the process. It was too slow. You write a book pretty much in isolation, you publish it, and then you never get to update it. I was never happy with that, and that's why I decided to do things differently this time.

Simply said, *ModSecurity Handbook* is a living book. Every time I make a change, a new digital version is made available to you. If I improve the book based on your feedback, you get the improvements as soon as I make them. If you prefer a paper book, you can still get it of course, through the usual channels. Although I can't do anything about updating the paper version of the book, we can narrow the gap slightly by pushing out book updates even between editions. That means that, even when you get the paper version (as most people seem to prefer to), it is never going to be too much behind the digital version.

Scope and Audience

This book exists to document every single aspect of ModSecurity and to teach you how to use it. It is as simple as that. ModSecurity is a fantastic tool, but it is let down by the poor quality of the documentation. As a result, the adoption is not as good as it could be; application security is difficult on its own and you don't really want to struggle with poorly documented tools too. I felt a responsibility to write this book and show how ModSecurity can compete with commercial web application firewalls, in spite of being the underdog. Now that the book is finished, I feel I've done a proper job with ModSecurity.

If you are interested in application security, you are my target audience. Even if you're not interested in application security as such, and only want to deal with your particular problems (it's difficult to find a web application these days that's without security problems), you are still my target audience.

You don't need to know anything about ModSecurity to get started. If you just follow the book from the beginning, you will find that every new chapter advances a notch. Even if you are a long-time ModSecurity user, I believe you will benefit from a fresh start. I will let you in on a secret—I have. There's nothing better for completing one's knowledge than having to write about a particular topic. I suspect that long-time ModSecurity users will especially like the second half of the book, which discusses many advanced topics and often covers substantial new ground.

But, there is only so much a book can cover. *ModSecurity Handbook* assumes you already know how to operate the Apache web server. You don't have to be an expert, but you do need to know how to install, configure, and run it. If you don't know how to do that already, you should get my first book, *Apache Security*. I wrote it five years ago, but it's still remarkably fresh. (Ironically, it is only the ModSecurity chapter in *Apache Security* that is completely obsolete. But that's why you have this book.)

On the other end, *ModSecurity Handbook* will teach you how to use ModSecurity and write good rules, but it won't teach you application security. In my earlier book, *Apache Security*, I included a chapter that served as an introduction to application security, but, even then, I was barely able to mention all that I wanted, and the chapter was still the longest chapter in the book. Since then, the application security field has exploded and now you have to read several books and dozens of research papers just to begin to understand it.

I am aware that many of you will want to see examples that go beyond what is in this book—for example to deal with problems such as cross-site scripting and SQL injection—and that's why I will be providing them in my rule writing workshop, which is part of this book's online companion. The workshop will combine rule writing and application security in a way that extends beyond the scope of this book.

Contents

Once you go past the first chapter, which is the introduction to the world of ModSecurity, the rest of the book consists of roughly three parts. In the first part, you learn how to install and configure ModSecurity. In the second part, you learn how to write rules. As for the third part, you could say that it contains the advanced stuff—a series of chapters each dedicated to one important aspect of ModSecurity.

At the end of the book is the official reference documentation, reproduced with the permission from Breach Security.

Chapter 1, *Introduction*, is the foundation of the book. It contains a gentle introduction to ModSecurity, and then explains what it can and cannot do. The main usage scenarios are listed to help you identify where you can use ModSecurity in your environment. The middle of the chapter goes under the hood of ModSecurity to give you an insight into how it works, and finishes with an overview of the key areas you will need to learn in order to deploy it. The end of the chapter lists a series of resources (sites, mailing lists, tools, etc.) that you will find useful in your day-to-day work.

Chapter 2, *Installation*, teaches you how to install ModSecurity, either compiling from source (using one of the released versions or downloading straight from the development repository), or by using one of the available binary packages, on Unix and Windows alike.

Chapter 3, *Configuration*, explains how each of the available configuration directives should be used. By the end of the chapter, you get a complete overview of the configuration options and will have a solid default configuration for all your ModSecurity installations.

Chapter 4, *Logging*, deals with the logging features of ModSecurity. The two main logging facilities explained are the debug log, which is useful in rule writing, and the audit log, which is used to log complete transaction data. Special attention is given to remote logging, which you'll need to manage multiple sensors, or to use any of the user-friendly tools for alert management. File interception and validation is covered in detail. The chapter ends with an advanced section of logging, which explains how to selectively log traffic, and how to use the sanitation feature to prevent sensitive data from being stored in the logs.

Chapter 5, *Rule Language Overview*, is the first of the three chapters that deal with rule writing. This chapter contains an overview of the entire rule language, which will get you started as well as give you a feature map to which you can return whenever you need to deal with a new problem.

Chapter 6, *Rule Language Tutorial*, teaches how to write rules, and how to write them well. It's a very fun chapter that adopts a gradual approach, introducing the features one by one. By the end of the chapter, you will know everything about writing individual rules.

Chapter 7, *Rule Configuration*, completes the topic of rule writing. It takes a step back to view the rules as the basic block for policy building. You first learn how to put a few rules together and add them to the configuration, as well as how the rules interact with Apache's ability to use different configuration contexts for different sites and different locations within sites. The chapter spends a great deal of time making sure you take advantage of the inheritance feature, which helps make ModSecurity configuration much easier to maintain.

Chapter 8, *Persistent Storage*, is quite possibly the most exciting chapter in the book. It describes the persistent storage mechanism, which enables you to track data and events over time and thus opens up an entire new dimension of ModSecurity. This chapter is also the most practical one in the entire book. It gives you the rules for periodic alerting, brute force attack detection, denial of service attack detection, session and user management, fixing session management weaknesses, and more.

Chapter 9, *Practical Rule Writing*, is, as the name suggests, a tour through many of the practical activities you will perform in your day-to-day work. The chapter starts by covering whitelisting, virtual patching, IP address reputation and blacklisting. You then learn how to integrate with other Apache modules, with practical examples that show how to perform conditional logging and fix insecure session cookies. Special attention is given to the topic of blocking; several approaches, starting from the simple to the very sophisticated, are presented. A section on regular expressions gets you up to speed with the most important ModSecurity operator. The chapter ends with a discussion of rule sets, discussing how to use the rule sets others have written, as well as how to write your own.

Chapter 10, *Performance*, covers several performance-related topics. It opens with an overview of where ModSecurity usually spends its time, a list of common configuration mistakes that should be avoided, and a list of approaches that result in better performance. The second part of the chapter describes how to monitor ModSecurity performance in production. The third part tests the publicly available rule sets in order to give you a taste of what they are like, as well as document a methodology you can use to test your own rules. The chapter then moves to rule set benchmarking, which is an essential part of the process of rule writing. The last part of this chapter gives very practical advice on how to use regular expressions and parallel matching, comparing several approaches and explaining when to use them.

Chapter 11, *Content Injection*, explains how to reach from ModSecurity, which is a server-side tool, right into a user's browser and continue with the inspection there. This feature makes it possible to detect the attacks that were previously thought to be undetectable by a server-side tool, for example DOM-based cross-site scripting attacks. Content injection also comes in handy if you need to communicate with your users—for example, to tell them that they have been attacked.

Chapter 12, *Writing Rules in Lua*, discusses a gem of a feature: writing rules using the Lua programming language. The rule language of ModSecurity is easy to use and can get a lot done, but for the really difficult problems you may need the power of a proper programming language. In addition, you can use Lua to react to events, and it is especially useful when integrating with external systems.

Chapter 13, *Handling XML*, covers the XML capabilities of ModSecurity in detail. You get to learn how to validate XML using either DTDs or XML Schemas, and how to combine XPath expressions with the other features ModSecurity offers to perform both whitelist- and blacklist-based validation. The XML features of ModSecurity have traditionally been poorly documented; here you will find details never covered before. The chapter ends with an validation framework you can easily adapt for your needs.

Chapter 14, *Extending Rule Language*, discusses how you can extend ModSecurity to in ment new functionality. It gives several step-by-step examples, explaining how to implei ..... a transformation function, an operator, and a variable. Of course, with ModSecurity being open source, you can extend it directly at any point, but when you use the official APIs, you avoid making a custom version of ModSecurity (which is generally time consuming because it prevents upgrades).

Updates and Online Companion

This book is continuously updated. If you've purchased the digital version from the Feisty Duck's web site [https://www.feistyduck.com], your purchase of *ModSecurity Handbook* in-cludes at least one year of updates. I will update the book whenever I have something new to say, whenever I realize that I can improve something, and whenever ModSecurity changes in some way that requires documenting. I want to make this book the first place to turn to whenever you need something from ModSecurity.

The digital versions of *ModSecurity Handbook* are updated automatically every time a change is made. At the moment, for example, there is a script that runs once every 15 minutes, and which rebuilds the book when necessary. Whenever you visit your personal digital download link, you get the most recent version of the book.

I use a dedicated Twitter account (@modsecuritybook) to announce every change I make to the book. By following that account you'll find out about the improvements pretty much as they happen. If you only care about major changes, follow my personal Twitter account instead (@ivanristic) or subscribe to my blog [http://blog.ivanristic.com].

The online companion, which you can find on the book's home page [http://www.modsecurityhandbook.com], contains the resources that I couldn't fit in the book. The most important part of the companion is the rule writing workshop, which contains many practical examples that show how to write rules to detect attacks such as cross-site scripting, SQL injection, remote file inclusion, and many more.

Feedback

To get in touch with me please write to *ivanr@webkreator.com*. I would like to hear from you very much, because I believe that a book can fulfill its potential only through the interaction among its author(s) and the readers. Your feedback is particularly important when a book is continuously updated, like this one is. When I change the book as a result of your feedback, all the changes are immediately delivered back to you. There is no more waiting for years to see the improvements!

About the Author

Ivan Ristić is a respected security expert and author, known especially for his contribution to the web application firewall field and the development of ModSecurity, the open source web application firewall. He is also the author of *Apache Security*, a comprehensive security guide for the Apache web server. A frequent speaker at computer security conferences, Ivan is an active participant in the application security community, a member of the Open Web Application Security Project (OWASP), and an officer of the Web Application Security Consortium (WASC).

About the Technical Reviewer

Brian Rectanus is the Director of Research Development at Breach Security, Inc., the current maintainer of the ModSecurity code base and an active developer for the Open Information Security Foundation's Suricata IDS/IPS engine. He spends his time developing Breach's commercial web application firewall, working on ModSecurity, and helping out on the Suricata engine when he can. Brian is an open source advocate and proud `NIX loving, non-Windows user who has been writing code on various `NIX platforms with vi since 1993. Today he does all his development on his trusty Ubuntu laptop using the more modern vim editor—like there is any other—and loves every bit of it. Brian has spent the majority of his career working with web technology from various perspectives, be it developer, administrator or security assessor. Brian holds GCIA and GCIH certification from the SANS Institute and a BS in computer science from Kansas State University.

Acknowledgments

To begin with, I would like to thank the entire ModSecurity community for their support, and especially all of you who used ModSecurity and sent me your feedback. ModSecurity wouldn't be what it is without you. Developing and supporting ModSecurity was a remarkable experience; I hope you enjoy using it as much as I enjoyed developing it.

I would also like to thank my former colleagues from Breach Security, who gave me a warm welcome, even though I joined them pretty late in the game. I regret that, due to my geographic location, I didn't spend more time working with you. I would especially like to thank —in no particular order—Brian Rectanus, Ryan Barnett, Ofer Shezaf, and Avi Aminov, who worked with me on the ModSecurity team. Brian was also kind to work with me on the book as a technical reviewer, and I owe special thanks to him for ensuring I didn't make too many mistakes.

I mustn't forget my copyeditor, Nancy Kotary, who was a pleasure to work with, despite having to deal with DocBook and Subversion, none of which is in the standard copyediting repertoire.

For some reason unknown to me, my dear wife Jelena continues to tolerate my long working hours. Probably because I keep promising to work less, even though that never seems to happen. To her I can only offer my undying love and gratitude for accepting me for who I am. My daughter Iva, who's four, is too young to understand what she means to me, but that's all right —I have the patience to wait for another 20 years or so. She is the other sunshine in my life.

User Guide

This part, with its 14 chapters, constitutes the main body of the book. The first chapter is the introduction to ModSecurity and your map to the rest of the book. The remaining chapters fall into roughly four groups: installation and configuration, rule writing, practical work, and advanced topics.

1 Introduction

ModSecurity is a tool that will help you secure your web applications. No, scratch that. Actually, ModSecurity is a tool that will help you sleep better at night, and I will explain how. I usually call ModSecurity a *web application firewall* (WAF), because that's the generally accepted term to refer to the class of products that are specifically designed to secure web applications. Other times I will call it an *HTTP intrusion detection tool,* because I think that name better describes what ModSecurity does. Neither name is entirely adequate, yet we don't have a better one. Besides, it doesn't really matter what we call it. The point is that web applications—yours, mine, everyone's—are terribly insecure on average. We struggle to keep up with the security issues and need any help we can get to secure them.

The idea to write ModSecurity came to me during one of my sleepless nights—I couldn't sleep because I was responsible for the security of several web-based products. I could see how most web applications were just slapped together with little time spent on design and little time spent on understanding the security issues. Furthermore, not only were web applications insecure, but we had no idea how insecure they were or if they were being attacked. Our only eyes were the web server access and error logs, and they didn't say much.

ModSecurity will help you sleep better at night because, above all, it solves the visibility problem: it lets you see your web traffic. That visibility is key to security: once you are able to see HTTP traffic, you are able to analyze it in real time, record it as necessary, and react to the events. The best part of this concept is that you get to do all of that without actually touching web applications. Even better, the concept can be applied to any application—even if you can't access the source code.

Brief History of ModSecurity

Like many other open source projects, ModSecurity started out as a hobby. Software development had been my primary concern back in 2002, when I realized that producing secure web applications is virtually impossible. As a result, I started to fantasize about a tool that would sit in front of web applications and control the flow of data in and out. The first version was released in November 2002, but a few more months were needed before the tool became useful. Other people started to learn about it, and the popularity of ModSecurity started to rise.

Initially, most of my effort was spent wrestling with Apache to make request body inspection possible. Apache 1.3.x did not have any interception or filtering APIs, but I was able to trick it into submission. Apache 2.x improved things by providing APIs that do allow content interception, but there was no documentation to speak of. Nick Kew released the excellent *The Apache Modules Book* (Prentice Hall) in 2007, which unfortunately was too late to help me with the development of ModSecurity.

By 2004, I was a changed man. Once primarily a software developer, I became obsessed with web application security and wanted to spend more time working on it. I quit my job and started treating ModSecurity as a business. My big reward came in the summer of 2006, when ModSecurity went head to head with other web application firewalls, in an evaluation conducted by Forrester Research, and came out very favorably. Later that year, my company was acquired by Breach Security. A team of one eventually became a team of many: Brian Rectanus came to work on ModSecurity, Ofer Shezaf took on the rules, and Ryan C. Barnett the community management and education. ModSecurity 2.0, a complete rewrite, was released in late 2006. At the same time we released ModSecurity Community Console, which combined the functionality of a remote logging sensor and a monitoring and reporting GUI.

The last major update of ModSecurity was 2.5, released in February 2008. That may seem like too long ago, but there have been many maintenance releases and many improvements since. ModSecurity 2.5.12 (released in February 2010) is the most recent version at the time of writing.

Since leaving Breach Security in January 2009, I am no longer in charge of ModSecurity, but it remains in the capable hands of Brian Rectanus and Ryan C. Barnett. I remain involved and contribute from time to time.

What Can ModSecurity Do?

ModSecurity is a toolkit for real-time web application monitoring, logging, and access control. I like to think about it as an enabler: there are no hard rules telling you what to do; instead, it is up to you to choose your own path through the available features. That's why the title of this section asks what ModSecurity can do, not what it does.

The freedom to choose what to do is an essential part of ModSecurity's identity and goes very well with its open source nature. With full access to the source code, your freedom to choose extends to the ability to customize and extend the tool itself to make it fit your needs. It's not a matter of ideology, but of practicality. I simply don't want my tools to restrict what I can do.

Back on the topic of what ModSecurity can do, the following is a list of the most important usage scenarios:

Real-time application security monitoring and access control

At its core, ModSecurity gives you access to the HTTP traffic stream, in real-time, along with the ability to inspect it. This is enough for real-time security monitoring. There's an added dimension of what's possible through ModSecurity's persistent storage mechanism, which enables you to track system elements over time and perform event correlation. You are able to reliably block, if you so wish, because ModSecurity uses full request and response buffering.

Virtual patching

Virtual patching is a concept of vulnerability mitigation in a separate layer, where you get to fix problems in applications without having to touch the applications themselves. Virtual patching is applicable to applications that use any communication protocol, but it is particularly useful with HTTP, because the traffic can generally be well understood by an intermediary device. ModSecurity excels at virtual patching because of its reliable blocking capabilities and the flexible rule language that can be adapted to any need. It is, by far, the activity that requires the least investment, is the easiest activity to perform, and the one that most organizations can benefit from straight away.

Full HTTP traffic logging

Web servers traditionally do very little when it comes to logging for security purposes. They log very little by default, and even with a lot of tweaking you are not able to get everything that you need. I have yet to encounter a web server that is able to log full transaction data. ModSecurity gives you that ability to log anything you need, including raw transaction data, which is essential for forensics. In addition, you get to choose which transactions are logged, which parts of a transaction are logged, and which parts are sanitized.

Continuous passive security assessment

Security assessment is largely seen as an active scheduled event, in which an independent team is sourced to try to perform a simulated attack. Continuous passive security assessment is a variation of real-time monitoring, where, instead of focusing on the behavior of the external parties, you focus on the behavior of the system itself. It's an early warning system of sorts that can detect traces of many abnormalities and security weaknesses before they are exploited.

Web application hardening

One of my favorite uses for ModSecurity is attack surface reduction, in which you selectively narrow down the HTTP features you are willing to accept (e.g., request methods, request headers, content types, etc.). ModSecurity can assist you in enforcing many similar restrictions, either directly, or through collaboration with other Apache modules. They all fall under web application hardening. For example, it is possible to fix many session management issues, as well as cross-site request forgery vulnerabilities.

Something small, yet very important to you

Real life often throws unusual demands to us, and that is when the flexibility of Mod-Security comes in handy where you need it the most. It may be a security need, but it may also be something completely different. For example, some people use ModSecurity as an XML web service router, combining its ability to parse XML and apply XPath expressions with its ability to proxy requests. Who knew?

Note

I often get asked if ModSecurity can be used to protect Apache itself. The answer is that it can, in some limited circumstances, but that it isn't what it is designed for. You may sometimes be able to catch an attack with ModSecurity before it hits a vulnerable spot in Apache or in a third-party module, but there's a large quantity of code that runs before ModSecurity. If there's a vulnerability in that area, ModSecurity won't be able to do anything about it.

What Are Web Application Firewalls, Anyway?

I said that ModSecurity is a web application firewall , but it's a little known fact that no one really knows what web application firewalls are. It is generally understood that a web application firewall is an intermediary element (implemented either as a software add-on or process, or as a network device) that enhances the security of web applications, but opinions differ once you dig deeper. There are many theories that try to explain the different views, but the best one I could come up with is that, unlike anything we had before, the web application space is so complex that there is no easy way to classify what we do security-wise. Rather than focus on the name, you should focus on what a particular tool does and how it can help.

If you want to learn more about the topic, there are two efforts that focus on understanding web application firewalls:

- *Web application firewall evaluation criteria [http://projects.webappsec.org/Web-Application-Firewall-Evaluation-Criteria]* (WAFEC) is a project of the Web Application Security Consortium [http://www.webappsec.org] (WASC). It's an older effort (which has been inactive for a couple of years now) that focuses on the technical features of web application firewalls.

- *Best practices: Web Application Firewalls [http://www.owasp.org/index.php/Best_Practices:_Web_Application_Firewalls]* is a project of Open Web Application Security Project [http://www.owasp.org] (OWASP) that focuses largely on the practicalities of WAF deployment, which is an important aspect that is often overlooked.

Guiding Principles

There are four guiding principles on which ModSecurity is based, as follows:

Flexibility

I think that it's fair to say that I built ModSecurity for myself: a security expert who needs to intercept, analyze, and store HTTP traffic. I didn't see much value in hard-coded functionality, because real life is so complex that everyone needs to do things just slightly differently. ModSecurity achieves flexibility by giving you a powerful rule language, which allows you to do exactly what you need to, in combination with the ability to apply rules only where you need to.

Passiveness

ModSecurity will take great care to never interact with a transaction unless you tell it to. That is simply because I don't trust tools, even the one I built, to make decisions for me. That's why ModSecurity will give you plenty of information, but ultimately leave the decisions to you.

Predictability

There's no such thing as a perfect tool, but a predictable one is the next best thing. Armed with all the facts, you can understand ModSecurity's weak points and work around them.

Quality over quantity

Over the course of six years spent working on ModSecurity, we came up with many ideas for what ModSecurity could do. We didn't act on most of them. We kept them for later. Why? Because we understood that we have limited resources available at our disposal and that our minds (ideas) are far faster than our implementation abilities. We chose to limit the available functionality, but do really well at what we decided to keep in.

There are bits in ModSecurity that fall outside the scope of these four principles. For example, ModSecurity can change the way Apache identifies itself to the outside world, confine the Apache process within a jail, and even implement an elaborate scheme to deal with a once-infamous universal XSS vulnerability in Adobe Reader. Although it was I who added those features, I now think that they detract from the main purpose of ModSecurity, which is a reliable and predictable tool that allows for HTTP traffic inspection.

Deployment Options

ModSecurity supports two deployment options: embedded and reverse proxy deployment. There is no one correct way to use them; choose an option based on what best suits your circumstances. There are advantages and disadvantages to both options:

Embedded

Because ModSecurity is an Apache module, you can add it to any compatible version of Apache. At the moment that means a reasonably recent Apache version from the 2.0.x branch, although a newer 2.2.x version is recommended. The embedded option is a great choice for those who already have their architecture laid out and don't want to change it. Embedded deployment is also the only option if you need to protect hundreds of web servers. In such situations, it is impractical to build a separate proxy-based security layer. Embedded ModSecurity not only does not introduce new points of failure, but it scales seamlessly as the underlying web infrastructure scales. The main challenge with embedded deployment is that server resources are shared between the web server and ModSecurity.

Reverse proxy

Reverse proxies are effectively HTTP routers, designed to stand between web servers and their clients. When you install a dedicated Apache reverse proxy and add ModSecurity to it, you get a "proper" network web application firewall, which you can use to protect any number of web servers on the same network. Many security practitioners prefer having a separate security layer. With it you get complete isolation from the systems you are protecting. On the performance front, a standalone ModSecurity will have resources dedicated to it, which means that you will be able to do more (i.e., have more complex rules). The main disadvantage of this approach is the new point of failure, which will need to be addressed with a high-availability setup of two or more reverse proxies.

Is Anything Missing?

ModSecurity is a very good tool, but there are a number of features, big and small, that could be added. The small features are those that would make your life with ModSecurity easier, perhaps automating some of the boring work (e.g., persistent blocking, which you now have to do manually). But there are really only two features that I would call missing:

Learning

Defending web applications is difficult, because there are so many of them, and they are all different. (I often say that every web application effectively creates its own communication protocol.) It would be very handy to have ModSecurity observe application traffic and create a model that could later be used to generate policy or assist with false positives. While I was at Breach Security, I started a project called ModProfiler [http://www.modsecurity.org/projects/modprofiler/] as a step toward learning, but that project is still as I left it, as version 0.2.

Passive mode of deployment

ModSecurity can be embedded only in Apache 2.x, but when you deploy it as a reverse proxy, it can be used to protect any web server. Reverse proxies are not everyone's cup of tea, however, and sometimes it would be very handy to deploy ModSecurity passively, without having to change anything on the network.

Although a GUI is not within the scope of the project, there are currently two options when it comes to remote logging and alert management. You will find them in the Resources section later in this chapter.

Getting Started

In this first practical section in the book, I will give you a whirlwind tour of the ModSecurity internals, which should help you get started.

Hybrid Nature of ModSecurity

ModSecurity is a hybrid web application firewall that relies on the host web server for some of the work. The only supported web server at the moment is Apache 2.x, but it is possible, in principle, to integrate ModSecurity with any other web server that provides sufficient integration APIs.

Apache does for ModSecurity what it does for all other modules—it handles the infrastructure tasks:

1. Decrypts SSL
2. Breaks up the inbound connection stream into HTTP requests
3. Partially parses HTTP requests
4. Invokes ModSecurity, choosing the correct configuration context (`<VirtualHost>`, `<Location>`, etc.)
5. De-chunks request bodies as necessary

There a few additional tasks Apache performs in a reverse proxy scenario:

1. Forwards requests to backend servers (with or without SSL)
2. Partially parses HTTP responses
3. De-chunks response bodies as necessary

The advantage of a hybrid implementation is that it is very efficient—the duplication of work is minimal when it comes to HTTP parsing. A couple of disadvantages of this approach are that you don't always get access to the raw data stream and that web servers sometimes don't process data in the way a security-conscious tool would. In the case of Apache, the hybrid approach works reasonably well, with a few minor issues:

Request line and headers are NUL-terminated

This is normally not a problem, because what Apache doesn't see cannot harm any module or application. In some very rare cases, however, the purpose of the NUL-byte evasion is to hide things, and this Apache behavior only helps with the hiding.

Request header transformation

Apache will canonicalize request headers, combining multiple headers that use the same name and collapsing those that span two or more lines. The transformation may make it difficult to detect subtle signs of evasion, but in practice this hasn't been a problem yet.

Quick request handling

Apache will handle some requests quickly, leaving ModSecurity unable to do anything but notice them in the logging phase. Invalid HTTP requests, in particular, will be rejected by Apache without ModSecurity having a say.

No access to some response headers

Because of the way Apache works, the Server and Date response headers are invisible to ModSecurity; they cannot be inspected or logged.

Main Areas of Functionality

The functionality offered by ModSecurity falls roughly into four areas:

Parsing

ModSecurity tries to make sense of as much data as available. The supported data formats are backed by security-conscious parsers that extract bits of data and store them for use in the rules.

Buffering

In a typical installation, both request and response bodies will be buffered. This means that ModSecurity usually sees complete requests before they are passed to the application for processing, and complete responses before they are sent to clients. Buffering is an important feature, because it is the only way to provide reliable blocking. The downside of buffering is that it requires additional RAM to store the request and response body data.

Logging

Full transaction logging (also referred to as *audit logging*) is a big part of what ModSecurity does. This feature allows you to record complete HTTP traffic, instead of just rudimentary access log information. Request headers, request body, response header, response body—all those bits will be available to you. It is only with the ability to see what is happening that you will be able to stay in control.

Rule engine

The rule engine builds on the work performed by all other components. By the time the rule engine starts operating, the various bits and pieces of data it requires will all be prepared and ready for inspection. At that point, the rules will take over to assess the transaction and take actions as necessary.

> **Note**
>
> There's one thing ModSecurity purposefully avoids to do: as a matter of design, ModSecurity does not support data sanitization. I don't believe in sanitization, purely because I believe that it is too difficult to get right. If you know for sure that you are being attacked (as you have to before you can decide to sanitize), then you should refuse

> to process the offending requests altogether. Attempting to sanitize merely opens a
> new battlefield where your attackers don't have anything to lose, but everything to
> win. You, on the other hand, don't have anything to win, but everything to lose.

What Rules Look Like

Everything in ModSecurity revolves around two things: configuration and rules. The configuration tells ModSecurity how to process the data it sees; the rules decide what to do with the processed data. Although it is too early to go into how the rules work, I will show you a quick example here just to give you an idea what they look like.

For example:

```
SecRule ARGS "<script>" log,deny,status:404
```

Even without further assistance, you can probably recognize the part in the rule that specifies what we wish to look for in input data (`<script>`). Similarly, you will easily figure out what will happen if we do find the desired pattern (`log,deny,status:404`). Things will become more clear if I tell you about the general rule syntax, which is the following:

```
SecRule VARIABLES OPERATOR ACTIONS
```

The three parts have the following meanings:

1. The `VARIABLES` part tells ModSecurity where to look. The `ARGS` variable, used in the example, means all request parameters.

2. The `OPERATOR` part tells ModSecurity how to look. In the example, we have a regular expression pattern, which will be matched against `ARGS`.

3. The `ACTIONS` part tells ModSecurity what to do on a match. The rule in the example gives three instructions: `log` problem, `deny` transaction and use the status 404 for the denial (`status:404`).

I hope you are not disappointed with the simplicity of this first rule. I promise you that by combining the various facilities offered by ModSecurity, you will be able to write very useful rules that implement complex logic where necessary.

Transaction Lifecycle

In ModSecurity, every transaction goes through five steps, or phases. In each of the phases, ModSecurity will do some work at the beginning (e.g., parse data that has become available), invoke the rules specified to work in that phase, and perhaps do a thing or two after the phase rules have finished. At first glance, it may seem that five phases are too many, but there's a reason why each of the phases exist. There is always one thing, sometimes several, that can only be done at a particular moment in the transaction lifecycle.

Request headers (1)

The request headers phase is the first entry point for ModSecurity. The principal purpose of this phase is to allow rule writers to assess a request before the costly request body processing is undertaken. Similarly, there is often a need to influence how ModSecurity will process a request body, and this phase is the place to do it. For example, ModSecurity will not parse an XML request body by default, but you can instruct it do so by placing the appropriate rules into phase 1. (If you care about XML processing, it is described in detail in Chapter 13, *Handling XML*).

Request body (2)

The request body phase is the main request analysis phase and takes place immediately after a complete request body has been received and processed. The rules in this phase have all the available request data at their disposal.

Response headers (3)

The response headers phase takes place after response headers become available, but before a response body is read. The rules that need to decide whether to inspect a response body should run in this phase.

Response body (4)

The response body phase is the main response analysis phase. By the time this phase begins, the response body will have been read, with all its data available for the rules to make their decisions.

Logging (5)

The logging phase is special in more ways than one. First, it's the only phase from which you cannot block. By the time this phase runs, the transaction will have finished, so there's little you can do but record the fact that it happened. Rules in this phase are run to control how logging is done.

Lifecycle Example

To give you a better idea what happens on every transaction, we'll examine a detailed debug log of one POST transaction. I've deliberately chosen a transaction type that uses the request body as its principal method to transmit data, because following such a transaction will exercise most parts of ModSecurity. To keep things relatively simple, I used a configuration without any rules, removed some of the debug log lines for clarity, and removed the timestamps and some additional metadata from each line.

> ### Note
>
> Please do not try to understand everything about the logs at this point. The idea is just to get a general feel about how ModSecurity works, and to introduce you to debug logs. Very quickly after starting to use ModSecurity, you will discover that the debug logs will be an indispensable rule writing and troubleshooting tool.

The transaction I am using as an example in this section is very straightforward. I made a point of placing request data in two different places, parameter *a* in the query string and parameter *b* in the request body, but there is little else of interest in the request:

```
POST /?a=test HTTP/1.0
Content-Type: application/x-www-form-urlencoded
Content-Length: 6

b=test
```

The response is entirely unremarkable:

```
HTTP/1.1 200 OK
Date: Sun, 17 Jan 2010 00:13:44 GMT
Server: Apache
Content-Length: 12
Connection: close
Content-Type: text/html

Hello World!
```

ModSecurity is first invoked by Apache after request headers become available, but before a request body (if any) is read. First comes the initialization message, which contains the unique transaction ID generated by mod_unique_id. Using this information, you should be able to pair the information in the debug log with the information in your access and audit logs. At this point, ModSecurity will parse the information on the request line and in the request headers. In this example, the query string part contains a single parameter (a), so you will see a message documenting its discovery. ModSecurity will then create a transaction context and invoke the REQUEST_HEADERS phase:

```
[4] Initialising transaction (txid SopXW38EAAE9YbLQ).
[5] Adding request argument (QUERY_STRING): name "a", value "test"
[4] Transaction context created (dcfg 8121800).
[4] Starting phase REQUEST_HEADERS.
```

Assuming that a rule didn't block the transaction, ModSecurity will now return control to Apache, allowing other modules to process the request before control is given back to it.

In the second phase, ModSecurity will first read and process the request body, if it is present. In the following example, you can see three messages from the input filter, which tell you what was read. The fourth message tells you that one parameter was extracted from the request body. The content type used in this request (application/x-www-form-urlencoded) is one of the types ModSecurity recognizes and parses automatically. Once the request body is processed, the REQUEST_BODY rules are processed.

```
[4] Second phase starting (dcfg 8121800).
[4] Input filter: Reading request body.
```

```
[9] Input filter: Bucket type HEAP contains 6 bytes.
[9] Input filter: Bucket type EOS contains 0 bytes.
[5] Adding request argument (BODY): name "b", value "test"
[4] Input filter: Completed receiving request body (length 6).
[4] Starting phase REQUEST_BODY.
```

The filters that keep being mentioned in the logs are parts of ModSecurity that handle request and response bodies:

```
[4] Hook insert_filter: Adding input forwarding filter (r 81d0588).
[4] Hook insert_filter: Adding output filter (r 81d0588).
```

There will be a message in the debug log every time ModSecurity sends a chunk of data to the request handler, and one final message to say that there isn't any more data in the buffers.

```
[4] Input filter: Forwarding input: mode=0, block=0, nbytes=8192 ⏎
(f 81d2228, r 81d0588).
[4] Input filter: Forwarded 6 bytes.
[4] Input filter: Sent EOS.
[4] Input filter: Input forwarding complete.
```

Shortly thereafter, the output filter will start receiving data, at which point the RESPONSE_HEADERS rules will be invoked:

```
[9] Output filter: Receiving output (f 81d2258, r 81d0588).
[4] Starting phase RESPONSE_HEADERS.
```

Once all the rules have run, ModSecurity will continue to store the response body in its buffers, after which it will run the RESPONSE_BODY rules:

```
[9] Output filter: Bucket type MMAP contains 12 bytes.
[9] Output filter: Bucket type EOS contains 0 bytes.
[4] Output filter: Completed receiving response body (buffered full - 12 bytes).
[4] Starting phase RESPONSE_BODY.
```

Again, assuming that none of the rules blocked, the accumulated response body will be forwarded to the client:

```
[4] Output filter: Output forwarding complete.
```

Finally, the logging phase will commence. The LOGGING rules will be run first to allow them to influence logging, after which the audit logging subsystem will be invoked to log the transaction if necessary. A message from the audit logging subsystem will be the last transaction message in the logs. In this example, ModSecurity tells us that it didn't find anything of interest in the transaction and that it sees no reason to log it:

```
[4] Initialising logging.
[4] Starting phase LOGGING.
```

```
[4] Audit log: Ignoring a non-relevant request.
```

File Upload Example

Requests that contain files are processed slightly differently. The changes can be best understood by again following the activity in the debug log:

```
[4] Input filter: Reading request body.
[9] Multipart: Boundary: ---------------------------2411583925858
[9] Input filter: Bucket type HEAP contains 256 bytes.
[9] Multipart: Added part header "Content-Disposition" "form-data; name=\"f\"; ↩
filename=\"eicar.com.txt\""
[9] Multipart: Added part header "Content-Type" "text/plain"
[9] Multipart: Content-Disposition name: f
[9] Multipart: Content-Disposition filename: eicar.com.txt
[4] Multipart: Created temporary file: ↩
/opt/modsecurity/var/tmp/20090819-175503-SowuZ38AAQEAACV-Agk-file-gmWmrF
[9] Multipart: Changing file mode to 0600: ↩
/opt/modsecurity/var/tmp/20090819-175503-SowuZ38AAQEAACV-Agk-file-gmWmrF
[9] Multipart: Added file part 9c870b8 to the list: name "f" file name ↩
"eicar.com.txt" (offset 140, length 68)
[9] Input filter: Bucket type EOS contains 0 bytes.
[4] Reqest body no files length: 96
[4] Input filter: Completed receiving request body (length 256).
```

In addition to seeing the multipart parser in action, you see ModSecurity creating a temporary file (into which it will extract the upload) and adjusting its privileges to match the desired configuration.

Then, at the end of the transaction, you will see the cleanup and the temporary file deleted:

```
[4] Multipart: Cleanup started (remove files 1).
[4] Multipart: Deleted file (part) ↩
"/opt/modsecurity/var/tmp/20090819-175503-SowuZ38AAQEAACV-Agk-file-gmWmrF"
```

The temporary file will not be deleted if ModSecurity decides to keep an uploaded file. Instead, it will be moved to the storage area:

```
[4] Multipart: Cleanup started (remove files 0).
[4] Input filter: Moved file from ↩
"/opt/modsecurity/var/tmp/20090819-175503-SowuZ38AAQEAACV-Agk-file-gmWmrF" to ↩
"/opt/modsecurity/var/upload/20090819-175503-SowuZ38AAQEAACV-Agk-file-gmWmrF".
```

In the example traces, you've observed an upload of a small file that was stored in RAM. When large uploads take place, ModSecurity will attempt to use RAM at first, switching to on-disk storage once it becomes obvious that the file is larger:

```
[9] Input filter: Bucket type HEAP contains 8000 bytes.
```

```
[9] Input filter: Bucket type HEAP contains 8000 bytes.
[9] Input filter: Bucket type HEAP contains 8000 bytes.
[9] Input filter: Bucket type HEAP contains 8000 bytes.
[9] Input filter: Bucket type HEAP contains 8000 bytes.
[9] Input filter: Bucket type HEAP contains 8000 bytes.
[9] Input filter: Bucket type HEAP contains 8000 bytes.
[9] Input filter: Bucket type HEAP contains 1536 bytes.
[9] Input filter: Bucket type HEAP contains 8000 bytes.
[9] Input filter: Bucket type HEAP contains 8000 bytes.
[9] Input filter: Bucket type HEAP contains 8000 bytes.
[9] Input filter: Bucket type HEAP contains 576 bytes.
[9] Input filter: Bucket type HEAP contains 8000 bytes.
[9] Input filter: Bucket type HEAP contains 8000 bytes.
[9] Input filter: Bucket type HEAP contains 8000 bytes.
[9] Input filter: Bucket type HEAP contains 8000 bytes.
[9] Input filter: Bucket type HEAP contains 8000 bytes.
[9] Input filter: Bucket type HEAP contains 8000 bytes.
[4] Input filter: Request too large to store in memory, switching to disk.
```

A new file will be created to store the entire raw request body:

```
[4] Input filter: Created temporary file to store request body: ⏎
/opt/modsecurity/var/tmp//20090819-180105-SowvOX8AAQEAACWAArs-request_body-4nZjqf
[4] Input filter: Wrote 129559 bytes from memory to disk.
```

This file is always deleted in the cleanup phase:

```
[4] Input filter: Removed temporary file: ⏎
/opt/modsecurity/var/tmp//20090819-180105-SowvOX8AAQEAACWAArs-request_body-4nZjqf
```

Impact on Web Server

The addition of ModSecurity will change how your web server operates. As with all Apache modules, you pay for the additional flexibility and security ModSecurity gives you with increased CPU and RAM consumption on your server. The exact amount will depend on your configuration of ModSecurity and the usage of your server. Following is a detailed list of the various activities that increase resource consumption:

- ModSecurity will add to the parsing already done by Apache, and that results in a slight increase of CPU consumption.

- Complex parsers (e.g., XML) are more expensive.

- The handling of file uploads may require I/O operations. In some cases, inbound data will be duplicated on disk.

- The parsing will add to the RAM consumption, because every extracted element (e.g., a request parameter) will need to be copied into its own space.

- Request bodies and response bodies are usually buffered in order to support reliable blocking.

- Every rule in your configuration will use some of the CPU time (for the operator) and RAM (to transform input data before it can be analyzed).

- Some of the operators used in the rules (e.g., the regular expression operator) are CPU-intensive.

- Full transaction logging is an expensive I/O operation.

In practice, this list is important because it keeps you informed; what matters is that you have enough resources to support your ModSecurity needs. If you do, then it doesn't matter how expensive ModSecurity is. Also, what's expensive to someone may not be to someone else. If you don't have enough resources to do everything you want with ModSecurity, you will need to monitor the operation of your system and remove some of the functionality to reduce the resource consumption. Virtually everything that ModSecurity does is configurable, so you should have no problems doing that.

It is generally easier to run ModSecurity in reverse proxy mode, because then you usually have an entire server (with its own CPU and RAM) to play with. In embedded mode, ModSecurity will add to the processing already done by the web server, so this method is more challenging on a busy server.

For what it's worth, ModSecurity generally uses the minimal necessary resources to perform the desired functions, so this is really a case of exchanging functionality for speed: if you want to do more, you have to pay more.

What Next?

The purpose of this section is to map your future ModSecurity activities and help you determine where to go from here. Where you will go depends on what you want to achieve and how much time you have to spend. A complete ModSecurity experience, so to speak, consists of the following elements:

Installation and configuration
   This is the basic step that all users must learn how to perform. The next three chapters will teach you how to make ModSecurity operational, performing installation, general configuration, and logging configuration. Once you are done with that, you need to decide what you want to do with it. That's what the remainder of the book is for.

Rule writing
   Rule writing is an essential skill. You may currently view rules as a tool to use to detect application security attacks. They are that, but they are also much more. In ModSecurity, you write rules to find out more about HTTP clients (e.g., geolocation and IP address reputation), perform long-term activity tracking (of IP addresses, sessions

and users, for example), implement policy decisions (use the available information to make the decisions to warn or block), write virtual patches, and even to check on the status of ModSecurity itself.

It is true that the attack detection rules are in a class of its own, but that's mostly because, in order to write them successfully, you need to know so much about application security. For that reason, many ModSecurity users generally focus on using third-party rule sets for the attack detection. It's a legitimate choice. Not everyone has the time and inclination to become an application security expert. Even if you end up not using any inspection rules whatsoever, the ability to write virtual patches is reason enough to use ModSecurity.

Rule sets

The use of existing rule sets is the easiest way to get to the proverbial low hanging fruit: invest small effort and reap big benefits. You don't have to go far to obtain a rule set to use—*Core Rule Set* comes with ModSecurity itself. On the other hand, if you are keen to get your hands dirty, I can tell you that I draw great pleasure from writing my own rules. It's a great way to learn about application security. The only drawback is that it requires a large time investment.

Remote logging and alert management GUI

ModSecurity is perfectly usable without a remote logging solution and without a GUI (the two usually go together). Significant error messages are copied to Apache's error log. Complete transactions are usually logged to the audit log. With a notification system in place, you will know when something happens, and you can visit the audit logs to investigate. For example, many installations will divert Apache's error log to a central logging system (via syslog).

The process does become more difficult with more than one sensor to manage. Furthermore, GUIs make the whole experience of monitoring much more pleasant. For that reason you will probably seek to install one of the available remote centralization tools and use their GUIs. The available options are listed in the Resources section, which follows.

Resources

This section contains a list of assorted ModSecurity resources that can assist you in your work.

Figure 2-1. The homepage of www.modsecurity.org

General Resources

The following resources are the bare essentials:

ModSecurity web site

ModSecurity's web site [https://www.modsecurity.org] is probably going to be your main source of information. You should visit the web site from time to time, as well as subscribe to receive the updates from the blog.

Official documentation

The official ModSecurity documentation [https://www.modsecurity.org/documentation/] consists of two files: the *Reference Manual*, which covers the Rule Language, and the *Data Formats Guide*, which explains the data formats used for storage and the error messages. Always keep a bookmark to the documentation of the same version of ModSecurity that you are working with. Although the ModSecurity web site keeps the links to the documentation of the most recent release only, the previous versions are all there. To access them you just need to replace the current version number with whatever earlier version number you need.

Issue tracker

The ModSecurity issue tracker [https://www.modsecurity.org/tracker/] is the place you will want to visit for one of two reasons: to report a problem with ModSecurity itself (e.g., when you find a bug) or to check out the progress on the next (major or minor) version. Before reporting any problems, go through the Support Checklist [http://www.modsecurity.org/documentation/support-request-checklist.html], which will help you assemble the information required to help resolve your problem. Providing as much information as you can will help the developers understand and replicate the problem, and provide a fix (or a workaround) quickly.

Users' mailing list

The users' mailing list [http://lists.sourceforge.net/lists/listinfo/mod-security-users] (mod-security-users@lists.sourceforge.net) is a general-purpose mailing list where you can discuss ModSecurity. Feel free to ask questions, propose improvements, and discuss ideas. That is the place where you'll hear first about new ModSecurity versions.

ModSecurity@Freshmeat

If you subscribe to the users' mailing list, you will generally find out about new versions of ModSecurity as soon as they are released. If you care only about version releases, however, you may consider subscribing to the new version notifications at the ModSecurity page at Freshmeat [http://freshmeat.net/projects/modsecurity].

Core Rules mailing list

Starting with version 2, the Core Rules [http://www.owasp.org/index.php/Category:OWASP_ModSecurity_Core_Rule_Set_Project] project is part of OWASP [http://www.owasp.org], and has a separate mailing list (owasp-modsecurity-core-rule-set@lists.owasp.org).

Developer Resources

If you are interested in development work, you will need these:

Developers' mailing list

The developers' mailing list [https://lists.sourceforge.net/lists/listinfo/mod-security-developers] is generally a lonely place, but if you do decide to start playing with the ModSecurity source code, this list is the place to go to discuss your work.

Source code access

The source code of ModSecurity is hosted at a Subversion repository at SourceForge [http://sourceforge.net/projects/mod-security/develop], which allows you to access it directly or through a web-based user interface.

FishEye interface

If you are not looking to start developing immediately but still want to have a look at the source code of ModSecurity, I recommend that you use the ModSecurity FishEye interface [https://www.modsecurity.org/fisheye/], which is much better than the stock interface available at SourceForge.

Related Projects

There is a number of projects and sites that are related to ModSecurity in one way or another. The most interesting ones are:

jwall.org

Christian Bockermann runs jwall.org [http://www.jwall.org] and provides several interesting application security projects and ModSecurity tools. The most useful tool is the AuditConsole, a web-based application that consolidates audit logs from multiple ModSecurity sensors.

ModSecurity Community Console

When Breach Security acquired ModSecurity, they decided to give away the then-commercial log consolidation tool for free, calling it ModSecurity Community Console [https://www.modsecurity.org/projects/console/]. The tool has seen little improvement since 2006, but it fulfills the elementary requirements of log aggregation and storage. It is limited to supporting up to three ModSecurity sensors.

REMO

REMO [http://www.netnea.com/cms/?q=remo] (short for Rule Editor for ModSecurity) is a web-based rule editor designed for whitelist creation. It is written by Christian Folini, and uses existing audit logs to assist you in creating a positive-security shield around an application.

WebDefend GEM

WebDefend GEM [http://www.breach.com/products/webdefend-global-event-manager.html] (Global Event Manager) is a commercial web application firewall event management solution from Breach Security that will accept audit logs from ModSecurity sensors, as well as from WebDefend and the Akamai web application firewall.

Summary

This chapter was your ModSecurity orientation. I introduced ModSecurity at a high level, discussed what it is and what it isn't, and what it can do and what it cannot. I also gave you a taste of what ModSecurity is like and described common usage scenarios, as well as covered some of the interesting parts of its operation.

The foundation you now have should be enough to help you set off on a journey of ModSecurity exploration. The next chapter discusses installation.

2 Installation

Before you can install ModSecurity, you need to decide if you want to compile it from source or use a binary version—either one included with your operating system or one produced by a third party. Each of the options comes with its advantages and disadvantages, as listed in Table 2.1, "Installation options".

Table 2.1. Installation options

Installation type	Advantages	Disadvantages
Operating system version	• Fully automated installation • Maintenance included	• May not be the latest version
Third-party binary	• Semi-automated installation	• May not be the latest version • Manual download and updates • Do you trust the third party?
Source code	• Can always use the latest version • Can use experimental versions • Can make changes, apply patches, and make emergency security fixes	• Manual installation and maintenance required • A lot of work involved with rolling your own version

In some cases, you won't have a choice. For example, if you've installed Apache from source, you will need to install ModSecurity from source too (you will be able to reuse the system packages, of course). The following questions may help you to make the decision:

- Do you intend to use ModSecurity seriously?

- Are you comfortable compiling programs from source?

- Do you have enough time to spend on the compilation and the successive maintenance of a custom-installed program?

- Will you need to make changes to ModSecurity, or write your own extensions?

I generally try to use binary packages when they are available (and they are available on Debian, which is currently my platform of choice). When I build dedicated reverse proxy installations, however, I tend to build everything from source, because that allows me access to the latest Apache and ModSecurity versions, and makes it easier to tweak things (by changing the source code of either Apache or ModSecurity) when I want to.

Installation from Source

Installing from source is the preferred approach to installing ModSecurity, mostly because that way you get the latest (and best) version, and because you are able to make any changes you want.

Downloading Releases

To download ModSecurity, go to its web site [https://www.modsecurity.org] or the Source-Forge project page [http://sourceforge.net/projects/mod-security/]. You will need both the main distribution and the cryptographic signature:

```
$ wget http://www.modsecurity.org/download/modsecurity-apache_2.5.10-dev2.tar.gz
$ wget http://www.modsecurity.org/download/modsecurity-apache_2.5.10-dev2.tar.gz.asc
```

Verify the signature before doing anything else. That will ensure that the package you've just downloaded does not contain a trojan horse planted by a third party and that it hasn't been corrupted during transport.

```
$ gpg --verify modsecurity-apache_2.5.10-dev2.tar.gz.asc
gpg: Signature made Wed 12 Aug 2009 23:27:06 BST using DSA key ID E77B534D
gpg: Can't check signature: public key not found
```

Your first attempt may not provide the expected results, but that can be solved easily by importing the referenced key from a key server:

```
$ gpg --recv-keys E77B534D
gpg: requesting key E77B534D from hkp server keys.gnupg.net
gpg: /home/guest/.gnupg/trustdb.gpg: trustdb created
gpg: key E77B534D: public key "Brian Rectanus (work) <brian.rectanus@breach.com>" ↵
imported
gpg: no ultimately trusted keys found
gpg: Total number processed: 1
gpg:               imported: 1
```

Now you can try again:

```
$ gpg --verify modsecurity-apache_2.5.10-dev2.tar.gz.asc
```

```
gpg: Signature made Wed 12 Aug 2009 23:27:06 BST using DSA key ID E77B534D
gpg: Good signature from "Brian Rectanus (work) <brian.rectanus@breach.com>"
gpg:              aka "Brian Rectanus <brian@rectanus.net>"
gpg:              aka "Brian Rectanus (personal) <brectanu@gmail.com>"
gpg: WARNING: This key is not certified with a trusted signature!
gpg:          There is no indication that the signature belongs to the owner.
```

While this warning might look serious, it generally isn't a problem, and has to do with the way gpg expects you to verify the identity of an individual. The warning basically tells you that you've downloaded Brian's key from somewhere, but that you don't *really know* that it belongs to him. The only way to be sure, as far as gpg is concerned, is to meet Brian in real life, or to meet someone else who knows him personally. If you want to learn more, look up *web of trust* on Wikipedia.

Downloading from Repository

If you want to be on the cutting edge, downloading the latest development version directly from the Subversion (the source code control system used by the ModSecurity project) repository is the way to go. When you do this, you'll get new features days and even months before they make it into an official stable release. Having said that, however, there is a reason why we call some versions "stable." When you use a repository version of ModSecurity, you need to accept that there is no guarantee whatsoever that it will work correctly. For what it's worth, I am currently running a development version in production, and I am confident that it will not bring my server down.

Before you can install a development version of ModSecurity, you need to know where to find it. The repository, which is hosted with SourceForge [http://mod-security.svn.sourceforge.net/viewvc/mod-security/], can be viewed with a browser. The view of the root of the repository is similar to that in Figure 2-1, "ModSecurity repository root".

Figure 2-1. ModSecurity repository root

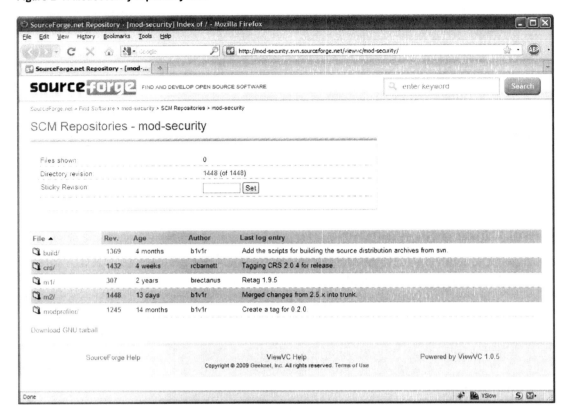

What you probably want is located in the m2/ directory, which houses ModSecurity 2.x. Within that directory, you will find a directory structure that you will find familiar if you've worked with Subversion before:

```
m2/
    branches/
        2.1.x/
        2.5.x/
    experimental/
        [some stuff you won't care about]
    tags/
        [all official releases, each in own directory]
    trunk/
```

The trunk directory always contains the most recent development version. The active branches (currently only 2.5.x) may sometimes contain a feature or a fix that has not been released yet. The branches will always be generally stable anyway, and the risk of something breaking is minimal.

Once you have determined the location of the version of ModSecurity that you wish to use, you can get it using the export command of Subversion, like this:

```
$ svn export https://mod-security.svn.sourceforge.net/svnroot/mod-security/↵
m2/trunk modsecurity-trunk
```

What you will get in the folder modsecurity-trunk is almost the same as what you get when you download a release. The only practical difference will be that you won't have the documentation in PDF or HTML (although the DocBook sources will be there, as usual, in the doc subdirectory). The documentation build scripts are not in the main repository, but I don't think that will be a problem, because you can always read the sources directly (e.g., using the free XMLmind XML editor [http://www.xmlmind.com/xmleditor/]), or generate the missing files yourself (e.g., using the free XMLmind XSL-FO Converter [http://www.xmlmind.com/foconverter/]).

Compilation under Unix

Before you can start to compile ModSecurity, you must ensure that you have a complete development toolchain installed. Refer to the documentation of the operating system you are using for instructions. If you'll be adding ModSecurity to an operating system–provided Apache, you are likely to need to install a specific Apache development package, too. For example, on Debian and Ubuntu, you need to use apache2-prefork-dev or apache2-threaded-dev, depending on which deployment model (process-based or thread-based) you chose.

In the next step, ensure that you have resolved all the dependencies before compilation. The dependencies are listed in Table 2.2, "ModSecurity 2.5.x dependencies".

Table 2.2. ModSecurity 2.5.x dependencies

Dependency	In Apache?	Purpose
Apache Portable Runtime [http://apr.apache.org]	Yes	Various
APR-Util [http://apr.apache.org]	Yes	Various
mod_unique_id	Yes, but may not be installed by default	Generate unique transaction ID
libcurl [http://curl.haxx.se/libcurl/]	No	Remote logging (mlogc)
libxml2 [http://xmlsoft.org]	No	XML processing
Lua 5.1 [http://www.lua.org]	No	Writing complex rules in Lua (optional)
PCRE [http://www.pcre.org]	Yes, but cannot be used by ModSecurity	Regular expression matching

If you already have Apache installed, you will only ever need to deal with libcurl, libxml2, and Lua. With Apache compiled from source, you will also need the PCRE library. Although Apache comes bundled with it, it is used in a way that does not allow other modules to access it. To work around this issue, install PCRE separately and then tell Apache to use the external copy. I explain how to do that later in this section.

If you're installing from source, go to the packages' web sites, and download and install the tarballs. If you're using managed packages, you just need to determine what the missing packages are called. On Debian Lenny, the following command installs the missing packages:

```
# apt-get install libcurl3-dev liblua5.1-dev libxml2-dev
```

Refer to the documentation of the package management system used by your platform to discover how to search the package database.

> **Note**
>
> Libcurl, which is used for remote logging, can be compiled to use OpenSSL or GnuTLS. You are advised to use OpenSSL because there have been complaints about remote logging problems when GnuTLS was used.

The process should be straightforward from here on. Execute the following commands in succession:

```
$ ./configure
$ make
$ make mlogc
```

This set of commands ensures that you don't need any compile-time options. If you do, they are explained in the next section. The second make command creates mlogc, which is the remote logging tool, which is run in a separate process.

> **Note**
>
> Running additional tests after compilation (make test and make test-regression) is always a good idea, and is an especially good idea when using a development version of ModSecurity. If you are going to have any problems, you want to have them before installation, rather than after.

After ModSecurity is built, all you need to do is copy the two generated binaries to the binaries folder. For example:

```
$ sudo cp ./.libs/mod_security2.so /opt/modsecurity/bin
$ sudo cp ./../tools/mlogc /opt/modsecurity/bin/
```

If you wish to keep the ModSecurity module along with the other Apache modules, just run the install target, which will produce the following output:

```
$ sudo make install
build/apxs-wrapper -i mod_security2.la
/usr/share/apache2/build/instdso.sh SH_LIBTOOL='/usr/share/apr-1.0/build/libtool' ⏎
```

```
mod_security2.la /usr/lib/apache2/modules
/usr/share/apr-1.0/build/libtool --mode=install cp mod_security2.la ↵
/usr/lib/apache2/modules/
cp .libs/mod_security2.so /usr/lib/apache2/modules/mod_security2.so
cp .libs/mod_security2.lai /usr/lib/apache2/modules/mod_security2.la
PATH="$PATH:/sbin" ldconfig -n /usr/lib/apache2/modules
----------------------------------------------------------------
Libraries have been installed in:
   /usr/lib/apache2/modules

If you ever happen to want to link against installed libraries
in a given directory, LIBDIR, you must either use libtool, and
specify the full pathname of the library, or use the '-LLIBDIR'
flag during linking and do at least one of the following:
   - add LIBDIR to the 'LD_LIBRARY_PATH' environment variable
     during execution
   - add LIBDIR to the 'LD_RUN_PATH' environment variable
     during linking
   - use the '-Wl,--rpath -Wl,LIBDIR' linker flag
   - have your system administrator add LIBDIR to '/etc/ld.so.conf'

See any operating system documentation about shared libraries for
more information, such as the ld(1) and ld.so(8) manual pages.
----------------------------------------------------------------
chmod 644 /usr/lib/apache2/modules/mod_security2.so
```

Installation does not activate or configure ModSecurity—you will need to do that manually, and I'll cover the process in the following sections.

Compile-time options

The configuration example from the previous section assumed that the dependencies were all installed as system libraries. It also assumed that the configure script will figure everything out on its own. It may or may not, but chances are good that you will occasionally need to do something different; this is where the compile-time options, listed in Table 2.3, "Compile-time options", come in handy.

Table 2.3. Compile-time options

Option	Description
--with-apr	Specify location of the Apache Portable Runtime library.
--with-apu	Specify location of the APR-Util library.
--with-apxs	Specify the location of Apache through the location of the apxs script.
--with-curl	Specify the location of libcurl.
--with-libxml	Specify the location of libxml2. Some older versions used --with-xml instead.
--with-pcre	Specify the location of PCRE.

Using ModSecurity with a custom-compiled version of Apache is more work than it should be, because of a dependency problem we have to resolve manually. PCRE, which ModSecurity uses for pattern matching, is a very popular library integrated into many operating systems. The problem is that Apache bundles PCRE and uses the bundled version by default when you compile it from source. Unless you take care to avoid conflicts, you'll probably end up with Apache using the bundled version of PCRE, and ModSecurity using the one provided by the operating system. The solution to this problem is to build Apache to use the external PCRE version too, which requires just one change to the way you build Apache.

The configure option you need (remember, this is the configure of Apache, not ModSecurity) is --with-pcre, and it is used like this:

```
$ ./configure --with-pcre=/usr/bin/pcre-config
```

After you compile and install Apache, you can confirm that the external PCRE library is used with ldd:

```
$ ldd ~/apache/bin/httpd | grep pcre
        libpcre.so.3 => /usr/lib/libpcre.so.3 (0xb7d3f000)
```

You should get the same result when you compile ModSecurity:

```
$ ldd ~/apache/modules/mod_security2.so | grep pcre
        libpcre.so.3 => /usr/lib/libpcre.so.3 (0xb7f4c000)
```

Installation from Binaries

As previously discussed, using a binary version of ModSecurity is often the easiest option. It is also the fastest way to get ModSecurity up and running. The list of the available binary packages is available from http://www.modsecurity.org/download/. Traditionally, the best support has been available on Debian, FreeBSD, and Windows, but Fedora Core is catching up. At the time of writing, you can get the latest version of ModSecurity in binary form on all these platforms.

Fedora Core, CentOS, and Red Hat Enterprise Linux

If you are a Fedora Core user and you are running version 10 or later, you can install ModSecurity directly from the official distribution, using yum:

```
# yum install mod_security
```

On CentOS and Red Hat Enterprise Linux, you have two options. One is to use the packages from EPEL [http://fedoraproject.org/wiki/EPEL] (Extra Packages for Enterprise Linux), which is a volunteer effort and part of the Fedora community. The other option is to use the custom packages built by Jason Litka [http://www.jasonlitka.com/yum-repository/]. Either way, the available packages support CentOS/RHEL 4.x and 5.x, on the i386 and x86_64 architectures. The installation process is the same as for Fedora Core.

Debian and Ubuntu

Debian was the first distribution to include ModSecurity, but also the first distribution to kick it out due to a licensing issue. (In a nutshell, the issue boils down to incompatibility between GPL v2 and ASL v2.) The ModSecurity license was clarified in version 2.5.6 with the addition of an open source exception, and that opened the door for it to get back into Debian. Alberto Gonzalez Iniesta has been a long-time supporter of ModSecurity on Debian, supporting ModSecurity in his own (unofficial) repository, and is now the official packager.

If you are running the current Debian testing (*squeeze*), then installing ModSecurity is as easy as typing:

```
# apt-get install libapache-mod-security
```

This single command will download the package and install it, then activate the module in the Apache configuration. If you are running the current Debian stable version (*lenny*), you can still get the binaries, but you will first need to configure your system to use the backports package repository [http://www.backports.org].

> **Note**
>
> Don't forget that Debian uses a special system to manage Apache modules and sites. To activate and deactivate modules, use a2emod and a2dismod, respectively. To manage Apache, use apache2ctl.

Installation on Windows

ModSecurity was ported to Windows early on, in 2003, and has run well on this platform ever since. Windows binary packages of ModSecurity are maintained by Steffen Land, who runs Apache Lounge [http://www.apachelounge.com], a community for those who run Apache on Windows. In addition to ModSecurity, Steffen maintains his version of Apache itself, as well as many third-party modules you might want to run on Windows. The ModSecurity binary packages are consistently up to date, so you will have little trouble if you want to run the latest version. The download includes ModSecurity (with embedded Lua 5.1) as well as the libxml2 dynamic library. At this time, however, there is no support for remote logging with mlogc.

> **Note**
>
> Although it might be possible to run Steffen's ModSecurity binaries with a version of Apache produced elsewhere, you should really use only the packages from a single

> location that are intended to be used together. If you don't, you may encounter un-
> usual behavior and web server crashes.

The installation is quite easy. First, download the package and copy the dynamic libraries into the modules/ folder (of the Apache installation). Then, modify your Apache configuration to activate ModSecurity:

```
LoadModule security2_module modules/mod_security2.so
```

You will also need to activate mod_unique_id. This module may not be already active, but there should already be a commented-out line in your configuration. You just need to find it and uncomment it. If it isn't there, just add the following:

```
LoadModule unique_id_module modules/mod_unique_id.so
```

Summary

It's never been easier to install ModSecurity, now that it is included with so many operating system and distributions. Although the installation from source code gives you guaranteed access to the most recent version, as well as access to the yet-unreleased code, it can be time-consuming if you are not used to it. It's not everyone's cup of tea. There is something to be said for using the provided version and not having to think about upgrading (and saving the time it takes to upgrade).

In the next chapter, I'll explain each of the configuration options, teaching you how to set every single option, step by step, so that everything is just the way you like it.

3 Configuration

Now that you have ModSecurity compiled and ready to run, we can proceed to the configuration. This section, with its many subsections, goes through every part of ModSecurity configuration, explicitly configuring every little detail:

- Going through all the configuration directives will give you a better understanding of how ModSecurity works. Even if there are features that you don't need immediately, you will learn that they exist and you'll be able to take advantage of them when the need arises.

- By explicitly configuring every single feature, you will foolproof your configuration against incompatible changes to default settings that may happen in future versions of ModSecurity.

In accordance with its philosophy, ModSecurity won't do anything implicitly. It won't even run unless you tell it to. There are three reasons for that:

1. By not doing anything implicitly, we ensure that ModSecurity does only what you tell it to. That not only keeps you in control, but it also makes you think about every feature before you add it to your configuration.

2. It is impossible to design a default configuration that works in all circumstances. We can give you a framework within which you can work (as I am doing in this section), but you still need to shape your configuration according to your needs.

3. Security is not free. You pay for it by the increased consumption of RAM, CPU, or the possibility that you may block a legitimate request. Incorrect configuration may cause problems, so we need you to think carefully about what you're doing.

The remainder of this section explains the proposed default configuration for ModSecurity. You can get a good overview of the default configuration simply by examining the configuration directives supported by ModSecurity, which are listed in Table 3.1, "Main configuration directives" (with the exception of the logging directives, which are listed in several tables in the Chapter 4, *Logging*).

Table 3.1. Main configuration directives

Directive	Description
SecArgumentSeparator	Sets the application/x-www-form-urlencoded parameter separator
SecCookieFormat	Sets the cookie parser version
SecDataDir	Sets the folder for persistent storage
SecRequestBodyAccess	Controls request body buffering
SecRequestBodyInMemoryLimit	Sets the size of the per-request memory buffer
SecRequestBodyLimit	Sets the maximum request body size ModSecurity will accept
SecRequestBodyNoFilesLimit	Sets the maximum request body size, excluding uploaded files
SecResponseBodyAccess	Controls response body buffering
SecResponseBodyLimit	Specifies the response body buffering limit
SecResponseBodyLimitAction	Controls what happens once the response body limit is reached
SecResponseBodyMimeType	Specifies a list of response body MIME types to inspect
SecResponseBodyMimeTypesClear	Clears the list of response body MIME types
SecRuleEngine	Controls the operation of the rule engine
SecTmpDir	Sets the folder for temporary files

Folder Locations

Your first configuration task is to decide where on the filesystem to put the various bits and pieces that every ModSecurity installation consists of. Installation layout is often a matter of taste, so it is difficult for me to give you advice. Similarly, different choices may be appropriate in different circumstances. For example, if you are adding ModSecurity to a web server and you intend to use it only occasionally, you may not want to use an elaborate folder structure, in which case you'll probably put the ModSecurity folder underneath Apache's. When you're using ModSecurity as part of a dedicated reverse proxy installation, however, a well–thought out structure is something that will save you a lot of time in the long run.

I prefer to always use an elaborate folder layout, because I like things to be neat and tidy, and because the consistency helps me when I am managing multiple ModSecurity installations. I start by creating a dedicated folder for ModSecurity (/opt/modsecurity) with multiple sub-folders underneath. The subfolders that are written to at runtime are all grouped (in /opt/modsecurity/var), which makes it easy to relocate them to a different filesystem using a symbolic link. I end up with the following structure:

Binaries
/opt/modsecurity/bin

Configuration files
/opt/modsecurity/etc

Audit logs
    /opt/modsecurity/var/audit

Persistent data
    /opt/modsecurity/var/data

Logs
    /opt/modsecurity/var/log

Temporary files
    /opt/modsecurity/var/tmp

File uploads
    /opt/modsecurity/var/upload

Getting the permissions right may involve slightly more effort, depending on your circumstances. Most Apache installations bind to privileged ports (e.g., 80 and 443), which means that the web server must be started as root, and that further means that root must be the principal owner of the installation. Because it's not good practice to stay root at runtime, Apache will switch to a low-privilege account (we'll assume it's apache) as soon as it initializes. You'll find the proposed permissions in Table 3.2, "Folder permissions".

Table 3.2. Folder permissions

Location	Owner	Group	Permissions
/opt/modsecurity	root	apache	rwxr-x---
/opt/modsecurity/bin	root	root	rwxr-x---
/opt/modsecurity/etc	root	root	rwx------
/opt/modsecurity/var	root	apache	rwxr-x---
/opt/modsecurity/var/audit	apache	root	rwx------
/opt/modsecurity/var/data	apache	root	rwx------
/opt/modsecurity/var/log	root	root	rwx------
/opt/modsecurity/var/tmp	apache	apache	rwxr-x---
/opt/modsecurity/var/upload	apache	root	rwx------

I've arrived at the desired permission layout through the following requirements:

1. As already discussed, it is root that owns everything by default, and we assign ownership to apache only where that is necessary.

2. In two cases (/opt/modsecurity and /opt/modsecurity/var), we need to allow apache to access a folder so that it can get to a subfolder; we do this by creating a group, also called apache, of which user apache is the only member.

3. One folder, `/opt/modsecurity/var/log`, stands out, because it is the only folder underneath `/opt/modsecurity/var` where apache is not allowed to write. That folder contains log files that are opened by Apache early on, while it is still running as root. On any Unix system, you *must* have only one account with write access to that folder, and it has to be the principal owner. In our case, that must be root. Doing otherwise would create a security hole, whereby the apache user would be able to obtain partial root privileges using symlink trickery. (Essentially, in place of a log file, the apache user creates a symlink to some other root-owned file on the system. When Apache starts it runs as root and opens for writing the system file that the apache user would otherwise be unable to touch. By submitting requests to Apache, one might be able to control exactly what is written to the log files. That can lead to system compromise.)

4. A careful observer will notice that I've allowed group folder access to `/opt/modsecurity/var/tmp` (which means that any member of the apache group is allowed to read the files in the folder) even though this folder is owned by apache, which already has full access. This is because you will sometimes want to allow ModSecurity to exchange information with a third user account—for example, if you want to scan uploaded files for viruses (usually done using ClamAV). To allow the third user account to access the files created by ModSecurity, you just need to make it a member of the apache group and relax the file permissions using the `SecUploadFileMode` directive.

> **Note**
>
> As an exception to the proposed layout, you may want to reuse Apache's log directory for ModSecurity logs. If you don't, you'll have the error log separate from the debug log (and the audit log if you choose to use the serial logging format). In a reverse proxy installation in particular, it makes great sense to keep everything integrated and easier to find. There may be other good reasons for breaking convention. For example, if you have more than one hard disk installed and you use the audit logging feature a lot, you may want to split the I/O operations across the disks.

Configuration Layout

If you have anything but a trivial setup, spreading configuration across several files is necessary in order to make maintenance easier. There are several ways to do that, and some have more to do with taste than anything else, but in this section I will describe an approach that is good enough to start with.

Whatever configuration design I use, there is usually one main entry point, typically named `modsecurity.conf`, which I use as a bridge between Apache and ModSecurity. In my bridge file, I refer to any other ModSecurity files I might have, such as those listed in Table 3.3, "Configuration files".

Table 3.3. Configuration files

Filename	Description
main.conf	Main configuration file
rules-first.conf	Rules that need to run first
rules.conf	Your principal rule file
rules-last.conf	Rules that need to run last

Somewhere in your Apache configuration, use the following line to include the ModSecurity configuration:

```
Include /opt/modsecurity/etc/modsecurity.conf
```

Your main configuration file (modsecurity.conf) may thus contain only the following lines:

```
<IfModule mod_security2.c>
Include /opt/modsecurity/etc/main.conf
Include /opt/modsecurity/etc/rules-first.conf
Include /opt/modsecurity/etc/rules.conf
Include /opt/modsecurity/etc/rules-last.conf
</IfModule>
```

The <IfModule> tag is there to ensure that the ModSecurity configuration files are used only if ModSecurity is active in the web server. This is common practice when configuring any nonessential Apache modules and allows you to deactivate a module simply by commenting out the appropriate LoadModule line.

Adding ModSecurity to Apache

As the first step, make Apache aware of ModSecurity, adding the needed components. Depending on how you've chosen to run ModSecurity, this may translate to adding one or more lines to your configuration file. This is what the lines may look like:

```
# Load libxml2
LoadFile /usr/lib/libxml2.so
# Load Lua
LoadFile /usr/lib/liblua5.1.so
# Finally, load ModSecurity
LoadModule security2_module modules/mod_security2.so
```

Now you just need to tell Apache where to find the configuration:

```
Include /opt/modsecurity/etc/modsecurity.conf
```

Powering Up

ModSecurity has a master switch—the SecRuleEngine directive—that allows you to quickly turn it on and off. This directive will always come first in every configuration. I generally recommend that you start in detection-only mode, because that way you are sure nothing will be blocked.

```
# Enable ModSecurity, attaching it to every transaction.
SecRuleEngine DetectionOnly
```

You will normally want to keep this setting enabled, of course, but there will be cases in which you won't be exactly sure whether ModSecurity is doing something it shouldn't be. Whenever that happens, you will want to set it to Off, just for a moment or two, until you perform a request without it running.

The SecRuleEngine directive is context-sensitive (i.e., it works with Apache's container tags <VirtualHost>, <Location>, and so on), which means that you are able to control exactly where ModSecurity runs. You can use this feature to enable ModSecurity only for some sites, parts of a web site, or even for a single script only. I discuss this feature in detail later.

Will ModSecurity Block in Detection-Only Mode?

You may expect ModSecurity never to block when you configure SecRuleEngine with DetectionOnly, but that's not actually the case. There are two edge cases in which ModSecurity will block, to the surprise of most users. In both cases, an error occurs while ModSecurity is handling inbound or outbound data. If ModSecurity sees more data than it was configured to handle, it will respond with a HTTP_REQUEST_ENTITY_TOO_LARGE (417) error code. The three directives to watch are: SecRequestLimit, SecRequestNoFilesLimit, and SecResponseBodyLimit.

Only the problems with response body limits can be worked around, by changing the SecResponseBodyLimitAction setting to ProcessPartial. For the other two directives, we will have to wait for a future version of ModSecurity. I submitted a proposal to fix this behavior (issue MODSEC-104), and I expect that we will see a true detection-only mode in the next major version.

Request Body Handling

Requests consist of two parts: the headers part, which is always present, and the body, which is optional. Use the SecRequestBodyAccess directive to tell ModSecurity to look at request bodies:

```
# Allow ModSecurity to access request bodies. If you don't,
# ModSecurity won't be able to see any POST parameters
```

```
# and that's generally not what you want.
SecRequestBodyAccess On
```

Once this feature is enabled, ModSecurity will not only have access to the content transmitted in request bodies, but it will also completely buffer them. The buffering is essential for reliable attack prevention. With buffering in place, your rules have the opportunity to inspect requests in their entirety, and only after you choose not to block will the requests be allowed through.

The downside of buffering is that, in most cases, it uses RAM for storage, which needs to be taken into account when ModSecurity is running embedded in a web server. There are three directives that control how buffering is done. The first two, SecRequestBodyLimit and SecRequestBodyNoFilesLimit, establish request limits:

```
# Maximum request body size we will accept for buffering.
# If you support file uploads then the value given on the
# first line has to be as large as the largest file you
# want to accept. The second value refers to the size of
# data, with files excluded. You want to keep that value
# as low as practical.
SecRequestBodyLimit 1310720
SecRequestBodyNoFilesLimit 131072
```

In the versions prior to 2.5, ModSecurity supported only SecRequestBodyLimit (which establishes an absolute limit on a request body), but that directive turned out to be impractical in combination with file uploads. File uploads generally do not use RAM (and thus do not create an opportunity for a denial of service attack), which means that it is safe to allow such large requests. Unfortunately, doing so also meant allowing large requests that are not file uploads, defying the purpose for which the directive was introduced in the first place. The second directive, SecRequestBodyNoFilesLimit, which was introduced in ModSecurity 2.5, calculates request body sizes slightly differently, ignoring the space taken up by files. In practice, this means that the maximum allowed request body size will be that specified in the SecRequestBodyNoFilesLimit directive, with the exception of file uploads, where the setting in SecRequestBodyLimit takes precedence.

> **Note**
>
> ModSecurity will respond with a 413 (Request Entity Too Large) response status code when a request body limit is reached. This response code was chosen to mimic what Apache would have done in similar circumstances.

The third directive that deals with buffering, SecRequestBodyInMemoryLimit, controls how much of a request body will be stored in RAM, but it only works with file upload (multipart/form-data) requests:

```
# Store up to 128 KB of request body data in memory. When
# the multipart parser reaches this limit, it will start
```

```
# using your hard disk for storage. That is generally slow,
# but unavoidable.
SecRequestBodyInMemoryLimit 131072
```

The request bodies that fit within the limit configured with SecRequestBodyInMemoryLimit will be stored in RAM. The request bodies that are larger will be streamed to disk. This directive allows you to trade performance (storing request bodies in RAM is fast) for size (the storage capacity of your hard disk is much bigger than that of your RAM).

Response Body Handling

Similarly to requests, responses consist of headers and a body. Unlike requests, however, most responses have bodies. Use the SecResponseBodyAccess directive to tell ModSecurity to observe (and buffer) response bodies:

```
# Allow ModSecurity to access response bodies. We leave
# this disabled because most deployments want to focus on
# the incoming threats, and leaving this off reduces
# memory consumption.
SecResponseBodyAccess Off
```

I prefer to start with this setting disabled, because many deployments don't care to look at what leaves their web servers. Keeping this feature disabled means ModSecurity will use less RAM and less CPU. If you care about output, however, just change the directive setting to On.

There is a complication with response bodies, because you generally only want to look at the bodies of some of the responses. Response bodies make the bulk of the traffic on most web sites, and the majority of that are just static files that don't have any security relevance in most cases. The response MIME type is used to distinguish the interesting responses from the ones that are not. The SecResponseBodyMimeType directive lists the response MIME types you are interested in.

```
# Which response MIME types do you want to look at? You
# should adjust the configuration below to catch documents
# but avoid static files (e.g., images and archives).
SecResponseBodyMimeType text/plain text/html
```

> **Note**
>
> To instruct ModSecurity to inspect the response bodies for which the MIME type is unknown (meaning that it was not specified in the response headers), use the special string (null) as a parameter to SecResponseBodyMimeType.

You can control the size of a response body buffer using the SecResponseBodyLimit directive:

```
# Buffer response bodies of up to 512 KB in length.
```

```
SecResponseBodyLimit 524288
```

The problem with limiting the size of a response body buffer is that it breaks sites whose pages are longer than the limit. In ModSecurity 2.5, we introduced the `SecResponseBodyLimitAction` directive, which allows ModSecurity users to choose what happens when the limit is reached:

```
# What happens when we encounter a response body larger
# than the configured limit? By default, we process what
# we have and let the rest through.
SecResponseBodyLimitAction ProcessPartial
```

If the setting is `Reject`, the response will be discarded and the transaction interrupted with a 500 (Internal Server Error) response code. If the setting is `ProcessPartial`, which I recommend, ModSecurity will process what it has in the buffer and allow the rest through.

At the first thought, it may seem that allowing the processing of partial response bodies creates a security issue. For the attacker who controls output, it seems easy to create a response that is long enough to bypass observation by ModSecurity. This is true. However, if you have an attacker with full control of output, it is impossible for any type of monitoring to work reliably. For example, such an attacker could encrypt output, in which case it will be opaque to ModSecurity. Response body monitoring works best to detect information leakage, configuration errors, traces of attacks (successful or not), and data leakage in the cases when an attacker does not have full control of output.

Other than that, response monitoring is most useful when it comes to preventing the data leakage that comes from low-level error messages (e.g., database problems). Because such messages typically appear near the beginning of a page, the `ProcessPartial` setting will work just as well to catch them.

> **Note**
>
> If you are using `mod_deflate` for response compression, it may, under some circumstances, cause ModSecurity to assess and log compressed data (which is not very useful, and may even cause false positives). It is not clear what causes the problem, but a fix to deal with the problem is in ModSecurity 2.5.11 and later.

Filesystem Locations

We've made the decisions regarding filesystem locations already, so all we need to do now is translate them into configuration. The following two directives tell ModSecurity where to create temporary files (`SecTmpDir`) and where to store persistent data (`SecDataDir`):

```
# The location where ModSecurity will store temporary files
# (for example, when it needs to handle a multipart request
# body that is larger than the configured limit). If you don't
# specify a location here your system's default will be used.
```

```
# It is recommended that you specify a location that's private.
SecTmpDir /opt/modsecurity/var/tmp/

# The location where ModSecurity will keep its data. This,
# too, needs to be a path that other users can't access.
SecDataDir /opt/modsecurity/var/data/
```

File Uploads

Next, we configure the handling of file uploads. We configure the folder where ModSecurity will store intercepted files, but we keep this functionality disabled for now. File upload interception slows down ModSecurity and can potentially consume a lot of disk space, so you'll want to enable this functionality only in the places where you really need it.

```
# The location where ModSecurity will store intercepted
# uploaded files. This location must be private to ModSecurity.
SecUploadDir /opt/modsecurity/var/upload/

# By default, do not intercept (nor store) uploaded files.
SecUploadKeepFiles Off
```

For now, we also assume that you will not be using external scripts to inspect uploaded files. That allows us to keep the file permissions more secure, by allowing access only to the apache user:

```
# Uploaded files are by default created with permissions that
# do not allow any other user to access them. You may need to
# relax that if you want to interface ModSecurity to an
# external program (e.g., an anti-virus).
SecUploadFileMode 0600
```

> ## Note
>
> You may experience permission-related issues in ModSecurity versions 2.5.10 and 2.5.11 (but not in 2.5.12 and better), in which process umask affects the permissions of newly created files. Thus, if you set SecUploadFileMode to 0660, but the umask is 022, the resulting permissions will be 0644 (0660 & ~022). If you need to change the process umask, edit the script that you use to control Apache (e.g., apachectl in my case). For example, assuming that you wish to set the umask to 002, add umask 002 to the end of the script.

If you are using ModSecurity 2.5.12 or later, you should lower the maximum number of files that ModSecurity will handle in a request:

```
# Limit the number of files we are willing
# to handle in any one request.
SecUploadFileLimit 32
```

Chapter 3: Configuration

The default value is 100, but that's usually too much. The issue here is that it is very easy for an attacker to include many embedded files in a single `multipart/form-data` request (for example, hundreds and even thousands), but also that you don't want ModSecurity to create that many files on the filesystem (which happens only if the storage or validation of uploaded files is required), because it would create a denial of service situation.

Debug Log

Debug logging is very useful for troubleshooting, but in production you want to keep it at minimum, because too much logging will affect the performance. The recommended debug log level for production is 3, which will duplicate in the debug log what you will also see in Apache's error log. This is handy, because the error log will grow at a faster rate and may be rotated. A copy of the ModSecurity messages in the debug log means that you always have all the data you need.

```
# Debug log
SecDebugLog /opt/modsecurity/var/log/debug.log
SecDebugLogLevel 3
```

Audit Log

In ModSecurity terminology, "audit logging" refers to the ability to record complete transaction data. For a typical transaction without a request body, this translates to roughly 1 KB. Multiply that by the number of requests you are receiving daily and you'll soon realize that you want to keep this type of logging to an absolute minimum.

Our default configuration will use audit logging only for the transactions that are *relevant*, which means those that have had an error or a warning reported against them. Other possible values for `SecAuditEngine` are `On` (log everything) and `Off` (log nothing).

```
# Log only what is really necessary.
SecAuditEngine RelevantOnly
```

In addition, we will also log the transactions with response status codes that indicate a server error (500–599). You should never see such transactions on an error-free server. The extra data logged by ModSecurity may help you uncover security issues, or problems of some other type.

```
# Also log requests that cause a server error.
SecAuditLogRelevantStatus ^5
```

By default, we log all transaction data except response bodies. This assumes that you will seldom log (as it should be), because response bodies can take up a lot of space.

```
# Log everything we know about a transaction.
```

```
SecAuditLogParts ABCDEFHKZ
```

Using the same assumption, we choose to use a single file to store all the recorded information. This is not adequate for the installations that will log a lot and prevents remote logging, but it is good enough to start with:

```
# Use a single file for logging.
SecAuditLogType Serial
SecAuditLog /opt/modsecurity/var/log/audit.log
```

As the final step, we will configure the path that will be used in the more scalable audit logging scheme, called *concurrent logging*, even though you won't need to use it just yet:

```
# Specify the path for concurrent audit logging.
SecAuditLogStorageDir /opt/modsecurity/var/audit/
```

Miscellaneous Options

The directives covered in this section are seldom needed, but having them will allow us to achieve complete coverage of the ModSecurity configuration options. You'll also be aware that they exist and will be able to use them in the rare cases where they are needed.

The SecArgumentSeparator directive allows you to change the parameter separator used for the application/x-www-form-urlencoded encoding, which is used to transport all GET parameters and most POST parameters.

```
SecArgumentSeparator &
```

Virtually all applications use an ampersand for this purpose, but some may not. The HTML 4.01 specification recommends that applications support the use of semicolons as separators (see section *B.2.2 Ampersands in URI attribute values*) for convenience. In PHP, for example, it is possible to use any character as a separator.

The SecCookieFormat directive selects one of the two cookie parsers available in ModSecurity. Virtually all applications use Netscape-style cookies (sometimes also known as version 0 cookies), so there will be little reason to change this setting:

```
SecCookieFormat 0
```

Default Rule Match Policy

As we're nearing the end of the configuration, you need to decide what you want to happen when a rule matches. It is recommended that you start without blocking, because that will allow you to monitor the operation of your installation over a period of time and ensure that legitimate traffic is not being marked as suspicious:

```
SecDefaultAction "phase:1,log,auditlog,pass"
```

This default policy will work for all rules that follow it in the same configuration context. For more information, turn to the section called "Configuration Contexts" in Chapter 7.

> **Note**
>
> It is possible to write rules that ignore the default policies. If you are using third-party rule sets and you are not sure how they will behave, consider switching the entire engine to detection only (using `SecRuleEngine`). No rule will block when you do that, regardless of how it was designed to work.

Handling Processing Errors

As you may recall from our earlier discussion, ModSecurity avoids making decisions for you. It will detect problems as they occur, but it will generally leave to you to deal with them. In our default configuration, we will have a couple of rules to deal with the situations that ModSecurity can't deal with on its own—processing errors.

> **Note**
>
> I am including these rules here because they should be an integral part of every configuration, but you shouldn't worry if you don't understand what it is that they do exactly. The rules will be explained in detail later in the book.

There are currently two types of processing errors:

- Parsing errors
- PCRE limit errors

ModSecurity parsers are designed to be as permissive as possible without compromising security. They will raise flags when they fail, but also when they encounter something suspicious. By checking the flags in your rules you detect the processing errors.

Currently the only parsing errors that can happen are the request body processor errors. We will use two rules to handle those.

The first rule will examine the `REQBODY_PROCESSOR_ERROR` flag for errors. This flag will be raised whenever a request body parsing error occurs, regardless of which parser was used for parsing:

```
# Verify that we've correctly processed the request body.
# As a rule of thumb, when failing to process a request body
# you should reject the request (when deployed in blocking mode)
# or log a high-severity alert (when deployed in detection-only mode).
SecRule REQBODY_PROCESSOR_ERROR "!@eq 0" \
    "phase:2,t:none,log,block,msg:'Failed to parse request body: ↵
%{REQBODY_PROCESSOR_ERROR_MSG}'"
```

The second rule is specific to the `multipart/form-data` parser, which is used to handle file uploads. If it detects a problem, it produces an error message detailing the flaws:

```
# By default be strict with what you accept in the multipart/form-data
# request body. If the rule below proves to be too strict for your
# environment consider changing it to detection-only. You are encouraged
# _not_ to remove it altogether.
SecRule MULTIPART_STRICT_ERROR "!@eq 0" \
"phase:2,t:none,log,block,msg:'Multipart request body \
failed strict validation: \
PE %{REQBODY_PROCESSOR_ERROR}, \
BQ %{MULTIPART_BOUNDARY_QUOTED}, \
BW %{MULTIPART_BOUNDARY_WHITESPACE}, \
DB %{MULTIPART_DATA_BEFORE}, \
DA %{MULTIPART_DATA_AFTER}, \
HF %{MULTIPART_HEADER_FOLDING}, \
LF %{MULTIPART_LF_LINE}, \
SM %{MULTIPART_SEMICOLON_MISSING}, \
IQ %{MULTIPART_INVALID_QUOTING}, \
IF %{MULTIPART_INVALID_HEADER_FOLDING}, \
FE %{MULTIPART_FILE_LIMIT_EXCEEDED}'"
```

Errors specific to the multipart parsers should never occur unless an attacker genuinely tries to bypass ModSecurity by manipulating the request body payload. Some versions of ModSecurity did have false positives in this area, but the most recent version should be false-positive-free. If you do encounter such a problem, feel free to post it to the mod-security-users mailing list. It will mean that you've encountered an interesting attacker or a ModSecurity bug.

PCRE limit errors are available starting with ModSecurity version 2.5.12, when the way PCRE is used was changed to significantly lower the match and recursion limits. SecPcreMatchLimit and SecPcreMatchLimitRecursion were also added to allow users to control these settings. The lower the PCRE limits, the more difficult it is to subvert PCRE and the regular expressions to commit denial of service attacks.

We will leave the PCRE limits defaults as they are, but add a rule to warn us when they are exceeded:

```
SecRule TX:MSC_PCRE_LIMITS_EXCEEDED "@eq 1" \
    "phase:5,t:none,log,pass,msg:'PCRE limits exceeded'"
```

I've used phase 5 for the rule, but if you are really paranoid and think that exceeding PCRE limits is grounds for blocking, switch to phase 2 (and change `pass` to something else).

Verifying Installation

After you're done installing and configuring ModSecurity, it is recommended that you undertake a short exercise to ensure everything is in order:

1. Add a simple blocking rule to detect something in a parameter. For example, the following rule will inspect all parameters for the word `script`, responding with a 503 (*Service Unavailable*) on a match:

```
SecRule ARGS MY_UNIQUE_TEST_STRING \
    "phase:1,log,deny,status:503"
```

2. Restart Apache, using the `graceful` restart option if your server is in production and you don't want any downtime.

3. Send a `GET` request, using your browser, to the ModSecurity-protected server, including the "attack payload" in a parameter (i.e., `http://www.example.com/?test=MY_UNIQUE_TEST_STRING`). ModSecurity should block the request.

4. Verify that the message has appeared in both the error log and the debug log, and that the audit log contains the complete transaction.

5. Submit a `POST` request that triggers the test rule. With this request, you are testing whether ModSecurity will see the request body, and whether it will be able to pass the data in it to your backend after inspection. For this test, in particular, it is important that you're testing with the actual application you want to protect. Only doing so will exercise the entire stack of components that make the application. This test is important because of the way Apache modules are written (very little documentation, so module authors generally employ any approach that "works" for them)—you can generally never be 100% certain that a third-party module was implemented correctly. For example, it is possible to write a module that will essentially hijack a request early on and bypass all the other modules, including ModSecurity. We are doing this test simply because we don't want to leave anything to chance.

6. If you want to be really pedantic (I have been, on many occasion—you can never be too sure), you may want to consider writing a special test script for your application, which will somehow record the fact that it has been invoked (mine usually writes to a file in `/tmp`). By sending a request that includes an attack—which will be intercepted by ModSecurity—and verifying that the script has not been invoked, you can be completely sure that blocking works as intended.

7. Remove the test rule and restart Apache again.

8. Finally, and just to be absolutely sure, examine the permissions on all Apache and ModSecurity locations and verify that they are correct.

You're done!

Summary

In this chapter, we took the time to look at every configuration option of ModSecurity. Strictly speaking, we could have left many of the options at their defaults and spent about a tenth of this time on configuration. But I've always found it better to explicitly define every setting, because with that approach, you end up with the configuration that's tailored to your needs. In addition to that, you get to know ModSecurity better, which might prove crucial at some point in the future.

We didn't pay much attention to logging in this chapter, opting to configure both the debug log and the audit log very conservatively. But there's a wealth of logging options in ModSecurity. In the next chapter, I'll discuss logging in detail, and conclude with the configuration topics.

4 Logging

This section covers the logging capabilities of ModSecurity in detail. Logging is a big part of what ModSecurity does, so it will not surprise you to learn that there are extensive facilities available for your use.

Debug Log

The debug log is going to be your primary troubleshooting tool, especially initially, while you're learning how ModSecurity works. You are likely to spend a lot of time with the debug log cranked up to level 9, observing why certain things work the way they do. There are two debug log directives, as you can see in Table 4.1, "Debug log directives".

Table 4.1. Debug log directives

Directive	Description
SecDebugLog	Path to the debug log file
SecDebugLogLevel	Debug log level

In theory, there are 10 debug log levels, but not all are used. You'll find the ones that are in Table 4.2, "Debug log levels". Messages with levels 1–3 are designed to be meaningful, and are copied to the Apache's error log. The higher-level messages are there mostly for troubleshooting and debugging.

Table 4.2. Debug log levels

Debug log level	Description
0	No logging
1	Errors (e.g., fatal processing errors, blocked transactions)
2	Warnings (e.g., non-blocking rule matches)
3	Notices (e.g., non-fatal processing errors)
4	Informational
5	Detailed
9	Everything!

You will want to keep the debug log level in production low (either at 3 if you want a copy of all messages in the debug log, or at 0 if you're happy with having them only in the error log). This is because you can expect in excess of 50 debug log messages (each message is an I/O operation) and at least 7 KB of data for an average transaction. Logging all that for every single transaction consumes a lot of resources.

This is what a single debug log line looks like:

```
[18/Aug/2009:08:18:08 +0100] [192.168.3.111/sid#80f4e40][rid#81d0588][/index.html]↩
[4] Initialising transaction (txid SopVsH8AAAEAAE8-NB4AAAAD).
```

The line starts with metadata that is often longer than the message itself: the time, client's IP address, internal server ID, internal request ID, request URI, and finally, the debug log level. The rest of the line is occupied by the message, which is essentially free-form. You will find many examples of debug log messages throughout this guide, which I've used to document how ModSecurity works.

Debugging in Production

There's another reason for avoiding extensive debug logging in production, and that's simply that it's very difficult. There's usually so much data that it sometimes takes you ages to find the messages pertaining to the transaction you wish to investigate. In spite of the difficulties, you may occasionally need to debug in production because you can't reproduce a problem elsewhere.

> **Note**
>
> ModSecurity 2.5 extended the audit logging functionality by being able to record in the audit log all the rules that matched. This feature is very helpful, as it minimizes the need for debugging in production, but it still can't tell you why some rules *didn't* match.

One way to make debugging easier is to keep debug logging disabled by default and enable it only for the part of the site that you wish to debug. You can do this by overriding the default configuration using the `<Location>` context directive. While you're doing that, it may be a good idea to specify a different debug log file altogether. That way you'll keep main debug log file free of your tests.

```
<Location /myapp/>
    SecDebugLogLevel 9
    SecDebugLog /opt/modsecurity/var/log/troubleshooting.log
</Location>
```

This approach, although handy, still does not guarantee that the volume of information in the debug log will be manageable. What you really want is to enable debug logging for the requests you send. ModSecurity provides a solution for this by allowing a debug log level to be changed at runtime, on a per-request basis. This is done using the special `ctl` action that allows some of the configuration to be updated at runtime.

All you need to do is somehow uniquely identify yourself. In some circumstances, observing the IP address will be sufficient:

```
SecRule REMOTE_ADDR "@streq 192.168.1.1" \
    phase:1,nolog,pass,ctl:debugLogLevel=9
```

Using your IP address won't work in the cases when you're hidden by a NAT of some sort, and share an IP address with a bunch of other users. One straightforward approach is to modify your browser settings to put a unique identifier in your User-Agent request header. (How exactly that is done depends on the browser you are using. In Firefox, for example, you can add a general.useragent.override setting to your configuration, or use one of the many extensions specifically designed for this purpose.)

```
SecRule REQUEST_HEADERS:User-Agent YOUR_UNIQUE_ID \
    phase:1,nolog,pass,ctl:debugLogLevel=9
```

This approach, although easy, has a drawback: all your requests will cause an increase in debug logging. You may think of an application in terms of dynamic pages, but extensive debug logging will be enabled for every single embedded object, too. Also, if you're dealing with an application that you're using frequently, you may want to avoid excessive logging.

The most accurate way of dynamically enabling detailed debug logging is to manually indicate, to ModSecurity, the exact requests on which you want it to increase logging. You can do this by modifying your User-Agent string on request-by-request basis, using one of the tools that support request interception and modification. (The Tamper Data extension does that for Firefox.) Armed with such a tool, you submit your requests in your browser, modify them in the tool, and then allow them through modified. It's a bit involved, but a time-saver overall. And, while you are at it, it is a good idea to make your identifiers similar enough for your rule to always detect them, but different enough to allow you to use a search function to quickly find the exact request in a file with thousands.

Audit Log

It is a little-known fact that I originally started to work on ModSecurity because I was frustrated with not being able to log full HTTP transaction data. The audit log, which does just that, was one of the first features implemented.

Table 4.3. Audit log directives

Directive	Description
SecAuditEngine	Controls the audit log engine; possible values On, Off, or RelevantOnly
SecAuditLog	Path to an audit log file
SecAuditLog2	Path to another audit log file (copy)
SecAuditLogParts	Specifies which part of a transaction will be logged
SecAuditLogRelevantStatus	Specifies which response statuses will be considered relevant
SecAuditLogStorageDir	Path there concurrent audit log files will be stored
SecAuditLogType	Specifies the type of audit log to use: Serial or Concurrent

A typical audit log entry (short, GET request without a body and no logging of the response body) consumes around 1.3 KB. Requests with bodies will increase the amount of data that needs to be logged, as well as the logging of response bodies.

Logically, each audit log entry is a single file. When serial audit logging is used, all entries will be placed within one file, but with concurrent audit logging, one file per entry is used. Looking at a single audit log entry, you'll find that it consists of multiple independent segments (parts):

```
--6b253045-A--
...
--6b253045-B--
...
--6b253045-C--
...
--6b253045-F--
...
--6b253045-E--
...
--6b253045-H--
...
--6b253045-Z--
```

A segment begins with a boundary and ends when the next segment begins. The only exception is the terminating segment (Z), which consists only of the boundary. The idea behind the use of multiple segments is to allow each audit log entry to contain potentially different information. Only the parts A and Z are mandatory; the use of the other parts is controlled with the SecAuditLogParts directive. Table 4.4, "Audit log parts"contains the list of all audit log parts, along with a description of their purpose.

Table 4.4. Audit log parts

Part letter	Description
A	Audit log header (mandatory)
B	Request headers
C	Request body
D	Reserved
E	Response body
F	Response headers
G	Reserved
H	Audit log trailer, which contains additional data
I	Compact request body alternative (to part C), which excludes files
J	Reserved
K	Contains a list of all rules that matched for the transaction
Z	Final boundary (mandatory)

Audit Log Entry Example

Every audit log entry begins with part A, which contains the basic information about the transaction: time, unique ID, source IP address, source port, destination IP address, and destination port:

```
--6b253045-A--
[18/Aug/2009:08:25:15 +0100] SopXW38EAAE9YbLQ 192.168.3.1 2387 192.168.3.111 8080
```

Part B contains the request headers and nothing else:

```
--6b253045-B--
POST /index.html?a=test HTTP/1.1
Host: 192.168.3.111:8080
User-Agent: Mozilla/5.0
Accept: text/html,application/xhtml+xml,application/xml;q=0.9,*/*;q=0.8
Accept-Language: en-us,en;q=0.5
Accept-Encoding: gzip,deflate
Accept-Charset: ISO-8859-1,utf-8;q=0.7,*;q=0.7
Keep-Alive: 300
Connection: keep-alive
```

```
Referer: http://192.168.3.111:8080/index.html?a=test
Content-Type: application/x-www-form-urlencoded
Content-Length: 6
```

Part C contains the raw request body, typically that of a POST request:

```
--6b253045-C--
b=test
```

Part F contains the response headers:

```
--6b253045-F--
HTTP/1.1 200 OK
Last-Modified: Tue, 18 Aug 2009 07:17:44 GMT
ETag: "6eccf-99-4716550995f20"
Accept-Ranges: bytes
Content-Length: 159
Keep-Alive: timeout=5, max=100
Connection: Keep-Alive
Content-Type: text/html
```

Part E contains the response body:

```
--6b253045-E--
<html><body><h1>It works!</h1></body></html>

<form action="index.html?a=test" method="POST">
<textarea name="b">test</textarea>
<input type=submit>
</form>
```

The final part, H, contains additional transaction information.

```
--6b253045-H--
Stopwatch: 1250580315933960 1902 (551* 580 978)
Response-Body-Transformed: Dechunked
Producer: ModSecurity for Apache/2.5.9 (http://www.modsecurity.org/).
Server: Apache/2.2.11 (Unix) DAV/2
```

Part K contains a list of rules that matched in a transaction. It is not unusual for this part to be empty, but if you have a complex rule set, it may show quite a few rules. Audit logs that record transactions on which there were warnings, or those that were blocked, will contain at least one rule here. In this example you'll find a rule that emits a warning on every request:

```
--6b253045-K--
SecAction "phase:2,auditlog,log,pass,msg:'Matching test'"
```

Every audit log file ends with the terminating boundary, which is part Z:

```
--6b253045-Z--
```

Concurrent Audit Log

Initially, ModSecurity supported only the serial audit logging format. Concurrent logging was introduced to address two issues:

- Serial logging is only adequate for moderate use, because only one audit log entry can be written at any one time. Serial logging is fast (logs are written at the end of every transaction, all in one go) but it does not scale well. In the extreme, a web server performing full transaction logging practically processes only one request at any one time.

- Real-time audit log centralization requires individual audit log entries to be deleted once they are dealt with, which is impossible to do when all alerts are stored in a single file.

Concurrent audit logging changes the operation of ModSecurity in two aspects. To observe the changes, switch to concurrent logging without activating mlogc by changing SecAuditLogType to Concurrent (don't forget to restart Apache).

First, as expected, each audit log entry will be stored in a separate file. The files will not be created directly in the folder specified by SecAuditLogStorageDir, but in an elaborate structure of subfolders whose names will be constructed from the current date and time:

```
./20090822
./20090822/20090822-1324
./20090822/20090822-1324/20090822-132420-SojdH8AAQEAAAugAQAAAAAA
./20090822/20090822-1324/20090822-132420-SojdH8AAQEAAAugAQEAAAAA
```

The purpose of the scheme is to prevent too many files from being created within one directory; many filesystems have limits that can be relatively quickly reached on a busy web server. The first two parts in each filename are based on time (YYYYMMDD and HHMMSS). The third parameter is the unique transaction ID.

In addition to each entry getting its own file, the format of the main audit log file will change when concurrent logging is activated. The file that previously stored the entries themselves will now be used as a record of all generated audit log files.

```
192.168.3.130 192.168.3.1 - - [22/Aug/2009:13:24:20 +0100] "GET / HTTP/1.1" 200 ↵
56 "-" "-" SojdH8AAQEAAAugAQAAAAAA "-" ↵
/20090822/20090822-1324/20090822-132420-SojdH8AAQEAAAugAQAAAAAA 0 1248 ↵
md5:8b097f4f880852e179e7b63b68a7fc92
192.168.3.130 192.168.3.1 - - [22/Aug/2009:13:24:20 +0100] "GET /favicon.ico ↵
HTTP/1.1" 404 267 "-" "-" SojdH8AAQEAAAugAQEAAAAA "-" ↵
/20090822/20090822-1324/20090822-132420-SojdH8AAQEAAAugAQEAAAAA 0 1226 ↵
md5:c76740f076a3cb759d62fb610ab39342
```

The index file is similar in principle to a web server access log. Each line describes one transaction, duplicating some of the information already available in audit log entries. The purpose of the index file is two-fold:

- The first part, which duplicates some of the information available in audit logs, serves as a record of everything that you have recorded so that you can easily search through it.
- The second part tells you where an audit log entry is stored (e.g., /20090822/20090822-1324/20090822-132420-SojdH8AAQEAAAugAQEAAAAA), where it begins within that file (always zero, because this feature is not used), how long it is, and gives you its MD5 hash (useful to verify integrity).

When real-time audit log centralization is used, this information is not written to a file. Instead, it is written to a pipe, which means that it is sent directly to another process, which deals with the information immediately. You will see how that works in the next section.

Remote Logging

ModSecurity comes with a tool called `mlogc` (short for ModSecurity Log Collector), which can be used to transport audit logs in real time to a remote logging server. This tool has the following characteristics:

Secure
The communication path between your ModSecurity sensors and the remote logging server is secured with SSL and authenticated using HTTP Basic Authentication.

Efficient
Remote logging is implemented with multiple threads of execution, which allow for many alerts to be handled in parallel. Existing HTTP connections are reused.

Reliable
An audit log entry will be deleted from the sensor only once its safe receipt is acknowledged by the logging server.

Buffered
The `mlogc` tool maintains its own audit entry queue, which has two benefits. First, if the logging server is not available the entries will be preserved, and submitted once the server comes back online. Second, `mlogc` controls the rate at which audit log entries are submitted, meaning that a burst of activity on a sensor will not result in an uncontrolled burst of activity on the remote logging server.

> **Note**
>
> Remote logging uses a simple but very effective protocol based on HTTP. You'll find it documented in the section called "Remote Logging Protocol" in Chapter 20.

If you've followed my installation instructions, you will have `mlogc` compiled and sitting in your `bin/` folder. To proceed, you will need to configure it, then add it to the ModSecurity configuration.

How Remote Logging Works

Remote logging in ModSecurity is implemented through an elaborate scheme designed to minimize the possibility of data loss. Here is how it's done:

1. ModSecurity processes a transaction and creates an audit log entry file on disk, as explained in the section called "Concurrent Audit Log".

2. ModSecurity then notifies the `mlogc` tool, which runs in a separate process. The notification contains enough information to locate the audit log entry file on disk.

3. The `mlogc` tool adds the audit log entry information to the in-memory queue and to its transaction log (file `mlogc-transaction.log` by default).

4. One of many worker threads that run within `mlogc` takes the audit log entry and submits it to a remote logging server. The entry is then removed from the in-memory queue and the transaction log is notified.

5. A periodic checkpoint operation, initiated by `mlogc`, writes the in-memory queue to the disk (file `mlogc-queue.log` by default) and erases the transaction log.

If `mlogc` crashes, Apache will restart it automatically. When an unclean shutdown is detected, `mlogc` will reconstruct the entry queue using the last known good point (the on-disk queue) and the record of all events since the moment the on-disk queue was created, which are stored in the transaction log.

Configuring Remote Logging

The `mlogc` configuration file is similar to that of Apache, only simpler. First we need to tell `mlogc` where its "home" is, which is where it will create its log files. Log files are very important, because—as it is Apache that starts `mlogc` and ModSecurity that talks to it—we never interact with `mlogc` directly. We'll need to look in the log files for clues in case of problems.

```
# Specify the folder where the logs will be created
CollectorRoot   /opt/modsecurity/var/log

# Define what the log files will be called. You probably
# won't ever change the names, but mlogc requires you
# to define it.
ErrorLog        mlogc-error.log

# The error log level is a number between 0 and 5, with
# level 3 recommended for production (5 for troubleshooting).
ErrorLogLevel 3

# Specify the names of the data files. Similar comment as
# above: you won't want to change these, but they are required.
```

```
TransactionLog mlogc-transaction.log
QueuePath       mlogc-queue.log
LockFile        mlogc.lck
```

Then we tell it where to find audit log entries. The value given to `LogStorageDir` should be the same as the one you provided to ModSecurity's `SecAuditLogStorageDir`:

```
# Where are the audit log entries created by ModSecurity?
LogStorageDir /opt/modsecurity/var/audit
```

Next, we need to tell `mlogc` where to submit the audit log entries. We identify a remote server with a URL and credentials:

```
# Remote logging server details.
ConsoleURI "https://REMOTE_ADDRESS:8888/rpc/auditLogReceiver"
SensorUsername "USERNAME"
SensorPassword "PASSWORD"
```

The remaining configuration directives aren't required, but it's always a good idea to explicitly configure your programs, rather than let them use their defaults:

```
# How many parallel connections to use to talk to the server,
# and how much to wait (in milliseconds) between submissions.
# These two directives are used to control the rate at which
# audit log entries are submitted.
MaxConnections      10
TransactionDelay    50

# How many entries is a single thread allowed to process
# before it must shut down.
MaxWorkerRequests   1000

# How long to wait at startup before really starting.
StartupDelay        5000

# Checkpoints are periods when the entries from the transaction
# log (which is written to sequentially) are consolidated with
# the entries in the main queue.
CheckpointInterval  15

# Back-off time after goes away or responds with a fatal error.
ServerErrorTimeout  60
```

> **Note**
>
> The mlogc tool will take audit log entries created by ModSecurity, submit them to a remote logging server and delete them from disk, but it will leave the empty folders (that were used to store the entries) behind. You will have to remove them yourself, either manually or with a script.

Activating Remote Logging

You will need to make two changes to your default configuration. First you need to switch to concurrent audit logging, because that's the only way mlogc can work:

```
SecAuditLogType Concurrent
```

Next you need to activate mlogc, which is done using the piped logging feature of Apache:

```
SecAuditLog "|/opt/modsecurity/bin/mlogc /opt/modsecurity/etc/mlogc.conf"
```

The pipe character at the beginning of the line tells Apache to treat what follows as a command line. As a result, whenever you start Apache from now on, it will start a copy of mlogc in turn, and keep it running in parallel, leaving a one-way communication channel that will be used by ModSecurity to inform mlogc of every new audit log entry it creates.

Your complete configuration should look like this now:

```
SecAuditEngine RelevantOnly
SecAuditLogRelevantStatus ^5
SecAuditLogParts ABCDEFHKZ
SecAuditLogType Concurrent
SecAuditLog "|/opt/modsecurity/bin/mlogc /opt/modsecurity/etc/mlogc.conf"
SecAuditLogStorageDir /opt/modsecurity/var/audit/
```

If you restart Apache now, you should see mlogc running:

```
USER      PID  COMMAND
root     11845 /usr/sbin/apache2 -k start
root     11846 /opt/modsecurity/bin/mlogc /opt/modsecurity/etc/mlogc.conf
apache   11847 /usr/sbin/apache2 -k start
apache   11848 /usr/sbin/apache2 -k start
apache   11849 /usr/sbin/apache2 -k start
apache   11850 /usr/sbin/apache2 -k start
apache   11851 /usr/sbin/apache2 -k start
```

If you go to the log/ folder, you should see two new log files:

```
dev:/opt/modsecurity/var/log# l
total 1684
drwx------ 2 root root      4096 2009-08-20 10:31 .
drwxr-x--- 7 root apache    4096 2009-08-18 20:01 ..
-rw-r----- 1 root root    926530 2009-08-20 08:09 audit.log
-rw-r----- 1 root root    771903 2009-08-20 08:09 debug.log
-rw-r--r-- 1 root root       696 2009-08-20 10:33 mlogc-error.log
-rw-r--r-- 1 root root         0 2009-08-20 10:31 mlogc-transaction.log
```

If you look at the mlogc-error.log file, there will be signs of minimal activity (the timestamps from the beginning of every line were removed for clarity):

```
[3] [11893/0] Configuring ModSecurity Audit Log Collector 2.5.10-dev2.
```

```
[3] [11893/0] Delaying execution for 5000ms.
[3] [11895/0] Configuring ModSecurity Audit Log Collector 2.5.10-dev2.
[3] [11895/0] Delaying execution for 5000ms.
[3] [11893/0] Queue file not found. New one will be created.
[3] [11893/0] Caught SIGTERM, shutting down.
[3] [11893/0] ModSecurity Audit Log Collector 2.5.10-dev2 terminating normally.
[3] [11895/0] Queue file not found. New one will be created.
```

It is normal for two copies of mlogc to have run, because that's how Apache treats all piped logging programs. It starts two (one while it's checking configuration), but leaves only one running. The second token on every line in the example is the combination of process ID and thread ID. Thus you can see how there are two processes running at the same time (PID 11893 and PID 11895). Because only one program can handle the data files, mlogc is designed to wait for a while before it does anything. Basically, if it still lives after the delay, that means it's the copy that's meant to do something.

What happens if you make an error in the configuration file, which is preventing mlogc from working properly? As previously discussed, mlogc can't just respond to you on the command line, so it will do the only thing it can. It will report the problem and shut down. (Don't be surprised if Apache continues with attempts to start it. That's what Apache does with piped logging programs.)

If you make a mistake in defining the error log, you may actually get an error message in response to the attempt to start Apache. Following is the error message you'd get if you left ErrorLog undefined:

```
dev:/opt/modsecurity/etc# apache2ctl start
[1] [12026/0] Failed to open the error log (null): Bad address
[3] [12026/0] ModSecurity Audit Log Collector 2.5.10-dev2 terminating with error 1
```

If mlogc managed to open its error log, it will do the expected and write all error messages there. For example:

```
[1] [11985/0] QueuePath not defined in the configuration file.
[3] [11985/0] ModSecurity Audit Log Collector 2.5.10-dev2 terminating with error 1
```

At this point, it is a good idea to delete the serial audit log file audit.log, or store it elsewhere. Having switched to concurrent logging, that file won't be updated anymore and it will only confuse you.

Troubleshooting Remote Logging

Assuming default logging configuration (level 3), a single audit log entry handled by mlogc will produce one line in the log file:

```
[3] [2435/693078] Entry completed (0.080 seconds, 9927 bytes): ↵
SsHOykMXI18AAAmnIgAAAABC
```

That's basically all you need to know—that an entry has been safely transmitted to the intended destination. The status codes 200 and 409 are taken to mean that an entry has been successfully processed. The response code 200 indicates that there were no problems with the entry; the response code 409 indicates that the entry is faulty, but that it has been accepted by the server (and that mlogc should delete it and move on).

You will get more information when something gets wrong, of course. For example, you will see the following message whenever your logging server goes down:

```
[2] [2435/693078] Flagging server as errored after failure to submit entry ⏎
SsHPNOMXI18AAAmLHucAAAAG (cURL code 7): couldn't connect to host
```

The message will appear on the first failed delivery, and then once every minute until the server becomes operational. This is because mlogc will shut down its operation for a short period whenever something unusual happens with the server. Only one thread of operation will continue to work to probe the server, with processing returning to full speed once the server recovers. You'll get the following information in the log:

```
[3] [2435/693078] Clearing the server error flag after successful entry ⏎
submission: SsHPNOMXI18AAAmLHucAAAAG
[3] [2435/693078] Entry completed (0.684 seconds, 9927 bytes): ⏎
SsHPNOMXI18AAAmLHucAAAAG
```

Going back to the error message, the first part tells you that there's a problem with the server; the second part tells you what the problem is. In the previous case, the problem was "couldn't connect to host", which means the server is down.

Table 4.5. Common remote logging problems

Error message	Description
couldn't connect to host	The server could not be reached. It probably means that the server itself is down, but it could also indicate a network issue. You can investigate the cURL return code to determine the exact cause of the problem.
Possible SSL negotiation error	Most commonly, this message will mean that you configured mlogc to submit over plain-text, but the remote server uses SSL. Make sure the ConsoleURI parameter starts with "https://".
Unauthorized	The credentials are incorrect. Check the SensorUsername and SensorPassword parameters.
For input string: "0, 0"	A remote server can indicate an internal error using any response status code other than 200 and 409, but such errors are treated as transient. ModSecurity Community Console has a long-standing problem where it responds with a 500 code to an audit log entry that is invalid in some way. The use of the 500 response code makes mlogc pause and attempt to deliver again, only to see the Console fail again. The process continues indefinitely and the only solution at the moment is to track down the offending audit log entry on the sensor and manually delete it.

If you still can't resolve the problem, I suggest that you increase the mlogc error log level from 3 (NOTICE) to 5 (DEBUG2), restart Apache (graceful will do), and try to uncover more information that would point to a solution. Actually, I advise you to perform this exercise even before you encounter a problem, because an analysis of the detailed log output will give you a better understanding of how mlogc works.

File Upload Interception

File upload interception is a special form of logging, in which the files being uploaded to your server are intercepted, inspected, and stored, and all that before they are seen by an application. The directives related to this feature are in Table 4.6, "File upload directives", but you've already seen them all in the section called "File Uploads".

Table 4.6. File upload directives

Directive	Description
SecUploadDir	Specifies the location where intercepted files will be stored
SecUploadFileMode	Specifies the permissions that will be used for the stored files
SecUploadKeepFiles	Specifies whether to store the uploaded files (On, Off, or RelevantOnly)

Storing Files

Assuming the default configuration suggested in this guide, you only need to change the setting of the SecUploadKeepFiles directive to On to start collecting uploaded files. If, after a few file upload requests, you examine /opt/modsecurity/var/upload, you'll find files with names similar to these:

```
20090818-164623-SorMz38AAAEAAFG2AOAAAAAA-file-okOc4T
20090818-164713-SorNAX8AAAEAAFG4AbUAAAAC-file-2ef1eC
```

You can probably tell that the first two parts of a filename are based on the time of upload, then follows the unique transaction ID, the -file- part that is always the same, and a random string of characters at the end. ModSecurity uses this algorithm to generate file names primarily to avoid filename collision and support the storage of a large number of files in a folder. In addition, avoiding the use of a user-supplied file name prevents a potential attacker from placing a file with a known name on a server.

When you store a file like this, it is just a file and it doesn't tell you anything about the attacker. Thus, for the files to be useful, you also need to preserve the corresponding audit log entries, which will contain the rest of the information.

> **Note**
>
> Storage of intercepted files can potentially consume a lot of disk space. If you're doing it, you should at least ensure that the filesystem that you're using for storage is not the root filesystem—you don't want an overflow to kill your entire server.

Inspecting Files

For most people, a more reasonable SecUploadKeepFiles setting is RelevantOnly, which enables the storage of only the files that have failed inspection in some way. For this setting to make sense, you need to have at least one external inspection script along with a rule that invokes it.

A file inspection rule is rather simple:

```
SecRule FILES_TMPNAMES "@inspectFile /opt/modsecurity/bin/file-inspect.pl" \
    phase:2,t:none,log,block
```

This example rule will invoke the script /opt/modsecurity/bin/file-inspect.pl for every uploaded file. The script will be given the location of the temporary file as its first and only parameter. It can do whatever it wants with the contents of the file, but it is expected to return a single line of output that consists of a verdict (1 if everything is in order and 0 for a fault), followed by an error message. For example:

```
1 OK
```

Or:

```
0 Error
```

Following are the debug log lines produced by the inspection file:

```
[4] Recipe: Invoking rule 99e6538; [file "/opt/modsecurity/etc/rules.conf"] ↵
[line "3"].
[5] Rule 99e6538: SecRule "FILES_TMPNAMES" "@inspectFile ↵
/opt/modsecurity/bin/file-inspect.pl" "phase:2,auditlog,t:none,log,block"
[4] Transformation completed in 2 usec.
[4] Executing operator "inspectFile" with param ↵
"/opt/modsecurity/bin/file-inspect.pl" against FILES_TMPNAMES:f.
[9] Target value: ↵
"/opt/modsecurity/var/tmp//20090819-181304-SowyoH8AAQEAACW1AIo-file-ZPtFAq"
[4] Executing /opt/modsecurity/bin/file-inspect.pl to inspect ↵
/opt/modsecurity/var/tmp//20090819-181304-SowyoH8AAQEAACW1AIoAAAAA-file-ZPtFAq.
[9] Exec: /opt/modsecurity/bin/file-inspect.pl
[4] Exec: First line from script output: "1 OK"
[4] Operator completed in 6969 usec.
[4] Rule returned 0.
```

If an error occurs, for example if you make a mistake in the name of the script, you'll get an error message that looks similar to this one:

```
[9] Exec: /opt/modsecurity/bin/file_inspect.pl
[1] Exec: Execution failed while reading output: ↵
/opt/modsecurity/bin/file_inspect.pl (End of file found)
```

> **Tip**
>
> If you write your inspection scripts in Lua, ModSecurity will be able to execute them directly using an internal Lua engine. The internal execution will not only be faster, but from the Lua scripts you will be able to access the complete transaction context (which is not available to any external programs).

Integrating with ClamAV

ClamAV (http://www.clamav.net) is a popular open source anti-virus program. If you have it installed, the following script will allow you to utilize it to scan files from ModSecurity:

```perl
#!/usr/bin/perl

$CLAMSCAN = "/usr/bin/clamscan";

if (@ARGV != 1) {
    print "Usage: modsec-clamscan.pl FILENAME\n";
    exit;
}

my ($FILE) = @ARGV;

$cmd = "$CLAMSCAN --stdout --disable-summary $FILE";
$input = `$cmd`;
$input =~ m/^(.+)/;
$error_message = $1;

$output = "0 Unable to parse clamscan output";

if ($error_message =~ m/: Empty file\.$/) {
    $output = "1 empty file";
}
elsif ($error_message =~ m/: (.+) ERROR$/) {
    $output = "0 clamscan: $1";
}
elsif ($error_message =~ m/: (.+) FOUND$/) {
    $output = "0 clamscan: $1";
}
elsif ($error_message =~ m/: OK$/) {
    $output = "1 clamscan: OK";
}
```

```
print "$output\n";
```

> **Note**
>
> If you need a file to test with, you can download one from http://www.eicar.org/
> anti_virus_test_file.htm. The files at this location contain a test signature that will
> be picked up by ClamAV.

The error message from the integration script will return either the result of the inspection
of the file or an error message if the inspection process failed. Following is an example that
shows a successful detection of a "virus":

```
[9] Exec: /opt/modsecurity/bin/modsec-clamscan.pl
[4] Exec: First line from script output: "0 clamscan: Eicar-Test-Signature"
[4] Operator completed in 2137466 usec.
[2] Warning. File ↵
"/opt/modsecurity/var/tmp//20090819-181833-Sowz6X8AAQEAACXQAWAAAAAB-file-logg59" ↵
rejected by the approver script "/opt/modsecurity/bin/modsec-clamscan.pl": 0 ↵
clamscan: Eicar-Test-Signature [file "/opt/modsecurity/etc/rules.conf"] [line "3"]
```

If you look carefully at the example output, you'll see that the inspection took in excess of
2 seconds. This is not unusual (even for my slow virtual server), because we're creating a
new instance of the ClamAV engine for every inspection. The scanning alone is fast, but the
initialization takes considerable time. A more efficient method would be to use the ClamAV
daemon (e.g., the clamav-daemon package on Debian) for inspection. In this case, the daemon
is running all the time, and the script is only informing it that it needs to inspect a file.

Assuming you've followed the recommendation for the file permissions settings given in the
section called "Folder Locations", this is what you need to do:

1. Change the name of the ClamAV script from clamscan to clamdscan (note the added d
   in the filename).

2. Add the ClamAV user (typically clamav) to the group apache.

3. Relax the default file permissions used for uploaded files to allow group read, by
   changing SecUploadFileMode from 0600 to 0640.

An examination of the logs after the change in the configuration will tell you that there's been
a significant improvement—from seconds to milliseconds:

```
[9] Exec: /opt/modsecurity/bin/modsec-clamscan.pl
[4] Exec: First line from script output: "0 clamscan: Eicar-Test-Signature"
[4] Operator completed in 13329 usec.
[2] Warning. File ↵
"/opt/modsecurity/var/tmp//20090819-182404-Sow1NH8AAQEAACiEAIcAAAAA-file-AMzbgK" ↵
rejected by the approver script "/opt/modsecurity/bin/modsec-clamscan.pl": 0 ↵
clamscan: Eicar-Test-Signature [file "/opt/modsecurity/etc/rules.conf"] [line "3"]
```

Advanced Logging Configuration

By now you have seen how you have many facilities you can use to configure logging to work exactly as you need it. The facilities can be grouped into four categories:

Static logging configuration
The various audit logging configuration directives establish the default (or static) audit logging configuration. You should use this type of configuration to establish what you want to happen in most cases. You should then use the remaining configuration mechanisms (listed next) to create exceptions to handle edge cases.

Setting of the relevant flag on rule matches
Every rule match, unless suppressed, increments the transaction's *relevant* flag. This handy feature, designed to work with the RelevantOnly setting of SecAuditEngine, allows you to trigger transaction logging when something unusual happens.

Per-rule logging suggestions
Rule matching and the actions auditlog and noauditlog do not control logging directly. They should be viewed as mere suggestions—it is up to the engine to decide whether to log a transaction. They are also ephemeral, affecting only the rules with which they are associated. They will be forgotten as the processing moves onto the next rule.

Dynamic logging configuration
Rules can make logging decisions that affect entire decisions (through the ctl action), but that functionality should not be used lightly. Most rules should be concerned only with event generation, restricting their decisions to the suggestions mentioned in the previous. The ability to affect transaction logging should be used by system rules placed in phase 5 and written specifically for the purpose of logging control.

Increasing Logging from a Rule

Using the SecAuditLogParts directive, you will configure exactly what parts (how much information) you want logged for every transaction, but one setting will not be adequate in all cases. For example, most configurations will not be logging response bodies, but that information is often required to determine whether certain types of attack (XSS, for example) were successful.

The following rule will detect only simple XSS attacks, but when it does, it will cause the transaction's response body to be recorded:

```
SecRule ARGS <script> phase:2,log,block,ctl:auditLogParts=+E
```

Dynamically Altering Logging Configuration

The feature discussed in the previous section is very useful, but you may not always like the fact that some rules are changing what you're logging. I know I would not. Luckily, it's a problem that can be resolved with an addition of a phase 5 rule that resets the logged audit log parts:

```
SecAction phase:5,nolog,pass,ctl:auditLogParts=ABCDFGH
```

You can then decide on your own whether the logging of part E is justified. If you are using full audit logging in particular, you will need to manually increase the amount you log per transaction. The HIGHEST_SEVERITY variable, which contains the highest severity of the rules that matched during a transaction, is particularly useful:

```
SecRule HIGHEST_SEVERITY "@le 2" phase:5,nolog,pass,ctl:auditLogParts=+E
```

Removing Sensitive Data from Audit Logs

Most web application programmers are taught to always use POST methods for the transactions that contain sensitive data. After all it is well known that request bodies are never logged, meaning that the sensitive data will never be logged, either. ModSecurity changes this situation, because it allows for full transaction logging. To deal with the sensitive data that may find its way into the logs, ModSecurity uses the sanitation actions sanitiseArg, sanitiseRequestHeader and sanitiseResponseHeader, and sanitiseMatched. You basically just need to tell ModSecurity which elements of a transaction you want removed and it will remove them for you, replacing their values in the log with asterisks. The first three actions all require parameters that you will typically know at configuration time, which means that you will invoke them unconditionally with SecAction. Sanitation works when invoked from any phase, but you should always use phase 5, which is designed for this type of activity.

Use sanitiseArg to prevent the logging of the parameters whose names you know. For example, let's assume that you have an application that uses the parameters password, oldPassword, and newPassword to transmit, well, passwords. This is what you'll do:

```
SecAction phase:5,nolog,pass,\
    sanitiseArg:password,\
    sanitiseArg:oldPassword,\
    sanitiseArg:newPassword
```

Similarly, use sanitiseRequestHeader and sanitiseResponseHeader to remove the contents of the headers whose names you know. For example, if you have an application that uses HTTP Basic Authentication, you will need the following rule to prevent the passwords from being logged:

```
SecAction phase:5,nolog,pass,\
    sanitiseRequestHeader:Authorization
```

The last action, sanitiseMatched, is used when you need to sanitize a parameter whose name you don't know in advance. My first example will sanitize the contents of every parameter that has the word password in the name:

```
SecRule ARGS_NAMES password phase:5,nolog,pass,\
    sanitiseMatched
```

In the following example, we look for anything that resembles a credit card number and then sanitize it:

```
SecRule ARGS @verifyCC phase:5,nolog,pass,\
    sanitiseMatched
```

Selective Audit Logging

Although full transaction logging (the logging of every single byte of every single transaction) sounds good in theory, in practice it is very difficult to use, because it slows down your sever and requires huge amounts of storage space. There are ways to get some of the same benefits for a fraction of cost by using partial full logging on demand.

The trick is to tie in logging to the tracking of IP addresses, users, or sessions. By default you will log only what is relevant, but when you spot something suspicious coming from (for example) an IP address, you may change your logging configuration to turn on full logging for the offending IP address only. Here's how.

First you need to set up IP address tracking. You do this only once for all your rules, so it should usually be part of your main configuration:

```
SecAction phase:1,nolog,pass,initcol:ip=%{REMOTE_ADDR}
```

Now you need to add a phase rule that will trigger logging when something else happens. In the following case, we want to start logging everything coming from an IP address after a single rule match. To achieve that, we set the flag ip.logflag for up to one hour (3600 seconds):

```
SecRule HIGHEST_SEVERITY "@gt 0" \
    phase:5,nolog,pass,setvar:ip.logflag=1,expirevar:ip.logflag=3600
```

Finally, we add a rule that detects the flag and forces logging:

```
SecRule IP:logflag "@gt 0" \
    phase:5,nolog,pass,ctl:auditLogEngine=On
```

Summary

This chapter, along with the two before it, covered the configuration of ModSecurity. You learned how to install ModSecurity and how to configure it, with special attention given to the logging facilities. Logging deserved its own chapter, because configuring a tool to perform certain actions is often only half of the entire story, with the other half consisting of tracking exactly what happened and why. Further, remote logging is a gateway to other systems, which may assist you in managing ModSecurity.

The next three chapters discuss a new topic: rule writing. You'll first read an overview of the entire rule language, followed by a tutorial in rule writing and then by a higher-level discussion on how to place ModSecurity configuration within Apache's own directives. Finally, the interesting bits are here!

5 Rule Language Overview

ModSecurity doesn't do anything implicitly, which is why it has the rule language to enable you to implement the inspection logic and policies exactly as you want them. The rule language may initially appear very simple to you—and it is simple—but it is amazing how powerful and flexible it actually is.

The rule language is implemented using 9 directives, which are listed in Table 5.1, "Rule language directives".

Table 5.1. Rule language directives

Directive	Description
SecAction	Performs an unconditional action. This directive is essentially a rule that always matches.
SecDefaultAction	Specifies the default action list, which will be used in the rules that follow.
SecMarker	Creates a marker that can be used in conjunction with the skipAfter action. A marker creates a rule that does nothing, but has an ID assigned to it.
SecRule	Creates a rule.
SecRuleInheritance	Controls whether rules are inherited in a child configuration context.
SecRuleRemoveById	Removes the rule with the given ID.
SecRuleRemoveByMsg	Removes the rule whose message matches the given regular expression.
SecRuleScript	Creates a rule implemented using Lua.
SecRuleUpdateActionById	Merges the action list of the rule with the given ID with the supplied action list.

The main directive to know is SecRule, which is used to create rules and thus does most of the work. The remainder of this section documents the individual elements that make the rules.

Anatomy of a Rule

Every rule defined by SecRule conforms to the same format, as follows:

```
SecRule VARIABLES OPERATOR [TRANSFORMATION_FUNCTIONS, ACTIONS]
```

You can see all 4 building blocks of the rule language on the list. The 2 building blocks at the end are optional; if they are not explicitly defined in a rule, the defaults (inherited from a previous SecDefaultAction directive) will be used. So what do those building blocks do? Here's what:

Variables

Identify parts of a HTTP transaction that a rule works with. ModSecurity will extract information from every transaction and make it available, through variables, to rules to use. The important thing about variables to remember is that they contain *raw bytes of data*, meaning that they can contain special characters and bytes of any value. They are not text. Your sites may be restricting themselves to using only text in parameters, but that does not mean that your adversaries will. In fact, your adversaries will use whatever helps them achieve their goals. A rule must specify one or more variables.

Operators

Specify how a (transformed) variable is to be analyzed. Regular expressions are the most popular choice, but ModSecurity supports many other operators, and you are even able to write your own. Only one operator is allowed per rule.

Transformation functions

A rule can specify one or more transformation functions. The transformation functions change input in some way before the rule operator is run. They are commonly used to counter evasion, but they can also be used to decode data when necessary.

Actions

Specify what should be done when a rule matches.

Variables

In ModSecurity, variables are used to identify the parts of a HTTP transaction that you wish to inspect. One of the main features of ModSecurity is the fact that it preprocesses raw transaction data and makes it easy for the rules to focus on the logic of detection. There are 77 variables in the most recent version of ModSecurity; they are listed in this section.

Scalar variables

Contain only one piece of information, which could be data or a number. For example, REMOTE_ADDR always contains the IP address of the client.

Collections

Groups of regular variables. Some collections (e.g., ARGS) allow enumeration, making it possible to use every member in a rule. Some other collections (e.g., ENV) are not as flexible, but there is always going to be some way to extract individual regular variables out of them.

Read-only collections

Many of the collections point to some data that cannot be modified, in which case the collection itself will be available only for reading.

Read/write collections

When a collection is not based on immutable data, ModSecurity will allow you to modify it. A good example of a read/write collection is TX, which is a collection that starts empty and exists only as long as the currently processed transaction exists.

Special collections

Sometimes a collection is just a handy mechanism to retrieve information from something that is not organized as a collection but can seem like one. This is the case with the XML collection, which takes an XPath expression as a (mandatory) parameter and allows you to extract values out of an XML file.

Persistent collections

Some collections can be stored into ModSecurity's internal database, where the data can live beyond the life of the current transaction. This feature allows you to adopt a wider view of your systems—for example, tracking access per IP address or per session, or per user account.

Request Variables

Request variables are those extracted from the request part of the transaction that is being inspected. The variables that describe the request line (request method, URI, and protocol information) and the request headers are available from the very beginning, but the complete information may not be available until phase 2 (REQUEST_BODY) begins.

Table 5.2. Request variables

Variable	Description
ARGS	Request parameters (read-only collection)
ARGS_COMBINED_SIZE	Total size of all request parameters combined
ARGS_NAMES	Request parameters' names (collection)
ARGS_GET	Query string parameters (read-only collection)
ARGS_GET_NAMES	Query string parameters' names (read-only collection)
ARGS_POST	Request body parameters (read-only collection)
ARGS_POST_NAMES	Request body parameters' names (read-only collection)
FILES	File names (read-only collection)
FILES_COMBINED_SIZE	Combined size of all uploaded files
FILES_NAMES	File parameter names (read-only collection)
FILES_SIZES	A list of file sizes (read-only collection)
FILES_TMPNAMES	A list of temporary file names (read-only collection)
PATH_INFO	Extra path information
QUERY_STRING	Request query string
REMOTE_USER	Remote user
REQUEST_BASENAME	Request URI basename
REQUEST_BODY	Request body
REQUEST_COOKIES	Request cookies (read-only collection)
REQUEST_COOKIES_NAMES	Request cookies' names (read-only collection)
REQUEST_FILENAME	Request URI file name/path
REQUEST_HEADERS	Request headers (collection, read-only)
REQUEST_HEADERS_NAMES	Request headers' names (read-only collection)
REQUEST_LINE	Request line
REQUEST_METHOD	Request method
REQUEST_PROTOCOL	Request protocol
REQUEST_URI	Request URI, convert to exclude hostname
REQUEST_URI_RAW	Request URI, as it was presented in the request

Server Variables

Server variables contain the pieces of information available to the server, but still related to the ongoing transaction.

Table 5.3. Server variables

Variable	Description
AUTH_TYPE	Authentication type
REMOTE_ADDR	Remote address
REMOTE_HOST	Remote host
REMOTE_PORT	Remote port
SCRIPT_BASENAME	Script basename
SCRIPT_FILENAME	Script file name/path
SCRIPT_GID	Script group ID
SCRIPT_GROUPNAME	Script group name
SCRIPT_MODE	Script permissions
SCRIPT_UID	Script user ID
SCRIPT_USERNAME	Script user name
SERVER_ADDR	Server address
SERVER_NAME	Server name
SERVER_PORT	Server port

Response Variables

Response variables are those extracted from the response part of the transaction that is being inspected. Most response variables will be available in phase 3. The arguably most important response variable, RESPONSE_BODY, is available only in phase 4 (the phase is also called RESPONSE_BODY).

Table 5.4. Response variables

Variable	Description
RESPONSE_BODY	Response body
RESPONSE_CONTENT_LENGTH	Response content length
RESPONSE_CONTENT_TYPE	Response content type
RESPONSE_HEADERS	Response headers (read-only collection)
RESPONSE_HEADERS_NAMES	Response headers' names (read-only collection)
RESPONSE_PROTOCOL	Response protocol
RESPONSE_STATUS	Response status code

Miscellaneous Variables

Miscellaneous variables are exactly what they are called: they are the variables that couldn't fit in any other category.

Table 5.5. Utility variables

Variable	Description
HIGHEST_SEVERITY	Highest severity encountered
MATCHED_VAR	Contents of the last variable that matched
MATCHED_VAR_NAME	Name of the last variable that match
MODSEC_BUILD	ModSecurity build version (e.g., 02050102)
SESSIONID	Session ID associated with current transaction
USERID	User ID associated with current transaction
WEBAPPID	Web application ID associated with current transaction
WEBSERVER_ERROR_LOG	Error messages generated by Apache during current transaction

Parsing Flags

Parsing flags are used by ModSecurity to signal important parsing events. The idea is to avoid taking implicit action (e.g., blocking in response to an invalid request), but allow the rules to decide what to do.

Table 5.6. Request body parsing variables

Variable	Description
MULTIPART_BOUNDARY_QUOTED	Multipart parsing error: quoted boundary encountered
MULTIPART_BOUNDARY_WHITESPACE	Multipart parsing error: whitespace in boundary
MULTIPART_CRLF_LF_LINES	Multipart parsing error: mixed line endings used
MULTIPART_DATA_BEFORE	Multipart parsing error: seen data before first boundary
MULTIPART_DATA_AFTER	Multipart parsing error: seen data after last boundary
MULTIPART_FILE_LIMIT_EXCEEDED	Multipart parsing error: too many files
MULTIPART_HEADER_FOLDING	Multipart parsing error: header folding used
MULTIPART_INVALID_HEADER_FOLDING	Multipart parsing error: invalid header folding encountered
MULTIPART_LF_LINE	Multipart parsing error: LF line ending detected
MULTIPART_SEMICOLON_MISSING	Multipart parsing error: missing semicolon before boundary
MULTIPART_STRICT_ERROR	At least one multipart error except unmatched boundary occurred
MULTIPART_UNMATCHED_BOUNDARY	Multipart parsing error: unmatched boundary detected
REQBODY_PROCESSOR	Request processor that handled request body
REQBODY_PROCESSOR_ERROR	Request processor error flag (0 or 1)
REQBODY_PROCESSOR_ERROR_MSG	Request processor error message

Collections

Collections are the special kind of variables that can contain other variables. With exception of the persistent collections, all collections are essentially one-offs—special variables that give access to the information to which ModSecurity has access.

Table 5.7. Special collections

Variable	Description
ENV	Environment variables (read-only collection, although it's possible to use setvar to change it)
GEO	Geo lookup information from the last @geoLookup invocation (read-only collection)
GLOBAL	Global information, shared by all processes (read/write collection)
IP	IP address data storage (read/write collection)
TX	Transient transaction data (read/write collection)
RULE	Current rule metadata (read-only collection)
SESSION	Session data storage (read/write collection)
USER	User data storage (read/write collection)
XML	XML DOM tree (read-only collection)

Time Variables

Time variables describe the moment in time when the current transaction began.

Table 5.8. Time variables

Variable	Description
TIME	Time (HH:MM:SS)
TIME_DAY	Day of the month (1–31)
TIME_EPOCH	Seconds since January 1, 1970 (e.g., 1251029017)
TIME_HOUR	Hour of the day (0–23)
TIME_MIN	Minute of the hour (0–59)
TIME_MON	Month of the year (0–11)
TIME_SEC	Second of the minute (0–59)
TIME_WDAY	Week day (0–6)
TIME_YEAR	Year

Operators

In ModSecurity, operators are invoked to inspect variables. Most rules will use regular expressions for the inspection, but there will be cases when other operators will be more suitable. Numerical operators, for example, make it possible to compare numerical values, which is difficult to achieve using regular expressions. Similarly, parallel matching, which matches any number of phrases in parallel, achieves much better performance than regular expressions.

There are four operator groups:

- String–matching operators
- Numerical operators
- Validation operators
- Miscellaneous operators

String Matching Operators

String matching operators all take a string on input and attempt to match it to the provided parameter. The @rx and @pm operators are the ones commonly used, because of their versatility (@rx) and speed (@pm), but the remaining operators are also useful, especially if you need variable expansion, which neither @rx nor @pm support.

Table 5.9. String matching operators

Operator	Description
@beginsWith	Input begins with parameter
@contains	Input contains parameter
@endsWith	Input ends with parameter
@rx	Regular pattern match in input
@pm	Parallel pattern matching
@pmFromFile (@pmf in trunk)	Parallel patterns matching, with patterns read from a file
@streq	Input equal to parameter
@within	Parameter contains input

Numerical Operators

Numerical operators, in Table 5.10, "Numerical operators" make comparing numerical values easy (previously, you had to resort to using complex regular expressions). Numerical operators support variable expansion as of ModSecurity 2.5.12.

Table 5.10. Numerical operators

Operator	Description
@eq	Equal
@ge	Greater or equal
@gt	Greater than
@le	Less or equal
@lt	Less than

Validation Operators

Validation operators, listed in Table 5.11, "Validation operators", all validate input in some way.

Table 5.11. Validation operators

Operator	Description
@validateByteRange	Validates that parameter consists only of allowed byte values
@validateDTD	Validates XML payload against a DTD
@validateSchema	Validates XML payload against a schema
@validateUrlEncoding	Validates an URL-encoded string
@validateUtf8Encoding	Validates an UTF-8-encoded string

Miscellaneous Operators

And, finally, there's the miscellaneous category (Table 5.12, "Miscellaneous operators"), which offers some very useful functionality.

Table 5.12. Miscellaneous operators

Operator	Description
@geoLookup	Determines the physical location of an IP address
@inspectFile	Invokes an external script to inspect a file
@rbl	Looks up the parameter against a RBL (real-time block list)
@verifyCC	Checks whether the parameter is a valid credit card number

Actions

Actions make ModSecurity tick. They make it possible to react to events, and, more importantly, they are the glue that holds everything else together and makes the advanced features possible. They are also the most overloaded element of the rule language. Because of the constraints of the Apache configuration syntax, within the rule language that exists, actions are used to carry everything other than variables and operators.

Actions can be split into 7 categories:

- Disruptive actions
- Flow actions
- Metadata actions
- Variable actions
- Logging actions
- Special actions
- Miscellaneous Actions

Disruptive Actions

Disruptive actions (Table 5.13, "Disruptive actions") specify what a rule wants to do on a match. Each rule must be associated with exactly one disruptive action. The pass action is the only exception, as it will allow processing to continue when a match occurs. All other actions from this category will block in some specific way.

Table 5.13. Disruptive actions

Action	Description
allow	Stop processing of one or more remaining phases
block	Indicate that a rule wants to block
deny	Block transaction with an error page
drop	Close network connection
pass	Do not block, go to the next rule
proxy	Proxy request to a backend web server
redirect	Redirect request to some other web server

Flow Actions

Flow actions (Table 5.14, "Flow actions") alter the way rules are processed within a phase.

Table 5.14. Flow actions

Action	Description
chain	Connect two or more rules into a single logical rule
skip	Skip over one or more rules that follow
skipAfter	Skip after the rule or marker with the provided ID

Metadata Actions

Metadata actions (Table 5.15, "Metadata actions") provide additional information about rules. The information is meant to accompany the error messages to make it easier to understand why they occurred.

Table 5.15. Metadata actions

Action	Description
id	Assign unique ID to a rule
phase	Phase for a rule to run in
msg	Message string
rev	Revision number
severity	Severity
tag	Tag

Variable Actions

Variable actions (Table 5.16, "Variable actions") deal with variables. They allow you to set, change, and remove variables.

Table 5.16. Variable actions

Action	Description
capture	Capture results into one or more variables
deprecatevar	Decrease numerical variable value over time
expirevar	Remove variable after a time period
initcol	Create a new persistent collection
setenv	Set or remove an environment variable
setvar	Set, remove, increment, or decrement a variable
setuid	Associate current transaction with an application user ID (username)
setsid	Associate current transaction with an application session ID

Logging Actions

Logging actions (Table 5.17, "Logging actions") influence the way logging is done. The actions that influence logging (auditlog, log, noauditlog, and nolog) only affect the rule in which they reside. To control logging for the transaction as a whole, use the ctl action.

Table 5.17. Logging actions

Action	Description
auditlog	Log current transaction to audit log
log	Log error message; implies auditlog
logdata	Log supplied data as part of error message
noauditlog	Do not log current transaction to audit log
nolog	Do not log error message; implies noauditlog
sanitiseArg	Remove request parameter from audit log
sanitiseMatched	Remove parameter in which a match occurred from audit log
sanitiseRequestHeader	Remove request header from audit log
sanitiseResponseHeader	Remove response header from audit log

Special Actions

Special actions (Table 5.18, "Special actions") are gateways of a sort; they provide access to another class of functionality. The ctl action has several sub-actions of its own and allows engine configuration to be changed (but the changes only affect the ongoing transaction). The multiMatch rule activates a special way of matching in which the rule operator is run after every transformation (normally, the operator is run only once after all transformations). The t action is used to specify zero or more transformations that will be applied to variables before an operator is run.

Table 5.18. Special actions

Action	Description
ctl	Change configuration of current transaction
multiMatch	Activate multi-matching, where an operator runs after every transformation
t	Specify transformation functions to apply to variables before matching

Miscellaneous Actions

Miscellaneous actions (Table 5.19, "Miscellaneous actions") contain the actions that don't belong in any of the groups.

Table 5.19. Miscellaneous actions

Action	Description
append	Append content to response body
exec	Execute external script
pause	Pause transaction
prepend	Prepend content to response body
status	Specify response status code to use with deny and redirect
xmlns	Specify name space for use with XPath expressions

Summary

This chapter gave you a complete overview of the rule language, but that does not mean that you won't need it again in the future. I like to think of this chapter as a map of all ModSecurity features. As with a map, whenever you need to do something with ModSecurity, you can come here to discover whether it's possible and how it can be done. For the details, though, visit one of the subsequent chapters.

The next chapter focuses on rule writing, and it's going to be the most interesting chapter of all you've seen so far. I'd like to think that it's setting a trend, with every new chapter being more interesting than the one before it.

6 Rule Language Tutorial

Now that you have a basic understanding of what the rules look like, I will walk you through some examples that demonstrate the most commonly used functionality.

Introducing Rules

The simplest possible rule will specify only a variable and a regular expression. In the example that follows, we look at the request URI, trying to match the regular expression pattern <script> against it:

```
SecRule REQUEST_URI <script>
```

This simple rule takes advantage of the fact that ModSecurity allows a rule to not specify an operator, in which case it assumes the regular expression operator. This feature is a leftover from ModSecurity 1.x, which supported only regular expressions—there were no operators at all. If you wish, you can always explicitly specify the operator. I usually do. The previous rule is functionally identical to this one:

```
SecRule REQUEST_URI "@rx <script>"
```

Note how I've had to use double quotes because the second parameter now contains a space.

ModSecurity supports a number of operators. Some are similar, but often have different performance characteristics. For example, the regular expression pattern I used for the examples (<script>) isn't much of a pattern. It's just a string, because it does not contain any special characters. I might have just as well written the same rule using the @contains operator:

```
SecRule REQUEST_URI "@contains <script>"
```

By now you are probably aware that the operators are very straightforward. They take a piece of a transaction and analyze it, typically comparing it in some way to the parameter you provided in the rule (<script> in the previous examples).

Working with Variables

You can specify as many variables as you wish in a rule, as long as you separate them using the pipe character:

```
SecRule REQUEST_URI|REQUEST_PROTOCOL <script>
```

Some variables, which we call *collections*, potentially contain more than one piece of information. This is the case with the ARGS variable, for example, which contains all request parameters in a transaction. You use the colon operator to specify only one member of a collection, as you can see in the following rule, which looks only at the parameter named p:

```
SecRule ARGS:p <script>
```

You can use the same collection more than once within the same rule, if you wish:

```
SecRule ARGS:p|ARGS:q <script>
```

The colon operator is actually quite potent and allows you to use a regular expression to specify the names, which is helpful when parameter names change at runtime. The following rule will target all parameters whose names begin with the letter p, catching parameters such as password or pea:

```
SecRule ARGS:/^p/ <script>
```

> **Warning**
>
> As always with regular expressions, take care not to forget to use the ^ and $ anchors when you intend to match complete request parameter names.

When you do not restrict a rule to only certain members of a collection, ModSecurity will assume that you want to use all of them. This is quite handy to use when you don't know what parameters a page uses. Not all collections can be used in this way (for example, ARGS can, but ENV cannot), but when they can, a reference to such a collection will be expanded into individual variables just before a rule is run. You can observe in the debug log how this works. For example, for a request that has the parameters p, q, and z, ARGS expands as follows:

```
[4] Expanded "ARGS" to "ARGS:p|ARGS:q|ARGS:z".
```

Now that you know how expansion works, parameter exclusion will make sense: to remove a parameter from a rule, just put an exclamation point before it. The following rule will look at all request parameters except the one named z:

```
SecRule ARGS|!ARGS:z <script>
```

Combining Rules into Chains

When you specify more than one variable in a rule, you are effectively combining them using the OR logical operator. The rule will match if any of the variables matches. It is also possible to use a logical AND, whereby you combine several rules into one. Let's say that you want to write a rule that matches when something is found in both the parameter p and the parameter q. You write:

```
SecRule ARGS:p <script> chain
SecRule ARGS:q <script>
```

This is called *rule chaining*. The `chain` action constructs a chain of two or more rules and effectively creates a single rule with more than one evaluation step. The first rule in a chain will always run, but the subsequent rules will run only if all the previous rules (in the same chain) ran. Whenever a rule that belongs to a chain does not match, the execution continues with the first rule that is not part of that chain.

Operator Negation

Operator result can be negated by placing an exclamation point right before it. For example, if you wanted to write a rule that matches on a username that is neither admin nor root (the opposite of the intent in the previous example), write this:

```
SecRule ARGS:username "!@rx ^(admin|root)$"
```

Operator negation should not be confused with rule negation. The two are the same only when a rule is used against only one variable, but the situation changes when there are more. Observe the following rule:

```
SecRule ARGS:p|ARGS:q "!@eq 5"
```

The previous rule will match if any one parameter does not equal 5. If you want to write a rule that matches when both parameters do not equal 5, you'll have to use rule chaining:

```
SecRule ARGS:p "!@eq 5" chain
SecRule ARGS:q "!@eq 5"
```

Variable Counting

Here's a question for you: how do you detect something that isn't there? Take the common rule that addresses all parameters in a request:

```
SecRule ARGS <script>
```

In a request without any parameters, ARGS will expand to zero variables. Without any variables to work with, any operator will fail and the rule (or a chain) will not match.

The answer is to use ModSecurity's ability to count how many variables there are in a collection. With the help of the ampersand operator, we can look into ARGS and detect a case in which there are no parameters:

```
SecRule &ARGS "@eq 0"
```

The ampersand operator can be applied to any collection, including a partial one. The following rule will match whenever it sees a request with more than one parameter named username:

```
SecRule &ARGS:username "!@eq 1"
```

Using Actions

Most of the examples in this tutorial, so far, haven't used any actions. I chose to initially focus only on the mechanics of detection. But it is practically impossible to write a rule without specifying a single action. Furthermore, it is good practice to write rules that are self-contained and do not rely on the defaults.

Actions are placed in the third parameter of SecRule and the first parameter of SecAction. A rule can have zero, one, or more actions. If there is more than one action, they are separated with a comma and any number of whitespace characters in between. The following rule specifies two actions:

```
SecRule ARGS K1 log,deny
```

Some actions have parameters, in which case you must place a colon after the action name and follow with the parameter. To deny with status 404, you could use:

```
SecRule ARGS K1 log,deny,status:404
```

Finally, if you want to supply a parameter that uses whitespace or contains a comma, enclose the value in single quotes. This way of parameter handling is often needed with messages:

```
SecRule ARGS K1 "log,deny,msg:'Acme attack detected'"
```

In addition to using single quotes around the parameter to the msg action, I enclosed the entire third directive parameter in double quotes. This is needed for Apache to correctly parse the directive line whenever there is whitespace in the directive parameters. You shall see later that some actions take complex parameters (e.g., ctl and setvar), but the same syntax discussed here applies to them too.

Understanding Action Defaults

You now know how to specify rule actions, but what happens if you don't? ModSecurity has a concept of *default action list*. Whenever a new rule is added to the configuration, the action list of the rule is merged with the default action list. The default action list is currently `phase:2,log,auditlog,pass`, but you can override that at any time using the `SecDefaultAc-tion` directive.

In the simplest case, when the rule being added has no action, the default action list is used instead. Take the following rule (and assume there are no other rules or defaults in the configuration):

```
SecRule ARGS K1
```

After the default action list is taken into consideration, the previous rule looks like this:

```
SecRule ARGS K1 phase:2,log,auditlog,pass
```

In a general case, when a rule has one or more actions, merging means one of two things:

Rule action replaces an action in the default action list
This will typically happen with disruptive actions, of which there can only be one per rule. If there's a disruptive action specified in both the default actions list and the rule, the one in the rule will prevail.

Rule action is appended to the ones in the default action list
Some actions can appear more than once in an action list. This is the case with many non-disruptive actions, such as `t`, `setvar`, `ctl`, and so on. In some cases, it is possible for the rule actions to completely remove the default actions, but how that's done depends on the action in question. With the transformation action, for example, using `t:none` clears the list of transformations and starts over.

The idea with `SecDefaultAction` was to make the job of rule writing easier by allowing you to specify the commonly used actions only once. For example, you could write something like this:

```
SecDefaultAction phase:2,log,deny,status:404
SecRule ARGS K1
SecRule ARGS K2
...
SecRule ARGS K99
```

This approach works well when you're in complete control of your configuration, but it complicates things, because the rules are no longer self-contained. The rules are perhaps easier to write initially, but at the price of being more difficult to understand when you come back to them in a couple of months. Furthermore, there's always a danger that there will be unforeseen interaction between the defaults and the rule. For example, suppose that you write a rule that relies on certain default values, but then you later change the defaults without realizing how you're affecting the rules. This is particularly true if you place any transformation functions in the default list:

```
SecDefaultAction phase:2,log,pass,t:lowercase
```

```
SecRule ARGS K1 t:urlDecode
```

> **Note**
>
> You should always write rules to specify the complete list of transformation functions
> that they depend on. To achieve this, always specify t:none as the first transformation
> function, which will reset the transformation pipeline.

Another peculiarity with the SecDefaultAction directive is that it can be used more than once.
Every time you use it, the default action list is changed. For example:

```
# First we have some rules that only warn
SecDefaultAction phase:2,log,pass
SecRule ARGS W1
SecRule ARGS W2
...
SecRule ARGS W19

# Now we have some rules that block
SecDefaultAction phase:2,log,deny,status:500
SecRule ARGS B1
...
SecRule ARGS B89
```

The bottom line is that even though SecDefaultAction is quite powerful and allows you to
specify any action, you should use it only to specify the default blocking method. Anything
other than that is asking for trouble! Because of that, and because of some other issues that
occur whenever SecDefaultAction is used in configuration with multiple contexts (which will
be explained in the section called "SecDefaultAction Inheritance Anomaly" in Chapter 7),
there is a good probability that SecDefaultAction will be deprecated and replaced with a safer
mechanism in the future.

Actions in Chained Rules

Special rules apply to the placement of actions in chained rules. Because several chained rules
form a single complex rule, there can only be one disruptive action for the entire chain. Similarly, there can only be one set of metadata rules. By convention, the disruptive action and
the metadata actions are placed with the first rule in a chain:

```
SecRule ARGS K1 chain,id:1001,log,deny
SecRule ARGS k2
```

That example looks innocent enough, but trouble begins once you start to write complex
chained rules (as most are), when you will have to mix non-disruptive actions with the disruptive ones. For example:

```
SecRule ARGS K1 chain,id:1001,log,deny,setvar:tx.score=+1
```

```
SecRule ARGS K2 setvar:tx.score=+1
```

Although the disruptive actions require special treatment when used in rule chains, the other actions don't. That means that a non-disruptive action associated with a rule executes as soon as the rule matches, even when the rule is a part of a chain. Only the disruptive actions execute at the end, when the last rule in the chain matches.

In hindsight, the last rule in a chain is a much better location for the disruptive and metadata rules, but it's too late to change that at this point.

Unconditional Rules

The actions that you specify in a SecRule execute when a match occurs, but you can use the SecAction directive to do something unconditionally. This directive accepts only one parameter, which is identical to the third parameter of SecRule, and it's a list of actions that you want to be executed:

```
SecAction nolog,pass,setvar:tx.counter=10
```

The SecAction directive is useful in the following cases:

- To initialize one or more variables before the rules that use them are processed.

- To initialize a persistent collection, most often using a client's IP address.

- In combination with skip, to implement an if-then-else construct (described later in this chapter).

Using Transformation Functions

You already know that rules typically work by taking some data determined by a variable name and applying an operator to it. But direct matching like that happens only in the simplest case. In a general case, the data processed by a rule will be transformed by one or more transformation functions before it is fed to an operator. The transformation functions are often referred to as a transformation pipeline.

As an example, take the following rule, which transforms input by converting all characters into lowercase, then compressing multiple consecutive whitespace characters:

```
SecRule ARGS "@contains delete from" \
    phase:2,t:lowercase,t:compressWhitespace,block
```

As a result, the rule will match all the following forms of input:

```
delete from
DELETE FROM
```

```
deLeTe fRoM
Delete   From
DELETE\tFROM -- \t represents a TAB character
```

> **Note**
>
> It is a good practice to always begin the list of transformation functions with t:none, which clears the transformation pipeline to start from scratch. If you don't do that, then you—as a rule writer—can never be completely sure that your user didn't specify a transformation function in his or her SecDefaultAction directive (on purpose or by mistake), in which case your rule will probably malfunction. Using t:none ensures that your rules use only the transformation actions you specified.

There are several reasons why you might want to apply operators to something other than the original variable values:

- Your input is not available in a form that is useful to you. For example, it might be Base64-encoded, in which case you won't be able to do anything useful with it. By applying the transformation function that decodes Base64 data (t:base64Decode), you "open" up the data for inspection.

- Similarly, you may need a piece of data in some other form. If you have some binary data that you need to record in a user-friendly manner, you will probably encode it as hex characters using t:hexEncode.

- Sometimes rules are difficult or impossible to write in order to deal with input in its original form. Take, for example, case sensitivity. Most ModSecurity operators are case-sensitive, but there are many occasions when case does not matter. If you attempt to match a nontrivial string using a case-sensitive matching function, you will soon discover that you need to write either a number or rules (each with a different combination of lowercase and uppercase letters) or a rule with a very ugly and difficult-to-decipher regular expression. You deal with this particular problem by transforming input into lowercase before matching.

- In the majority of cases, however, you will use transformation functions to counter evasion. Evasion is a technique often used by attackers to bypass existing detection and protection mechanisms. They will take advantage of the specific context in which attack payload data is processed to modify it in such a way as to evade detection, but remain effective.

Blocking

Regardless of whether you use actions, every ModSecurity rule is always associated with one (and only one) disruptive action. The disruptive actions are those that interrupt rule processing within a phase. A disruptive action can do one of three things:

Continue with the next rule

This is a special case of a disruptive action that doesn't disrupt. Use the `pass` action whenever you want to only warn about a potential issue, or if you want to have a rule that changes something else in the transaction or persistent state (e.g., increments a counter).

Stop processing phase but continue with transaction

The `allow` action is used for whitelisting. It allows transactions to proceed without further inspection. Depending on how you use `allow`, you may choose to skip just the current phase, the request inspection phases (phases 1 and 2) or all remaining inspection phases (the logging phase always runs). Whitelisting is so often used that I dedicate the section called "Whitelisting" in Chapter 7 to it.

Stop processing phase and block transaction

Blocking is a last-resort measure you undertake to either protect your web applications or turn away undesirable clients (e.g., worms, bots, and the like). The best way for a rule to block is by using the `block` action, which indicates blocking but does not state how it is to be done. Another advantage of `block` is that it can be overridden by the rule administrator. If you use any of the other blocking actions (`deny`, `drop`, `redirect`, or `proxy`), you are essentially hard-coding policy in rules. That may be all right if you are writing one-off rules for yourself, but be warned that for others to use your rules, they will probably have to change them to suit their circumstances.

If you are very interested in blocking, head to the section called "Advanced Blocking" in Chapter 9, which covers the topic in detail.

Changing Rule Flow

The assumption with ModSecurity rules is that they will be processed one by one, starting with the first rule in a phase and ending with the last. If a match occurs somewhere in the phase and blocking takes place, phase processing will stop, but the execution of the rules is still linear. But there is only so much you can achieve by executing rules in that fashion. Sometimes you will want to form rule groups and create if-then-else constructs, and for that you will need the actions that change the way rules flow.

Historically, the first skipping action supported by ModSecurity was `skip`, which takes one parameter and skips over as many rules as you specify. Rule skipping does not make any sense when used with a disruptive action, which means that you will use `skip` only in combination with `pass`. The following example demonstrates `skip`:

```
SecRule ARGS K1 id:1,nolog,pass,skip:2
SecRule ARGS K2 id:2,nolog,pass
SecRule ARGS K3 id:3,log,block
```

In this example, when rule 1 matches, it will skip the next two rules. It is as simple as that.

You should have the following in mind:

- When you form a chain of two or more individual rules, the entire chain counts as one rule for the sake of skipping.

- You can use skip in a chain, but the same rules as for the disruptive actions apply: only one skip is allowed and it has to be placed within the chain starter rule.

- Skipping only works within the same phase as the rule that initiated it. As far as ModSecurity is concerned, the rule in other phases simply do not exist.

Skipping is often used as an optimization technique. Sometimes executing a group of rules makes sense only under a specific condition and executing them otherwise is a waste of CPU power. In such cases, you will typically precede the group with a single rule that tests for the condition and jumps over the entire group of rules if the condition is not true.

Over time, several problems were identified with the skip action. First, counting the rules you wish to skip over is not very interesting, and it's easy to make a mistake. It also makes maintenance difficult. Every time you want to make changes to your rules you have to first remember that you have a skipping rule in the neighborhood, then look at it and figure out whether you need to update the skip parameter. There is also a potentially big problem that occurs when you use SecRuleRemoveById or SecRuleRemoveByMsg to remove a rule that is skipped over. With one fewer rule to skip over, the skip action will consume the intended next rule. The following example demonstrates this problem:

```
SecRule ARGS K1 id:1,nolog,pass,skip:1
SecRule ARGS K2 id:2,nolog,pass
SecRule ARGS K3 id:3,nolog,pass

...

SecRuleRemoveById 2
```

Rule 1 wants to skip over rule 2 on a match, but because we remove rule 2 later in the configuration, rule 1 will skip over rule 3 instead.

Smarter Skipping

After identifying the problems with skip, we decided to improve the rule language slightly and added skipAfter and SecMarker to the rule language. The first example, rewritten to use the new facilities, looks like this:

```
SecRule ARGS K1 id:1,nolog,pass,skipAfter:4
SecRule ARGS K2 id:2,nolog,pass,skipAfter:4
SecRule ARGS K3 id:3,log,block
SecMarker 4
```

When you use `skipAfter`, it will start to examine all the rules to follow to find the one with the specified ID. Once found, rule execution will continue with the next rule. This really means that you don't always need to use `SecMarker`. In many cases, `skipAfter` alone will work just fine. The same example can be rewritten like this:

```
SecRule ARGS K1 id:1,nolog,pass,skipAfter:3
SecRule ARGS K2 id:2,nolog,pass,skipAfter:3
SecRule ARGS K3 id:3,log,block
```

If-Then-Else

You can implement a primitive if-then-else construct if you use `skip` and `SecAction` together:

```
SecRule ARGS K1 id:1,nolog,pass,skip:2
SecRule ARGS K2 id:2,block
SecAction nolog,pass,skip:1
SecRule ARGS K3 id:3,block
```

The first rule in the example determines which of the two paths will be processed. If it matches, the `skip` action is executed to skip to rule 3. However, if the first rule doesn't match, the next rule, rule 2, will be processed. The unconditional match in `SecAction`, which follows rule 2, ensures that rule 3 is not processed if there is no match in rule 1.

Skipping using markers doesn't make the rules easier to read, although it makes large rule groups easier to maintain:

```
SecRule ARGS K1 id:1,nolog,pass,skipAfter:11
SecRule ARGS K2 id:2,block
SecAction nolog,pass,skipAfter:12
SecMarker 11
SecRule ARGS K3 id:3,block
SecMarker 12
```

Controlling Logging

There are several logging actions that a rule can use, and they fall into two groups. (As a reminder, you can find the list of all logging rules in Table 5.17, "Logging actions".) The first group consists of the actions that influence only what happens during the processing of the current rule; such actions are used in virtually every rule and I cover them in this section. The actions in the second group influence how logging is done on a transaction level, and they are normally only used in configuration rules. I will not cover the second group here, because the common use cases are already covered in the section called "Advanced Logging Configuration".

Going back to the first group, the most common usage is as follows:

```
SecRule ARGS K1 log,auditlog,block
```

If that rule matches, the actions `log` and `auditlog` tell the engine to emit an alert and log the transaction to the audit log, respectively. I will let you in on a secret. The `log` action actually implies `auditlog`, so it is always safe to use only the first. (The same is true for the actions that ask for no logging: `nolog`, the opposite of `log`, implies `noauditlog`, which is the opposite of `auditlog`.) There are two things to consider:

1. An alert is a record of a rule match that will appear in the debug log, in the Apache's error log, and in the H section of an audit log entry. Because there are two pairs of actions (`log` and `nolog`, and `auditlog` and `noauditlog`) you can decide exactly what happens, logging-wise, when a rule matches. Most rules will want both, but you may also log a match only to the error log and not have an entire audit log entry (which you achieve with `log,noauditlog`).

2. When a rule specifies `auditlog`, that does not mean that an audit log will be created. You should think about auditlog as *asking* for a transaction to be recorded, but a detection rule will not normally have full control over what will actually happen. ModSecurity classifies transactions as relevant or not relevant. When a rule matches and when it specifies `auditlog` (either explicitly, or implicitly through `log` without `noauditlog`), ModSecurity will set the relevancy flag. This will normally cause the transaction to be recorded, but, as we have seen in the section called "Advanced Logging Configuration", a subsequent rule can override that decision. This separation of concerns is intentional. Rules should only indicate what they want to achieve, but it is the administrator who should have the final say.

Capturing Data

The TX collection has 10 variables whose names are just digits from 0 to 9. Those variables are reserved for *data capture*, which is primarily a feature of the @rx operator. To make use of this feature, you have to do two things:

1. Use capturing parentheses within regular expression patterns to specify where capture should take place

2. Add the `capture` action to the rule in which you wish data capture to take place

Suppose you are dealing with a web application that places session identifiers in the request line. In order to support session state, you must extract the session information and initialize session state. The URI used in the application and containing a session identifier could look like this:

```
http://www.example.com/69d032331009e7b0/index.html
```

Your rule to extract the session identifier will use a regular expression data capture:

```
# Initialize session state from the session identifier in URI
SecRule REQUEST_URI ^/([0-9a-fA-f]{16})/ phase:1,nolog,pass,capture,setsid:%{TX.1}
```

> **Note**
>
> Although the previous example neatly demonstrates the data capture mechanism, that one rule alone is not enough for a correct implementation of session management. For complete coverage refer to the section called "Session Management" in Chapter 8.

Here is what happens on a successful match:

```
[4] Recipe: Invoking rule 8e8b5c8; [file "/home/ivanr/apache/conf/httpd.conf"] ↵
[line "479"].
[5] Rule 8e8b5c8: SecRule "REQUEST_URI" "@rx ^/([0-9a-fA-f]{16})/" ↵
"phase:1,auditlog,nolog,pass,capture,setsid:%{TX.1}"
[4] Transformation completed in 2 usec.
[4] Executing operator "rx" with param "^/([0-9a-fA-f]{16})/" against REQUEST_URI.
[9] Target value: "/69d032331009e7b0/index.html"
[9] Added regex subexpression to TX.0: /69d032331009e7b0/
[9] Added regex subexpression to TX.1: 69d032331009e7b0
[4] Operator completed in 63 usec.
```

The TX.0 variable will always contain the entire part of the input that was matched (/69d032331009e7b0/ in the example; note the forward slashes at the beginning and at the end of the value). If your regular expression uses the ^ and $ anchors, TX.0 will contain the entire input. In the example, I used only one of the anchors, so TX.0 contains the data from the beginning of input, but only until the end of the matching part (the second forward slash). The TX.1 variable will contain just the part that was enclosed in the first parentheses set that appeared in the pattern. The TX.2 variable will draw its contents from the second set of parentheses, and so on. Up to 9 captures will be created.

> **Note**
>
> If there is no match, the data capture variables will not be changed. However, if there is a match, the unused data capture variables will be unset.

The @pm and @pmFromFile operators have limited support for data capture: if the capture action was specified, the TX.0 variable will be populated with the input data matched. There is no need to use parentheses in the patterns anywhere.

Variable Manipulation

Although most of the data you'll be dealing with will be read-only, generated by Apache and ModSecurity as they parse transaction data, there are certain variables and collections that you are allowed to change. The TX collection is a private, per-transaction space that rules can use to collaborate. The variables placed in TX can be retrieved using the same approach as for other collections. The setvar action, however, allows the values to be changed.

To create a new variable, simply set its value to something:

```
SecAction nolog,pass,setvar:tx.score=1
```

To delete a variable, place an exclamation point before the name:

```
SecAction nolog,pass,setvar:!tx.score
```

Numerical values can be incremented or decremented. The following example first increments a variable by 2 then decrements it by 1:

```
SecAction nolog,pass,setvar:tx.score=+2
SecAction nolog,pass,setvar:tx.score=-1
```

Although collaboration within the same transaction is very interesting and useful, variable manipulation becomes more exciting when combined with the persistent storage functionality and the expirevar and deprecatevar actions (covered in Chapter 8, *Persistent Storage*).

Variable Expansion

In many text contexts, ModSecurity supports a feature known as variable expansion. The reference manual refers to it as macro expansion, but I think that is rather ambitious, at least at this time. Variable expansion enables you to put data into text, which can be very useful. You may recall that I used variable expansion in the system rules in the section called "Handling Processing Errors":

```
SecRule REQBODY_PROCESSOR_ERROR "!@eq 0" \
    "phase:2,t:none,log,block,msg:'Failed to parse request body: ↩
%{REQBODY_PROCESSOR_ERROR_MSG}',severity:2"
```

The idea is that when a fault occurs during request body parsing, you are able to see what the actual error was. Variable expansion takes place whenever ModSecurity encounters a variable name enclosed in %{...}, which is a syntax that ModSecurity adopted from mod_rewrite. The variable name can be anything, and you are able to access collections using the familiar syntax %{COLNAME.VARNAME}.

> **Note**
>
> The difference between COLNAME:VARNAME and COLNAME.VARNAME is that the former potentially returns more than one result, whereas the latter will always return one result (or no result at all).

Most parts of the rule language support variable expansion; many features actually require it. For example, session or IP address tracking would be impossible without the ability to somehow handle a piece of data received from a client. Having said that, don't be surprised if you encounter a part of the rule language that does not support this feature. If that happens, you are advised to report the problem to the issue tracker. Initially, the support for this feature was added only to the places where it was needed. By popular demand, the support expanded over time, but there may still be places where variable expansion does not work.

Here's an interesting example that uses variable expansion, where one piece of a request is compared to another one, from the same request:

```
# If an absolute URI (containing hostname) was given on the request
# line, check that the same hostname is used in the Host header
SecRule REQUEST_URI_RAW "@beginsWith http" "chain,phase:2,block,msg:'Hostname ↵
mismatch'"
    SecRule REQUEST_URI_RAW "!@beginsWith http://%{REQUEST_HEADERS.Host}"
```

Variable expansion is not supported by the regular expression and parallel matching operators, for performance reasons. Both @rx and @pm split their work into two steps. They do as much work as possible up front, compiling patterns into more efficient internal representations. Then, in the second step, they perform matching. The compilation of patterns is done only once, at configuration time, thus requiring the patterns to be static. On the upside, the matching is much faster. Variable expansion is where the string operators other than @rx and @pm have a rare advantage.

Recording Data in Alerts

The one remaining unmentioned log action is logdata, whose purpose is to take a piece of data you specify and include it along with other alert information.

Consider the following rule, which looks for JavaScript event handlers in input:

```
SecRule ARGS "\bon(abort|blur|change|click|dblclick|dragdrop|end|error|\
focus|keydown|keypress|keyup|load|mousedown|mousemove|mouseout\
mouseover|mouseup|move|readystatechange|reset|resize|select|submit|unload)\b\W*?=" \
    phase:1,t:none,t:lowercase,log,deny,capture,logdata:%{TX.0}
```

This rule may seem a bit intimidating at first glance, although it is conceptually simple. If you read the regular expression pattern carefully, you will see that all the patterns we are looking for share the beginning, have a part in the middle that is different, and share the end. So it's not that difficult after all. However, consider the following:

- Alert messages do not display input data. Thus, looking at an alert message alone, you will not be able to tell which part of the pattern matched, and you will have to seek access to the entire audit log. Even when it's possible to get it, it will still be time-consuming.

- Even with access to the audit log, tracking down the part of the input that matched may not be simple. When this sort of rule matches, it typically happens with request parameters that are quite long. So what you'd need to do first is understand what the

rule does and then effectively perform manual pattern matching by reading through
every parameter.

- Matching takes place against potentially transformed input, so often the raw input will
not contain the data in the form used for matching.

These problems are resolved when you use the logdata action. Have a look at the following
alert (just the emphasized part):

```
[Fri Dec 04 17:00:01 2009] [error] [client 192.168.3.1] ModSecurity: Access denied
with code 403 (phase 1). Pattern match "\\bon(abort|blur|change|click|dblclick
|dragdrop|end|error|focus|keydown|keypress|keyup|load|mousedown|mousemove
|mouseoutmouseover|mouseup|move|readystatechange|reset|resize|select
|submit|unload)\\b\\W*?=" at ARGS:p. [file "/home/ivanr/apache/conf/httpd.conf"]
[line "472"] [data "onload="] [hostname "192.168.3.100"] [uri "/"]
[unique_id "SxlAEcCoA2QAABLXHEAAAAAB"]
```

The capture action from the rule told the regular expression operator (@rx) to place the entire
matching area into the variable TX.0. The logdata:%{TX.0} part of the rule told the engine to
include the value of the TX.0 variable in the alert. The end result is that you now know, at a
glance, exactly what matched.

> ### Note
>
> At this point you may ask why we have logdata, when it is perfectly possible to use
> variable expansion in the msg action. There's only one reason: when you place a piece
> of data as part of the message, a programmatic parser will not know about that. To
> a computer, the entire message is just some text. But if you include the same data in
> an alert with logdata, the same parser will know that it is something that originated
> in input, and it can do something useful with it. It could, for example, highlight the
> piece of data on the alert page.

Adding Metadata

Although some rules are simple and do not require much thought to understand them, many
aren't. Also, even when the rule itself is simple, that does not mean that it will be easy to
understand what it does and why it does it. ModSecurity will generally try to add as much
metadata to alerts as possible. Consider the following rule, which gets the job done:

```
SecRule REQUEST_METHOD "!^(GET|HEAD)$" \
    phase:1,t:none,log,block
```

It restricts request methods to either GET or HEAD, which is suitable only for a static web site.
The rule will, on a match, produce the following alert:

```
[Thu Dec 03 20:02:50 2009] [error] [client 127.0.0.1] ModSecurity: ↵
Warning. Match of "rx ^(GET|HEAD)$" against "REQUEST_METHOD" required.↵
```

```
[file "/home/ivanr/apache/conf/httpd.conf"] [line "464"]↵
[hostname "192.168.3.100"] [uri "/"] [unique_id "SxgbacCoA2QAABC7HMgAAAAB"]
```

Alert messages contain quite a lot of information by default, but they do not provide enough. For example, the default message generated by ModSecurity gives you some idea about what the rule looks like, but it doesn't tell you what the rule writer wanted to accomplish. This is where metadata actions come into play. They are primarily used to document rules and make them easier to handle. Here is the same rule as earlier, but with additional metadata:

```
SecRule REQUEST_METHOD "!^(GET|HEAD)$" \
    "phase:1,t:none,log,block,id:1001,rev:2,\
    severity:WARNING,msg:'Request method is not allowed'"
```

I have added four metadata actions:

- The `id` action assigns a unique identifier to the rule, making it possible to match an alert to the rule that caused it. The addition of the ID also makes it possible for the rule to be manipulated, either at configuration time or at runtime. The IDs are very important, because they allow rule sets to be customized while leaving the original configuration files intact (for example, using the `SecRuleUpdateById` and `SecRuleRemoveById` directives), which, in turn, allows for the automated upgrades of rule sets.

- The `rev` action (short for revision) is essentially a change counter, or a serial number: it starts at 1 and increments by one every time a rule changes. The idea is to make it possible to determine, at a glance, whether a rule changed and, even better, to make it possible for a program (which wouldn't be able to understand the differences between two rule versions anyway) to do that.

- The `severity` action tells you how serious a detected problem is. ModSecurity adopted the *syslog* system of severities, which are listed in Table 18.1, "Severity values". The least serious severity is `DEBUG` (7) and the most serious one is `EMERGENCY` (1). However, there are no clear guidelines for how to assign severities to rules, leaving each author to adopt his or her own system.

- The `msg` action adds another message to the rule, which should explain the goal of a rule, or its result.

The information in metadata actions is always used in alerts. The improved rule produces the following alert:

```
[Thu Dec 03 20:11:25 2009] [error] [client 127.0.0.1] ModSecurity: Warning. ↵
Match of "rx ^(GET|HEAD)$" against "REQUEST_METHOD" required. ↵
[file "/home/ivanr/apache/conf/httpd.conf"] [line "465"] [id "1001"] [rev "2"] ↵
[msg "Request method is not allowed"] [severity "EMERGENCY"] ↵
[hostname "192.168.3.100"] [uri "/"] [unique_id "SxgZZsCoA2QAABCYL9IAAAAA"]
```

That's much better, but the alert still does not explain why we do not allow any request method other than GET or HEAD. Let's try again:

```
# Do not allow request methods other than GET or HEAD. Allow
# site does not currently use any other methods; restricting
# the methods allowed reduces the attack surface.
SecRule REQUEST_METHOD "!^(GET|HEAD)$" \
    "phase:1,t:none,log,block,id:1001,rev:2,\
    severity:WARNING,msg:'Request method is not allowed because \
it is not used by the application',tag:HARDENING"
```

This latest batch of improvements added a long description of the rule functionality and also improved the alert message. In addition, I also used the tag action to categorize the rule. Tags are pieces of text that can be attached to rules. It is possible to attach one or more tags. By convention, the first tag defines rule's primary category, and all other tags define secondary categories. Knowing the category for a rule helps you understand what the rule does. Categories also enable monitoring systems that collect alerts to construct pretty alert pie charts with little effort (e.g., displaying how many alerts of each category occurred in a time period). There are no clear guidelines for how to use tags, either. The Core Rule Set does use them to categorize rules, but it does not document the categories (and does not guarantee that the categories won't change).

Embedded vs. Reverse Proxy Mode

ModSecurity doesn't care whether it is deployed in embedded or reverse proxy mode. In the reverse proxy mode, Apache takes care of the transfer of data to the backend server and back, so there is very little for ModSecurity to worry about. There are only few small differences, which I am listing here for reference:

1. In an embedded scenario, there will typically be a resource (a script or a file) that is used to fulfill each request. ModSecurity rules can inspect the properties of such files (the SCRIPT_* family of variables allows access). In the reverse proxy mode, virtually all requests will be fulfilled by backend servers, which means that local resources won't be used and that the use of the variables that reference them makes little sense.

2. When embedded, ModSecurity gives access to the web server environment and error log. When used in a reverse proxy, you still get access to both the environment and the error log, but to those of the reverse proxy. The backend servers will have their own environments and error logs, which ModSecurity can't access.

3. Apache's <Directory>, <DirectoryMatch>, <Files> and <FileMatch> configuration contexts never match when used in a reverse proxy.

4. There are potential evasion issues when a reverse proxy is used in front of a backend system that interprets URIs differently (e.g., if you have a Unix box in front of a Windows box). In such cases, you have to be very careful if you're using the <Location> configuration context. The <Location> configuration context is case-sensitive and rec-

ognizes only forward slashes, whereas other platforms may have filesystems that are case-insensitive, or web servers that support the backslash as the URI path separator.

Table 6.1. Variables sensitive to operating mode

Variable	Availability in reverse proxy mode
AUTH_TYPE	Reverse proxy authentication
PATH_INFO	Not available
ENV	Reverse proxy environment
SCRIPT_BASENAME	Not available
SCRIPT_FILENAME	Not available
SCRIPT_GID	Not available
SCRIPT_GROUPNAME	Not available
SCRIPT_MODE	Not available
SCRIPT_UID	Not available
SCRIPT_USERNAME	Not available
SERVER_ADDR	Reverse proxy address
SERVER_NAME	Reverse proxy name
SERVER_PORT	Reverse proxy port
WEBSERVER_ERROR_LOG	Reverse proxy error log

Summary

Now that you've completed the rule tutorial, you should have a good understanding of rule writing. I thoroughly enjoyed working on this chapter, because it reminded me of every single rule feature—even the ones I don't use very often. It also reminded me of what it was like to add all of these features to ModSecurity, one by one, across a period of several years.

In the next chapter, we turn our attention to ModSecurity's existence within Apache. You'll learn the minimum necessary about how Apache handles its configuration files, which will help you organize your rules effectively. You'll also learn about configuration contexts and inheritance, concepts that will allow you to both simplify your configuration and use different configuration for different sites and applications in the same server.

7 Rule Configuration

This chapter is the last in the series of chapters that cover the core language. Whereas the previous chapter focused on how to write individual rules, this chapter focuses on the higher-level concepts:

- Apache configuration syntax
- How ModSecurity fits into Apache configuration files
- Configuration contexts and inheritance
- Rule manipulation

Apache Configuration Syntax

In the first instance, you should view Apache configuration as a single file that consists of many lines of text. In reality, any configuration can be split among many files, but that's only for our convenience. To Apache, it's just line after line after line.

If you take a look at a typical configuration file, you will find that every line falls into one of three groups:

Empty lines

Empty lines (either those that are genuinely empty, or those that contain only whitespace characters) have no function as far as Apache is concerned, but they help us make configuration files easier to read.

Comment lines

Comment lines have the # character as the first non-whitespace character; any text can follow. Comment lines are often used to make configuration files user-friendly, providing documentation. They are also used to deactivate parts of configuration without deletion, which is handy if you ever want to put the deactivated parts into use again.

Data lines

If a line is neither empty nor a comment line, it is a data line, and Apache will use it in configuration building.

With all this in mind, let's have a look at an example configuration fragment:

```
# It's always useful to begin configuration with a comment.
# Perhaps you have something important to say, for
# example, what is this configuration for?

# The one empty line above helps separate one comment from another.

# What follows is a single data line.
SecRuleEngine On
```

Breaking Lines

In practice, configuration lines can be as long as you need them to be. There is an absolute limit of 8192 bytes, but I've never encountered it and you probably won't either. You will want your lines to be on the short side anyway. Most configuration tweaking and maintenance takes place remotely, so for best results, your lines need to fit within your shell window. Otherwise you'll have to do a lot of scrolling or use the automated word-wrapping facility, if your editor supports it.

To split a long line into two, use a single backslash character followed by a newline:

```
SecRule ARGS KEYWORD \
    phase:1,t:none,block
```

Apache will interpret the previous two-line configuration snippet as a single line. You can use this trick as many times as you wish, creating single logical lines that consist of multiple actual lines.

You can place a break at any location, but some places are better than others. I prefer to indent continued lines, but although my eye does not see the indentation, the whitespace actually ends up in the line. Unless you break the line in a place where whitespace does not matter, you will end up with a gap somewhere. The best place for a continuation is between directive parameters, like in the previous example. With rules, the first two parameters are generally short, so in most cases you will place the continuation after the second parameter, again like in the example. The third parameter, action lists, is often too long to fit even on a broken line —I often find myself breaking the parameter across lines. When you do that, the best place for a break is just after a comma (that's where whitespace does not matter).

Directives and Parameters

Every data line begins with a directive name, followed by zero or more parameters. Apache supports the following directive parameter styles:

- No parameters.

- A single boolean parameter, which allows for only On or Off values (e.g., SecRuleInheritance).

- One, two, or three free-form parameters, where each parameter has a separate meaning; parameters other than the first one can be optional (e.g., SecRule and SecRuleScript).

- Any number of free-form parameters, but all must have the same meaning (e.g., SecResponseBodyMimeType).

Directive parameter values are separated one from another using whitespace:

```
SecRule ARGS script
```

Exceptionally, if you have a value that contains one or more whitespace characters, you will have to enclose the entire value in question marks, a signal that will enable Apache to understand that there's only one parameter inside:

```
SecRule RESPONSE_BODY "Error has occurred"
```

When there are no whitespace characters inside parameter values, you don't have to use question marks (even when the value contains a lot of unusual characters), but you can. Whatever you do, just be consistent and always use the same approach.

Spreading Configuration Across Files

As your configuration keeps growing, you will find it more difficult to find your way around. That is especially true with ModSecurity, because not only will you have the configuration, but there'll be many rules, some of which you may be writing yourself and some of which you may be downloading from an external source.

Apache configuration always begins with a single file, but you are allowed to include other configuration files using the Include directive. The following, for example, could be a skeleton for your ModSecurity configuration:

```
Include conf/modsecurity/main.conf
Include conf/modsecurity/preamble.conf
Include conf/modsecurity/rules1.conf
Include conf/modsecurity/rules2.conf
Include conf/modsecurity/rules3.conf
Include conf/modsecurity/epilogue.conf
```

The paths I used in this example are all relative; Apache will resolve them using its main installation path (e.g., /usr/local/apache) as a starting point. Of course, you can use absolute paths if you wish, but that usually means more typing.

The Include directive can also include several files in one go, when you use the Unix shell-style wildcard characters. They are:

- ?: any one character
- *: zero or more characters
- \: escapes the character that follows
- []: exactly one character from the range (e.g., [0-9] for a digit)

The most common way to use this feature is to include all files that end with a particular suffix:

```
Include conf/modsecurity/*.conf
```

If an Include line resolves to multiple files, they will be included in alphabetical order. That's quite logical, but does not always work as desired, because we tend to choose names based on the purpose the files serve. A common strategy is to use numbers in file names to control the order in which they are included. The example Include line, used with the previously discussed hypothetical ModSecurity configuration, wouldn't include the files in the correct order. But the inclusion will be done in the correct order if we rename the files to the following ones:

```
00-main.conf
10-preamble.conf
20-rules1.conf
30-rules2.conf
40-rules3.conf
90-epilogue.conf
```

I have intentionally selected a larger range than needed (0–99) and left gaps between numbers, because that will allow me to insert new files in between the existing ones.

> **Note**
>
> If you point Include to a directory, it will include all files in it, as well as all the files in all the subdirectories. This particular feature is not very useful, because you will virtually never have a directory that will contain just the configuration files; there'll always be something else, and that something will eventually break your configuration. For example, if your text editor automatically creates backup files, you may not get an error when a backup file is included, but your configuration may fail in unexpected ways.

Container Directives

Apache supports two directive types. The standard variant, which you have already seen, is defined by a single configuration line (which may be split across several physical lines). The other variant, container directives, uses a syntax similar to XML:

- They always come in pairs, which we call tags.
- The starting tag begins with < and ends with >.

- When it comes to parameters, the starting tag uses the same format as all other directives.

- The ending tag begins with </ and ends with >.

- The ending tag cannot have parameters.

- The directives enclosed in the pair of tags (including, possibly, other container directives) are nested in a new configuration context.

Have a look at the following example:

```
# This is the main configuration context

<VirtualHost demo1.example.com>
    # This is the configuration context
    # used by demo1.example.com

    <Location /special/>
        # This is the configuration context
        # used by demo1.example.com/example
    </Location>
</VirtualHost>

<VirtualHost demo2.example.com>
    # This is the configuration context
    # used by demo2.example.com
</VirtualHost>
```

The main configuration context exists in every configuration. There are two further Virtual-Host contexts, nested in the main configuration context, and one Location context, nested in one of the virtual hosts.

ModSecurity does not define any container directives itself (modules are allowed to create such directives, too), but it relies heavily on all the container directives used by Apache.

Configuration Contexts

Apache allows for several types of configuration context using container directives. Configuration contexts are a mechanism that allows you to apply configuration to only parts of the server. The example in the previous section already demonstrated the three most commonly used configuration contexts, the main configuration context, VirtualHost and Location, but there are others. Following is the complete list:

Main

> The main (implicit) configuration context is used by default. Unless a configuration uses explicit configuration contexts, the entire server will use the single configuration context.

VirtualHost

The VirtualHost configuration context is used to create a new virtual host, possibly using a configuration unique to it. Apache will automatically choose the correct virtual host to use for a request, based on the host information supplied in every request.

Location and LocationMatch

The Location and LocationMatch directives both create a location-specific configuration context. Apache will automatically choose the correct location configuration context to use, based on the active virtual host and the information provided in every request's URI.

Directory and DirectoryMatch

The Directory and DirectoryMatch directives both create a directory-specific configuration context. This type of context makes sense only when there is no proxying, because proxies typically don't interact with the local filesystems. This type of context will be used, but Apache determines which file on the local filesystem will be used to serve a request.

Files and FilesMatch

The Files and FilesMatch directives both create a file-specific configuration context. Apache automatically chooses the correct file-specific configuration context to serve a request, but only after it determines which file will be used.

> **Note**
>
> There is practically no difference between the Location, Directory, and Files directives and their respective LocationMatch, DirectoryMatch, and FilesMatch counterparts. They each provide a different way to achieve the same effect. You should invest some time in studying the Apache documentation to understand how and why these directives are different.

Configuration Merging

When configuration is simple, a request will use only one configuration context, but when configuration is complex, configuration contexts may overlap. For example, you may define some rules for a specific virtual host and some further rules for a specific location. Those two configuration contexts have to be merged into a single configuration context before a request that triggers both of them can be handled. Merging always takes place between two contexts at one time. Multiple merging operations will be performed when there are three or more configuration contexts to merge.

There are two aspects to understanding merging:

- The parent-child relationship is significant, as is the order in which contexts are merged. For example, if you define a setting in both contexts, one of the two values may be overwritten by the other. If there are three contexts to be merged, with a different value for the same setting in each context, you need to understand the order in which merging operations will happen.

- Apache initiates the process, but every individual module handles the merging of its configuration. Thus, to understand merging, you need to study the documentation of each module you are using. Some simpler modules may not support merging at all, while complex modules (e.g., ModSecurity) will use different merging strategies for different configuration directives.

The order in which contexts are merged can be quite complex to understand if you want to use every possible combination, but my advice is to simplify:

- Use only the `VirtualHost` and `Location` container directives.
- Remember that multiple `Location` containers (in the same virtual host) are processed in the order in which they appear in the configuration file.

If you follow my advice, your configuration will start with rules in the main configuration context, which will then be overwritten by the per-virtual-host configuration, which will then be overwritten by the per-location configuration.

Configuration and Rule Inheritance

ModSecurity uses two inheritance (configuration merging) strategies. The first strategy is used for the non-rule directives (e.g., `SecRuleEngine`); the second applies to the rules.

Configuration Inheritance

When it comes to the configuration settings, ModSecurity implements a straightforward merging strategy:

- The child context inherits all configuration settings from the parent configuration context.
- The settings explicitly defined in the child context will overwrite those defined in the parent context.

Consider the following example:

```
SecRuleEngine On
SecAuditEngine RelevantOnly

<VirtualHost www.example.com>
    SecRuleEngine DetectionOnly
</VirtualHost>
```

The effective configuration of the main context is exactly as it appears in the configuration file:

```
SecRuleEngine On
SecAuditEngine RelevantOnly
```

As for the configuration of the one virtual host, you can work it out using the two previously mentioned rules. First start with the configuration of the parent configuration context, then use the value of the SecRuleEngine with DetectionOnly instead of the inherited On.

> **Warning**
>
> The only exception to the above rules is SecDefaultAction, whose values are not inherited across configuration contexts. The default action list will always revert to default in every new configuration context.

Rule Inheritance

Because rules cannot overwrite one another in the way predefined settings can, different merging rules apply to them:

1. The child context inherits the rules from the parent context.

2. The rules defined in a child context are added after the rules defined in the parent context.

This, too, should be intuitive. For example:

```
SecRule ARGS K1 id:1001

<VirtualHost www.example.com>
    SecRule ARGS K2 id:1002
</VirtualHost>
```

In the previous example, there will be one rule defined in the main configuration context (the rule 1001), but two in the virtual host (1001 first, then 1002).

The positioning of a child context within the parent context does not influence the configuration of either context. The following segment, which uses a different layout, arrives at the same configuration as the previous example:

```
<VirtualHost www.example.com>
    SecRule ARGS K2 id:1002
</VirtualHost>

SecRule ARGS K1 id:1001
```

This is because, in Apache, configuration processing is a two-step process: all configuration contexts are created in the first step, with merging following in the second. From that point of view, the two previous configuration snippets are practically identical.

Rule inheritance is a desired feature in most circumstances, because you will generally specify your configuration in the main configuration context or in the virtual host container, and then use more specific per-location contexts for tweaking. In such circumstances, it makes sense to begin with the rules specified in the parent configuration context. If you ever need to completely redefine the rules that run in a specific location, ModSecurity allows you to disable rule inheritance using the SecRuleInheritance directive:

```
SecRule ARGS K1 id:1001

<VirtualHost www.example.com>
    SecRuleInheritance Off
    SecRule ARGS K2 id:1002
</VirtualHost>
```

In the previous example, in the virtual host context, the configuration will contain only the rule 1002, because rule inheritance was disabled.

Location-Specific Configuration Restrictions

There is a significant problem related to how the inheritance (of both configuration and rules) is implemented in the current stable versions of ModSecurity: phase 1 takes place before anything specified in a <Location> configuration container is evaluated. It's an implementation detail, but one with significant consequences:

- Phase 1 rules must be placed in the main configuration context, or within <Virtual-Host> contexts.
- Any phase 1 rules placed in <Location> will be silently ignored.
- Any configuration changes made in <Location> will take effect, but only for whatever happens in phase 2 and later.

The execution phases were implemented in this way in order to enable ModSecurity to act as early as possible in the transaction lifecycle, the reasoning being that acting early might help protect against flaws within Apache itself. Since the 2.0.0 release of ModSecurity, however, there was no case in which the early activation helped, but there were many cases of users suffering from unexpected inheritance behavior. The early activation turned out to be a bad decision.

> **Note**
>
> The good news is that this problem was fixed in the main development branch. In the next major version of ModSecurity, there probably won't be any restrictions on what you can change in a <Location> configuration container.

SecDefaultAction Inheritance Anomaly

There is one exception to the configuration merging rules outlined in the previous sections: the SecDefaultAction setting is not inherited. The exception is more a bug than anything else, and can lead to some very subtle problems and unexpected behavior. For example:

```
SecDefaultAction phase:2,log,auditlog,deny
SecRule ARGS K1 id:1001

<VirtualHost www.example.com>
    SecRule ARGS K2 id:1002
</VirtualHost>
```

In this example, the first line of the configuration will change the built-in default action list to activate blocking. The change will be picked up by the rule 1001, which follows in the same configuration context. The rule 1001 will thus block. In the nested configuration context for the www.example.com virtual host, because there is no inheritance of SecDefaultAction, the default action list will revert to the built-in value (phase:2,log,auditlog,pass). The rule 1002 will thus only warn, although it would be more intuitive if it blocked.

Rule Manipulation

When you write your own rules, it is logical to change them directly whenever you want to make a change. There are cases where changing the rules directly is not desired. For example, changing a third-party rule set effectively creates a fork and makes upgrades difficult. ModSecurity has a mechanism or two that you can use to change rules without actually changing them at their original location. Instead, you are either changing the rules after they are loaded, at configure time, or as transactions are evaluated, at runtime.

Whenever possible, you should choose configure-time manipulation, because this approach results with best performance. On the other hand, configure-time manipulation is quite limited, because it is unconditional; it results with a permanent modification of the rule within a context. Runtime manipulation is slower, but flexible: with it, you can use the rule language to evaluate a transaction in any way you choose and then make your modifications.

Removing Rules at Configure Time

ModSecurity supports a configure-time mechanism that allows the removal of a rule whose ID you know. Alternatively, you can also remove the rule whose message you know. That is achieved using SecRuleRemoveById and SecRuleRemoveByMsg, respectively. This example demonstrates both directives:

```
SecRule ARGS K1 log,deny,id:123
SecRuleRemoveById 123

SecRule ARGS K2 "log,deny,msg:'Strange error occurred'"
SecRuleRemoveByMsg "Strange error occurred"
```

The SecRuleRemoveById is quite flexible, because it allows you to list any number of rule IDs and rule ranges (e.g., 123–129), and it will remove all the rules that match. The SecRuleRemoveByMsg directive is similar in flexibility, because its one parameter is a regular expression and also supports removing multiple rules at once.

Removing rules at configuration time as presented in the examples thus far of course does not make any sense. But it will once I change the example to be slightly different. Imagine that you have a third-party rule set that you want to use:

```
Include /opt/modsecurity/etc/thirdPartyRules.conf
```

When you deploy the rule set, you discover that there's one rule that produces a high volume of false positives. You are now faced with a dilemma: do you remove the offending rule or do you live with it? If you do the former, you will be forced to assume the maintenance of the rule set and you won't be able to update it automatically. If you do the latter, you will have to tolerate the false positives.

But, armed with SecRuleRemoveById and SecRuleRemoveByMsg and the IDs (or messages) extracted from the false positives, you can now remove the offending rule without actually modifying the third-party rule set:

```
Include /opt/modsecurity/etc/thirdPartyRules.conf
SecRuleRemoveById 123
```

Thus, we've established that removing rules at configuration time can be very useful if you are unable, for some reason, to modify the original rule sets. You will find another application for this technique if you ever need to customize your rule sets for parts of application, which is done by creating a more specific configuration context in Apache:

```
<VirtualHost www.example.com>
    # Your ModSecurity configuration directives and rules here
    # ...

    # A more-specific configuration context in which
    # you don't want to run the rule 123
    <Location /moreSpecific/>
        SecRuleRemoveById 123
    </Location>
</VirtualHost>
```

Updating Rules at Configure Time

Speaking of changing rules at runtime, sometimes you'll encounter a rule that is not a false positive, but that just does something you don't want. For example, there may be a rule that was hard-coded to block in a particular way, but you want to warn, or block in another way. You can change what rule does on a match, at runtime, using the SecRuleUpdateActionById directive:

```
SecRule ARGS K1 log,deny,id:123
```

```
SecRuleUpdateActionById 123 pass
```

For simplicity, the previous example showed two rules in the same configuration context, but —as discussed in the previous section—changing rule actions like that is only useful when you can't change the rules themselves, or when you don't want to.

Excluding Rules at Runtime

Armed with one or more rule IDs (or rule ID ranges), a rule that runs first can prevent other rules from running, as in this example:

```
SecRule ARGS K1 nolog,pass,ctl:ruleRemoveById=123
# ...other rules here
SecRule ARGS K2 log,deny,id:123
```

If the first rule matches, the associated ctl action runs. Because the ctl action specifies ruleRemoveById with 123 as parameters, the engine will make a note that it should not run rule 123. Later in the phase, if the engine reaches rule 123, it will skip over it.

Configuration Tips

As described in this chapter, ModSecurity gives you great flexibility in how you can organize your rules. There isn't one best way, so you should use the approach that makes maintenance easy for you. The following tips may help you to decide:

- The simplest approach is to define all your rules in the main server body. Then, if there's a need to do something differently in a particular site, you can take one of the following actions:

    - Append new rules, by placing them into the correct <VirtualHost> tag.

    - Override the rules from the main server body using the techniques described earlier in this chapter.

    - Turn off rule inheritance completely, and then implement a new policy from scratch.

- The same advice applies equally to those cases in which you need to use different policies within one site, the only difference being that you will be using the <Location> tags instead of <VirtualHost>.

- A different approach to rule organization is to leave the main server configuration empty, configuring only the individual sites. That is fine too, as long as you understand that there may be some requests that won't fall within any of the sites (e.g., bad requests), which ModSecurity won't be able to see. In most cases it won't matter, but your view of web server activity may no longer be complete.

- If your sites require significantly different policies, define each policy in a separate file (or several files, if the policy is really complex) and use the Include directive to activate it. By doing that, you maximize reuse and minimize maintenance.

- Third-party rule sets are best left in their own files, allowing you to easily replace them with a newer version. If they are well-written, you will be able to use the exclusion techniques described earlier to change how they work without having to change the files directly.

Summary

This chapter is the last in the series of chapters that discuss rule writing, a three-part journey that started with an overview, followed with a step-by-step explanation of every rule feature, and concluded with the high-level "glue" to tie everything together.

The rule writing was the second main topic of the book, after configuration. The following seven chapters provide an in-depth look at the most important features, with each chapter generally focusing on only one aspect of ModSecurity. The only exception is Chapter 9, *Practical Rule Writing*, which contains a collection of topics that, although important, are not big enough to be in chapters of their own.

The next chapter discusses persistent storage, quite possibly the single most important facility in ModSecurity. You'll soon see why.

8 Persistent Storage

This chapter is about the persistent storage mechanism, which adds long-term memory to ModSecurity. Without persistent storage, you are condemned to look at only one transaction at a time without knowledge of what came before it, and of whether what came before it is important. With persistent storage, you are able to construct data models that mirror the main elements of the models used in applications. Some of the elements you will want to track are IP addresses, application sessions, and application users.

The persistent storage mechanism in ModSecurity can be described as a free-form database. You can have any number of tables, and within each table you can have any number of records. There is no need for the records to be uniform. You don't need to know in advance what you will store, and you can even store different data in different records. The storage mechanism was designed with ultimately transient data in mind, so each record has an expiry mechanism built in, which enables the database to essentially keep itself in shape, automatically removing expired records over time.

That's all fine, I hear you say, but what is the persistent storage for? Here are a couple of things that you can do, and which I will show you how to do in the remainder of this chapter:

- Track IP address activity, attack, and anomaly scores

- Track session activity, attack, and anomaly scores

- Track user behavior over a long period of time

- Monitor for session hijacking

- Enforce session inactivity timeouts and absolute life span

- Implement periodic alerting

- Detect denial of service and brute force attacks

I am sure that you will find plenty of additional scenarios in your own environment.

Manipulating Collection Records

In this section, I will cover the basics of collection manipulation. In most cases, the creation is all you need to do and ModSecurity will take care of everything else. The rest of the section will tell you the details you need to know when you want full control of the persistent storage mechanism.

Creating Records

Creating a record is a matter of deciding on a key and invoking the initcol action. The IP collection, for example, is almost always initialized unconditionally using the remote IP address. Because the REMOTE_ADDR variable is always available, it is a good idea to initialize the IP collection early, in phase 1:

```
# Track IP addresses
SecAction phase:1,nolog,pass,initcol:IP=%{REMOTE_ADDR}
```

A collection can be initialized with a record only once per transaction. If there are multiple invocations of the initcol action for the same collection (IP in the example), the first invocation will be processed and all the subsequent invocations will be ignored.

> **Note**
>
> The case of the collection names used in initcol should not matter (i.e., IP should be equivalent to ip, Ip, or iP), but, due to a bug in ModSecurity, it does. Or, rather, it does on all systems that use case-sensitive filesystems, but that's probably the majority of deployments anyway. To work around this problem until it is fixed, choose a style for collection names and stick to it.

Although most collections use single variables for their keys, it's perfectly possible to create a key out of two or more variables. For example, sometimes you may get a large number of users behind the same IP address but you may still want to attempt to track them individually. Although there's not a way to do that reliably, a more granular way would be to generate record keys using a combination of IP address and a hash of the User-Agent field:

```
# Generate a readable hash out of the User-Agent
# request header and store it in TX.uahash
SecRule REQUEST_HEADERS:User-Agent ^(.+)$ \
    phase:1,pass,t:none,t:sha1,t:hexEncode,capture,setvar:tx.uahash=%{TX.0}

# Initialize the IP collection using a
# combination of IP address and User-Agent hash
SecAction phase:1,nolog,pass,initcol:IP=%{REMOTE_ADDR}_%{TX.uahash}
```

In ModSecurity 2.5.x, you are allowed to create only the predefined collections listed in Table 8.1, "Allowed collections in ModSecurity 2.5.x". A future version of ModSecurity may allow you to use any name (that does not clash with the built-in variables).

Table 8.1. Allowed collections in ModSecurity 2.5.x

Collection	Create with	Description
GLOBAL	initcol	Global (per-server) data store
IP	initcol	Per-IP address data store
RESOURCE	initcol	Per-resource (URL) data store
SESSION	setsid	Per-session data store
USER	setuid	Per-user data store

The collection names are chosen to give clue to the intended usage and I trust you won't have any difficulty figuring out what it is. In any case, the rest of this section will show you how to use each of the collections.

You will notice that not all collections can be created using the initcol action. The SESSION and USER collections have a special initialization action each in order to support application namespaces (described in the section called "Application Namespaces" in this chapter).

> **Note**
>
> There is no practical difference between creating a record and retrieving an existing record. The initcol action will automatically create a new record if one does not already exist.

Application Namespaces

A single server running ModSecurity can serve many different sites with their own separate session IDs and user accounts. Although the session IDs will overlap only very rarely (assuming that the ID generation algorithm is solid), there's a good chance that the username collisions will be quite frequent. For example, I imagine that every other application uses admin for the main administration account.

ModSecurity uses *application namespaces* to deal with this problem, whereby you are able to manually specify application boundaries. Each application then receives a private space for its SESSION and USER collections, preventing overlaps. Applications are defined using the SecWebAppId directive. Your goal should be to use one unique application ID per application.

For example:

```
<VirtualHost www.ssllabs.com>
    SecWebAppId ssllabs
```

```
    </VirtualHost>

    <VirtualHost www.feistyduck.com>
        SecWebAppId feistyduck
    </VirtualHost>
```

The method in which application namespaces are implemented is very simple. For normal collections, the collection name is used to name the file in which its data will be stored. For namespace-aware collections, the namespace is part of the name. Assuming the configuration as in the previous example, the data persistence directory may contain the following files:

```
default_SESSION.dir
default_SESSION.pag
feistyduck_SESSION.dir
feistyduck_SESSION.pag
IP.dir
IP.pag
ssllabs_SESSION.dir
ssllabs_SESSION.pag
```

You can see that there is one global database for the IP collection, but three databases for sessions: one each for ssllabs and feistyduck applications, and one (default) for all other applications together. Each database uses two files: the .dir files contains indexes, whereas the .pag files contain data.

Initializing Records

The transparent record creation makes it difficult to perform record initialization, which you will need if you're writing a complex rule. The special record variable IS_NEW can be used to determine whether a record is new. The idea is to allow you to test whether this variable is set, and perform the initialization if it is:

```
# Track IP addresses
SecAction phase:1,nolog,pass,initcol:IP=%{REMOTE_ADDR}

# Set the default reputation value for new IP records
SecRule IP:IS_NEW "@eq 1" \
    phase:1,nolog,pass,setvar:IP.reputation=100
```

Controlling Record Longevity

The number of records in a collection can grow very quickly, especially in the cases where you use one or more records per IP address and you have many users. To preserve space and improve performance, you want your records to be deleted as soon as you no longer need them, but no sooner.

The principal way to control the removal of records is through the *inactivity timeout mechanism* that is built into the collections subsystem. This mechanism ensures the removal of the records that are no longer updated. Its operation is straightforward:

1. An inactivity timeout value associated with every record.
2. Records are scheduled for deletion as soon as they are created.
3. If a record is written to, the expiry time is recalculated using the current timeout value. This means that every activity prolongs the lifetime of a record.
4. The default inactivity timeout value is 3600 seconds, but can be changed by setting the special TIMEOUT collection variable on the record (e.g., setvar:IP.TIMEOUT=300).

It is a best practice to configure the desired inactivity timeout value only once, in a separate rule that checks IS_NEW before making any changes (as demonstrated in the previous section).

Choose the correct value depending on what your collection does. Use the following list as guidance:

- IP tracking: hours
- Session tracking: days
- User tracking: months

Deleting Records

In most cases, you will not need to delete collection records explicitly, because it's much better to configure the correct timeout period and let the garbage collection process deal with the records after they expire. There are currently two ways in which records are deleted:

- A special garbage collection process runs periodically to examine all records in all known collections (i.e., the collections that have been activated during the transaction using initcol, setsid, or setuid). This process will remove all expired records.
- When an attempt to retrieve an expired record is made, the record is deleted and replaced with a new one.

If you know that you no longer need a record, it is more efficient to delete it immediately. That's possible to do, in a roundabout sort of way: you force the deletion by unsetting the special KEY collection variable:

```
# Delete record
SecAction phase:1,nolog,pass,setvar:!IP.KEY
```

Detecting Very Old Records

Because the expiry time of a record can potentially be reset indefinitely, it is not impossible to have a record survive for a very long time. Although ModSecurity won't complain about a record that is too old, it does record the creation time, making it possible to write a custom rule to inspect it. My first attempt at detecting very old records was with the following Lua rule (because I thought the calculations would be impossible to do in the rule language):

```
function main()
    -- Retrieve CREATE_TIME of the current IP record
    local createTime = m.getvar("IP.CREATE_TIME");

    -- If the variable is available and if the record is older
    -- than 24 hours, report the problem back
    if ((createTime ~= nil) and (os.time() - createTime > 86400)) then
        -- Retrieve the record key, which will
        -- make the error message more useful
        local key = m.getvar("IP.KEY");
        -- Match
        return "IP record older than 24 hours (" ..
            (os.time() - createTime) .. "s): " .. key;
    end

    -- No match
    return nil;
end
```

To use the rule, place it in a file called check_ip_create_time.lua, and call it with the following:

```
# Check the CREATE_TIME of the IP collection
SecRuleScript check_ip_create_time.lua phase:5,log,pass
```

If you wish, you can delete such old records (using the technique described in the previous section), use the following rule instead:

```
# Delete very old IP collection records
SecRuleScript check_ip_create_time.lua phase:5,nolog,pass,setvar:!IP.KEY
```

To learn more about writing rules in Lua, go to Chapter 12, *Writing Rules in Lua*.

After seeing my Lua rule, Brian Rectanus came up with the following rule language equivalent:

```
# Detect very old IP records
SecAction "phase:5,log,pass,chain,\
    msg:'IP record older than 24 hours',\
    setvar:tx.exp=%{TIME_EPOCH},\
    setvar:tx.exp=-%{IP.CREATE_TIME}"
SecRule TX:exp "@gt 86400"
```

Although the rule language does not support arithmetic operations in operators, it does support addition and subtraction in the setvar action. The previous example starts with an unconditional rule that uses two setvar actions to calculate the age of an IP record. The second rule then checks it.

Collection Variables

What makes collections beautiful is the fact that they allow you to store any variable, and on a whim. Once you initialize a collection (and thus obtain a record), you can use the setvar action to create, modify, and delete collection variables. This section covers three additional features that persistent collections support, but ordinary collections don't:

- Built-in variables, which give you insight into how the record is used
- Variable expiry, which allows you to remove (expire) a variable at some point in the future
- Variable value depreciation, which allows you to reduce the value of a variable over time

Built-in Variables

Every persistent collection contains certain built-in variables, as seen in Table 8.2, "Built-in collection variables". The use of these variables is explained throughout this section, but they are generally populated using the information provided by the underlying persistence mechanism, allowing you to understand how individual records are used.

Table 8.2. Built-in collection variables

Name	Access	Description
CREATE_TIME	Read-only	Record creation time, in seconds since January 1, 1970 (also known as *Unix epoch*).
IS_NEW	Read-only	Flag that is set on a record that is yet to be persisted for the first time.
KEY	Read/delete	Record key. Can be unset, in which case the record will be deleted.
LAST_UPDATE_TIME	Read-only	The last record update time, in seconds (as above).
TIMEOUT	Read/write	The current timeout value, which will be used to extend the life of the record on the next write. The timeout is initially set to 3600 seconds.
UPDATE_COUNTER	Read-only	Incremented every time a record is persisted.
UPDATE_RATE	Read-only	Record update rate, in requests per second. This value is calculated using the CREATE_TIME, LAST_UPDATE_TIME, and UPDATE_COUNTER values.

Variable Expiry

The variable expiry mechanism enables you to schedule a variable to be expired (unset) at some point in the future. It is a feature you can use whenever you want to execute an action that will remain active for a period of time (long after the HTTP transaction that initiated it is gone).

A good example for this feature is IP address blocking. Assuming that you have the IP collection initialized, IP address blocking requires two rules:

1. One rule that will decide when to block an IP address, and set the appropriate flag in the IP collection (let's use IP.blocked).

2. The second rule that will block transactions originating from the flagged IP addresses.

For example:

```
# Detect attack and install a persistent IP address block
SecRule ARGS attack \
    "phase:2,log,block,msg:'Blocking IP address for 60s',\
    setvar:IP.blocked,\
    expirevar:IP.blocked=60"

# Enforce a persistent IP address block
SecRule IP:blocked "@eq 1" \
    "phase:2,block,msg:'Enforcing earlier IP address block'"
```

> **Note**
>
> If you want blocking to remain active for a very long period of time, make sure that the IP collection timeout value is longer than the blocking period. If an IP collection record expires, the block will expire with it.

Variable Value Depreciation

Variable expiry works well for things that are black or white, right or wrong. But when you have shades of gray, you'll need to use variable value depreciation (action deprecatevar), which is designed to work with the variables that contain numerical values. When you employ depreciation, the numerical value of your choice is gradually reduced over time until it reaches zero. This mechanism is usually used to work with anomaly or attack scores.

> **Note**
>
> The deprecatevar action is implemented in a different way from expirevar. Whereas expirevar uses a "fire-and-forget approach" and needs to run only once, the deprecatevar action needs to be invoked continuously—in most cases on every request—for as long as you need the depreciation to remain active. The recommended approach for expirevar is to use it in the same rule that creates (or updates) a variable. The recommended approach for deprecatevar is to use it unconditionally (with SecAction) in phase 5.

The deprecatevar action takes two positive integer parameters, separated by a forward slash. The first number defines by how much variable value will be reduced in a single change. The second number defines the duration between changes. Together, the parameters define the speed of depreciation. In the following example, the value of the IP.score variable will be reduced by 1 every 5 seconds:

```
SecAction phase:5,nolog,pass,deprecatevar:IP.score=1/5
```

The way in which you choose the numbers matters, because the reduction in value is made at the discrete intervals defined by the duration parameter. That means that although both 1/5 and 60/300 will both result in the same variable value after 300 seconds, in the first case there would be 60 decrements of 1 at 5-second intervals, whereas in the second case you will get just one decrement of 60 after 300 seconds.

For a complete example using depreciation, consider the following implementation of IP address attack scoring:

```
# Increment IP address attack score with every attack
SecRule ARGS attack \
    phase:2,log,pass,setvar:IP.score=+1

# Block IP addresses whose attack score is greater than 10
SecRule IP:score "@gt 10" \
    "phase:2,log,block,msg:'IP address anomaly score over 10 (%{IP.score})'"

# Decrement attack score by 1 every 5 seconds
SecAction phase:5,nolog,pass,deprecatevar:IP.score=1/5
```

If you look at the debug log, you may find the following two lines for each variable being depreciated:

```
[9] Deprecating variable: IP.score=1/5
[4] Deprecated variable "IP.score" from 17 to 15 (10 seconds since last update).
```

As you would expect, depreciation does not occur when there is no change in the value. In that case, you would see the following message in the debug log:

```
[9] Not deprecating variable "IP.score" because the new value (1) is the same as
the old one (1) (2 seconds since last update).
```

Implementation Details

Persistent storage in ModSecurity is implemented using the SDBM library, which is part of the Apache Portable Runtime (APR). SDBM was selected because it was already available (ModSecurity depends on APR anyway) and because it allows for the control of concurrent access. The latter is very important, because in ModSecurity we deal with potentially many concurrent transactions.

Retrieving Records

Collection records are retrieved when the initcol action is encountered. Assuming that the collection was not previously initialized, ModSecurity will look for the appropriate SDBM database and fetch the record with the corresponding key. You can examine the process when you increase the debug log level to 9:

```
[9] Resolved macro %{REMOTE_ADDR} to: 192.168.3.1
[9] Read variable: name "__expire_KEY", value "1263975870".
[9] Read variable: name "KEY", value "192.168.3.1".
[9] Read variable: name "TIMEOUT", value "3600".
[9] Read variable: name "__key", value "192.168.3.1".
[9] Read variable: name "__name", value "IP".
[9] Read variable: name "CREATE_TIME", value "1263970741".
[9] Read variable: name "UPDATE_COUNTER", value "21".
[9] Read variable: name "counter", value "21".
[9] Read variable: name "LAST_UPDATE_TIME", value "1263972270".
[4] Retrieved collection (name "IP", key "192.168.3.1").
[9] Recorded original collection variable: IP.UPDATE_COUNTER = "21"
[4] Added collection "IP" to the list.
```

The first line is the clue as to what the key used was. Following will be one line for every variable retrieved from the database. You will notice that some variable names begin with two underscore characters. Those variables are internal to ModSecurity, and you can probably guess from their names what they do. The variables with names that begin with the __expire_ prefix are created by the expirevar action to keep track of when individual variables need to be expired.

Storing a Collection

All the records initialized during a transaction will be persisted after the transaction completes. In the simpler of the two cases, persistence will be a straightforward write to the database:

```
[9] Wrote variable: name "__expire_KEY", value "1263975870".
[9] Wrote variable: name "KEY", value "192.168.3.1".
[9] Wrote variable: name "TIMEOUT", value "3600".
[9] Wrote variable: name "__key", value "192.168.3.1".
[9] Wrote variable: name "__name", value "IP".
[9] Wrote variable: name "CREATE_TIME", value "1263970741".
[9] Wrote variable: name "UPDATE_COUNTER", value "22".
[9] Wrote variable: name "counter", value "22".
[9] Wrote variable: name "LAST_UPDATE_TIME", value "1263972270".
[4] Persisted collection (name "IP", key "192.168.3.1").
```

> **Note**
>
> If, while looking at your debug logs, you discover that an initialized collection is not being persisted, that's because nothing was changed in it. When there are no changes in the record, the copy in storage will be identical to that in memory, so there is no need to perform the expensive write operation.

Because the writing is delayed until the end of a transaction and because there's no record locking (there can't be any, because it would create a terrible bottleneck), there's always a race condition, because of the time gap between the moment a rule retrieves a record and the moment it writes it back to storage. By the time a record is persisted, some other request may have changed the stored record values.

ModSecurity uses a double-retrieval mechanism with write-locking to deal with the concurrent access problem. It performs the following operations:

1. Locks database

2. Retrieves the record again to obtain the up-to-date values

3. For every numerical value that was changed, calculates the difference between what it originally saw and what it has

4. Updates the numerical values in the record retrieved in step 2 by making relative changes using the calculation from the previous step

5. Writes record to disk

6. Unlocks database

The debug log will show something similar to the following (note the delta calculations in between the read and write operations):

```
[9] Re-retrieving collection prior to store: IP
[9] Read variable: name "__expire_KEY", value "1263975870".
[9] Read variable: name "KEY", value "192.168.3.1".
[9] Read variable: name "TIMEOUT", value "3600".
[9] Read variable: name "__key", value "192.168.3.1".
[9] Read variable: name "__name", value "IP".
[9] Read variable: name "CREATE_TIME", value "1263970741".
[9] Read variable: name "UPDATE_COUNTER", value "21".
[9] Read variable: name "counter", value "21".
[9] Read variable: name "LAST_UPDATE_TIME", value "1263972270".
[4] Retrieved collection (name "IP", key "192.168.3.1").
[9] Delta applied for IP.UPDATE_COUNTER 21->22 (1): 21 + (1) = 22 [22,2]
[9] Delta applied for IP.counter 21->22 (1): 21 + (1) = 22 [22,2]
[9] Wrote variable: name "__expire_KEY", value "1263975870".
[9] Wrote variable: name "KEY", value "192.168.3.1".
[9] Wrote variable: name "TIMEOUT", value "3600".
[9] Wrote variable: name "__key", value "192.168.3.1".
[9] Wrote variable: name "__name", value "IP".
[9] Wrote variable: name "CREATE_TIME", value "1263970741".
[9] Wrote variable: name "UPDATE_COUNTER", value "22".
[9] Wrote variable: name "counter", value "22".
[9] Wrote variable: name "LAST_UPDATE_TIME", value "1263972270".
[4] Persisted collection (name "IP", key "192.168.3.1").
```

The locking and the delta calculations are necessary in order to ensure the integrity of the persisted numerical values. Without them, multiple concurrent transactions would overwrite one another's values, and the numerical values would be incorrect. By remembering the changes, rather than absolute values, ModSecurity ensures that numerical values are always correctly persisted. Unfortunately, there is no way to ensure the integrity of nonnumerical values in the concurrent access scenario (not without severe performance degradation, that is). On the positive side, nonnumerical values are not frequently used in persistent storage and, when they are, they are used in situations when there is little concurrent access.

Record Limits

The SDBM library imposes an arbitrary limit of 1008 bytes on the combined size of key length and record length. If you break this limit, the persistence operation will fail and you'll get the following message in your logs:

```
[1] Failed to write to DBM file "/tmp/IP": Invalid argument
```

ModSecurity uses about 200 bytes for its needs (mostly the built-in collection variables), which means that you practically have about 800 bytes left. Although 800 bytes does not sound like much, it's enough in most situations, because rules generally only use numerical values in persistent storage.

> **Note**
>
> If you are running out of space, avoid using very long keys. Keys are stored in three copies: two copies are used by ModSecurity and one copy by SDBM itself. If everything else fails, you can always resort to "brute force" and recompile the APR to increase the size limit to a much higher value.

As a rule of thumb, you should avoid to store anything user-controlled in persistent storage. For example, you might want to store the value of the User-Agent request header in a SESSION collections to check for possible session hijacking attacks, but that value can be up to 8190 bytes long (that's Apache's default request header limit). In such situations, it is better to store a value derived from the User-Agent value, instead of the value itself.

Practically speaking, you can use the md5 and sha1 transformation functions, which will "compress" input of any size to a fixed-length output. Because the output of those two transformation functions is binary, it is a good idea to follow with a hexEncode transformation, making the final value printable. Following is the rule from an earlier example, which takes the value of the User-Agent request header and transforms it into a value (stored in TX.uahash) that can be used with persistent storage:

```
SecRule REQUEST_HEADERS:User-Agent !^(.+)$ \
    phase:1,t:none,t:sha1,t:hexEncode,capture,setvar:tx.uahash=%{TX.0}
```

Applied Persistence

In this section, I will apply the previously discussed persistence techniques to several real-life problems:

- Periodic alerting
- Denial of service attack detection
- Brute force attack detection

The combination of the persistence facilities and the rule language is what makes the examples that follow particularly interesting. The techniques you learn in the remainder of this chapter will help you take your own rules to the next level!

Periodic Alerting

Periodic alerting is a technique useful in the cases when it is enough to see one alert about a particular situation, and when further events would only create clutter. You can implement periodic alerting to work once per IP address, session, URL, or even an entire application. First you choose the collection you want to work with, and then you create a special flag whose presence will tell you that an alert needs to be suppressed.

The best case for periodic alerting can be made when you're dealing with problems that are not caused by an external factor, which typically happens with rules that perform *passive vulnerability scanning*. Such rules detect traces of vulnerabilities in output, and alert on them. They are quite handy because they can alert about problems before they are exploited. If passive scanning rules are stateless, they may cause far too many alerts, because they will report a problem whenever they see it, which may happen very frequently on busy sites. If you are faced with such a problem, you will have probably seen the first couple of alerts, and, even if you are not doing anything to deal with the discovered issue, you don't really want to be reminded about it. That annoyance can be solved by updating passive vulnerability scanning rules to alert only once, as I will demonstrate.

To start with, here's a simple rule that detects PHP version leakage in the X-Powered-By response header:

```
SecRule RESPONSE_HEADERS:X-Powered-By !^$ \
    "phase:3,log,pass,msg:'X-Powered-By information leakage'"
```

PHP version leakage is a minor issue that is good to know about, but not with an alert on every web server hit. The leakage is caused by a site-wide problem in the configuration of the PHP engine, which means that we can use the GLOBAL collection. The idea is to create a special record (in the GLOBAL collection) just for this one problem and use it to keep track of the previous activity.

The following rule will detect X-Powered-By information leakage, but warn about the problem only once every 60 seconds:

```
SecRule RESPONSE_HEADERS:X-Powered-By !^$ \
    "chain,phase:5,log,pass,id:1001,\
    msg:'X-Powered-By information leakage(%{TX.temp} hits since last alert)',\
    initcol:GLOBAL=1,\
    setvar:GLOBAL.id1001_counter=+1"
SecRule &GLOBAL:id1001_flag "@eq 0" \
    "setvar:GLOBAL.id1001_flag,\
    expirevar:GLOBAL.id1001_flag=60,\
    setvar:TX.temp=%{GLOBAL.id1001_counter},\
    setvar:GLOBAL.id1001_counter=0"
```

I will walk you through what the rule does:

1. The first rule checks whether the problem exists by looking for a nonempty X-Powered-By response header.

2. Upon successful detection, two actions are carried out:

   a. A record in the GLOBAL collection is initialized, using the constant key 1. By performing the initialization only after a match, we enhance performance of the requests that do not have the leakage problem.

   b. The counter value is increased by 1. Even if we don't alert on the problem, we keep track of how many violations there were.

3. The second rule—which, being part of the same chain, is tested only after the first rule matches—tests the GLOBAL.id1001_flag variable, which will tell us if we've alerted in the previous period of time. The presence of the variable is a sign that we shouldn't alert (and you will see why in the next step). If the variable is not present, the rule will match, and the following three actions will be carried out:

   a. The GLOBAL.id1001_flag variable will be created.

   b. The GLOBAL.id1001_flag will be set to expire 60 seconds in the future.

   c. The value of the GLOBAL.id1001_counter variable is preserved in the temporary variable TX.temp.

   d. The counter (GLOBAL.id1001_counter) is then reset to zero.

   e. The match of the second rule will cause the entire chain to match and create an alert. Note how the chain message makes use of the temporary variable TX.temp, which stored the earlier value of the counter (which we've reset since).

> **Note**
>
> If you don't need to track how many alerts were suppressed, omit the incrementation of the GLOBAL.id1001_counter, which will save you a write to disk for every sup-

> pressed alert (which could be a write for every request to your site, depending on the nature of the problem being detected).

Even with this elaborate scheme to implement periodic alerting, it is possible to get more than one alert for a problem that occurs very often (e.g., on every request). This is because processing a request takes time, so it is entirely possible for two requests to execute so close to each other that they don't realize the alert has already taken place. We are minimizing the chances of that happening by choosing phase 5 for the rule and using late initialization. Collections are persisted right after the rules in phase 5 complete, which means that the window of opportunity for the collision is minimized.

If you need suppression to work per application script, use the RESOURCE collection. The following rule is identical to the previous example, except that the collection initialization is slightly different:

```
SecRule RESPONSE_HEADERS:X-Powered-By !^$ \
    "chain,phase:5,log,pass,id:1002,\
    msg:'X-Powered-By information leakage(%{TX.temp} hits since last alert)',\
    initcol:RESOURCE=%{SCRIPT_FILENAME},\
    setvar:RESOURCE.id1002_counter=+1"
SecRule &RESOURCE:id1002_flag "@eq 0" \
    setvar:RESOURCE.id1002_flag,\
    expirevar:RESOURCE.id1002_flag=60,\
    setvar:TX.temp=%{RESOURCE.id1002_counter},\
    setvar:RESOURCE.id1002_counter=0
```

The idea with the RESOURCE collection is that it will give you access to a record that is unique for the script that will be processing the request. When ModSecurity is embedded in a web server, initialize the RESOURCE collection in phase 2 using SCRIPT_FILENAME (which will map to the actual script on disk, no matter what the request URI looks like). In a proxy situation, you can use only the REQUEST_FILENAME variable, but bear in mind that there are situations in which a single script is used for an unlimited number of request URIs. A proxy cannot differentiate between /index.php/1001 and /index.php/1002 and sees them as two different request URIs. A web server would see them as only one script (when you use SCRIPT_FILENAME). Furthermore, it is possible that you will have two locations (e.g., /index.php in two different virtual hosts). To avoid the chances for collision, you should also use the current hostname as part of the key.

Denial of Service Attack Detection

Generally speaking, reacting to denial of service attacks from within a web server is less than ideal. When the target of an attack is the web server itself (e.g., the attacker is trying to overwhelm it by sending a large number of requests or keeping a large number of connections open), by the time a request reaches the web server, it will have already caused the damage.

Denial of service attacks based on brute force should be handled by the network layer, where you are able to minimize the attack impact.

When it comes to attacks against applications, that's another story, and you may actually find ModSecurity very useful. Application attacks rely on being able to send cheap requests (in terms of resources needed to send them) to applications which will use disproportionately more resources (CPU, I/O, and RAM) to process them. Any application function that performs intensive work is a good attack choice. For example, most simple database-backed sites exercise no control over how many database connections they open and are easy prey. Send more than a handful requests to such a site, and it will suddenly start to malfunction.

The simplest approach to detecting DoS attacks is to check the value in the UPDATE_RATE variable of a collection. But because collections are persisted only when there's a change to record, you need to ensure that the collection you are using is written to on every request that matters. A simple way to do that is to increment a counter on every request. Here's an example using the IP collection:

```
SecAction phase:1,nolog,pass,setvar:IP.counter=+1
SecRule IP:UPDATE_RATE "@gt 10" \
    "phase:1,block,msg:'Request rate too high for IP address: %{IP.UPDATE_RATE}'"
```

I have one concern about this approach, though: I don't like the fact that the IP collection is written to on every request. Unless you are already doing something with the IP collection, the constant updating of the collection will add to your overall resource consumption. That does not mean that it's not going to work well, but it does mean that you need to watch it.

It is possible to improve the performance by focusing only on those requests that really matter. If you examine your access logs, chances are good that you will find that only a fraction of all requests are forwarded to the application, with the rest being requests for static resources, such as images, JavaScript, and CSS files. Static files are delivered efficiently by the web server and you can probably avoid tracking them in ModSecurity. By amending the first rule in the previous example to increment only on a non-static request (using an unreliable method of checking the file extension, which will be sufficiently good in this case), we increase the efficiency of our application DoS detection.

For example:

```
# Only increment the counter if the
# request is for a non-static resource
SecRule REQUEST_FILENAME "!\.(jpg|png|gif|js|css|ico)$" \
    phase:1,nolog,pass,setvar:IP.counter=+1
```

A recent addition to ModSecurity is the DURATION variable (not yet released, but available in the development trunk), which you can use to discover how long a transaction has been running. You can use that information to keep track of how much time the web server is spending, per IP address, session, or user.

The following example keeps track of the resources spent on every IP address:

```
# Block the IP addresses that use too
# much of the web server's time
SecRule IP.load "@gt 10000" \
    "phase:1,t:none,block,\
    msg:'IP address load too high: %{IP.load}'"

# Keep track of how much web server
# time is consumed by each IP address
SecAction "phase:5,nolog,pass,\
    setvar:IP.load=+%{DURATION},\
    deprecatevar:IP.load=250/1"
```

You mustn't forget to use the deprecatevar action to ensure that the load value goes down during the periods of inactivity. Otherwise, the load will keep increasing and the block will never drop. Please note that the values I used in the example are completely arbitrary. They are not likely to work on your sites. Use the trial and error approach until you arrive at the values that work for you. Similarly, keep in mind that a client's communication speed may affect the time he or she spends with a transaction. Excessively large pages may have skewed DURATION values. If you are buffering response bodies, I suggest that you move the tracking rule from phase 5 (which occurs after a transaction is complete) to phase 4 (which occurs just before a response body is sent).

Finally, if you get tired looking at the debug log as you test your persistent rules, consider writing a content injection rule (see Chapter 11, *Content Injection*, for more information) to append the IP address update rate (or load) to the end of each site page. You can even use such a rule in production if you make the appended content invisible by putting it inside a HTML comment. Then just view the HTML source whenever you need to find out the value.

Brute Force Attack Detection

Brute force attack detection is conceptually similar to the approach used to detect denial of service attacks. You keep track of the authentication failures and you react when you feel an

---

attack is taking place. Performance-wise, brute force detection uses less resources, because the rules only have to work when authentication takes place.

To start with, you need to understand how authentication failure is manifested, because the condition will be different for every application. You do that by using the application, recording all traffic to the logging script, and performing both successful and unsuccessful authentication. Your goal is to write a rule that will trigger on a failure, but not on success.

Let's assume that we're dealing with an application that uses the URL /login.php for all authentication requests: on success, the application redirects the user to /index.php. On failure, the application redirects back to /login.php, asking the user to try again. Our brute force attack detection rule could thus begin with:

```
<Location /login.php>
    # Check for authentication failure
    SecRule RESPONSE_HEADERS:Location ^/login.php \
        "phase:5,t:none,log,pass,msg:'Failed authentication'"
</Location>
```

Once we verify that this works as expected, we can move to manage the counters. Let's start with the IP collection first. The following rule will keep a per-IP address counter and alert only after seeing 25 authentication attempts, when it will clear the counter and start over:

```
<Location /login.php>
    # Check for authentication failure, maintaining
    # a counter that keeps track of how many failures were
    SecRule RESPONSE_HEADERS:Location ^/login.php \
        "phase:5,chain,t:none,setvar:IP.bf_counter=+1,nolog,pass,\
        msg:'Multiple authentication failures from IP address'"
    SecRule IP:bf_counter "@gt 25" t:none,setvar:!IP.bf_counter
</Location>
```

What we really want to do is block access for a period of time when too many authentication attempts are seen. We can do that with an additional flag and a rule that checks for it:

```
<Location /login.php>
    # Enforce an existing IP address block
    SecRule IP:bf_block "@eq 1" "phase:2,block,\
        msg:'IP address blocked because of suspected brute force attack'"

    # Check for authentication failure
    SecRule RESPONSE_HEADERS:Location ^/login.php \
        "phase:5,chain,t:none,nolog,pass, \
        msg:'Multiple authentication failures from IP address',\
        setvar:IP.bf_counter=+1"
    SecRule IP:bf_counter "@gt 25" "t:none,\
        setvar:IP.bf_block,\
        setvar:!IP.bf_counter,\
        expirevar:IP.block=3600"
```

```
</Location>
```

And there, we have our brute force detection rules, which will block anyone who misbehaves
for one hour. I will now proceed to implement another layer of brute force attack defence,
keeping track of the per-username authentication failures. This is possible, but with some
restrictions, as you shall soon see.

For the second layer of defense, we need a place to store the second counter, of which we need
to keep track no matter which IP address is used for access. It is only natural to use the USER
collection, which was designed for that sort of thing—keeping track of information on a per-
user basis:

```
<Location /login.php>
    # Enforce an existing IP address block
    SecRule IP:bf_block "@eq 1" \
        "phase:2,deny,\
        msg:'IP address blocked because of suspected brute force attack'"

    # Retrieve the per-username record
    SecAction phase:2,nolog,pass,initcol:USER=%{ARGS.username}

    # Enforce an existing username block
    SecRule USER:bf_block "@eq 1" \
        "phase:2,deny,\
        msg:'Username blocked because of suspected brute force attack'"

    # Check for authentication failure and increment counters
    SecRule RESPONSE_HEADERS:Location ^/login.php \
        "phase:5,t:none,nolog,pass,\
        setvar:IP.bf_counter=+1,\
        setvar:USER.bf_counter=+1"

    # Check for too many failures from a single IP address
    SecRule IP:bf_counter "@gt 25" \
        "phase:5,pass,t:none,\
        setvar:IP.bf_block,\
        setvar:!IP.bf_counter,\
        expirevar:IP.block=1800"

    # Check for too many failures for a single username
    SecRule USER:bf_counter "@gt 25" \
        "phase:5,t:none,pass,\
        setvar:USER.bf_block,\
        setvar:!USER.bf_counter,\
        expirevar:USER.block=1800"
        </Location>
```

This example uses a user-supplied value (whatever is in the username parameter) as a collection key. In such situations, you are advised to always check that the user-supplied data is safe.

You will find more information about the dangers of using user-supplied data in the rest of this chapter.

Session Management

Session management is one of the more fun aspects of ModSecurity, and is an area where ModSecurity can be truly useful. The reason for that is simple: unlike with other methods, with sessions you get to understand and monitor in practice what one single user does. The usefulness of session tracking will vary depending on what you're protecting, but it's best used with applications that use sessions to enable the users to establish a "relationship" with the application. Because sessions are required to use an application in a meaningful way, the adversaries are compelled to use them, too, and that makes monitoring easier.

Initializing Sessions

Before you start to think about session initialization, think about how many applications you have on the same server. If you have more than one, you must create a separate application namespace using the SecWebAppId directive. Even if you have only one application, it doesn't hurt to use SecWebAppId, because it causes the application ID to be recorded in audit logs. Over time, you may add more applications, in which case it would be useful to know which audit log entries belong to which application.

To initialize a session, you need to do two things:

Extract session token from request

Most applications use cookies to transmit session tokens. Session cookies' names vary, but they should be easy to identify, because they usually contain a large, random-looking string (for example, 64c24d4e35dc753cd085ca574def4131). A small number of applications embed session tokens in their URLs, and they are even easier to identify, because the large string can be seen in your browser's URL bar.

Configure sufficient session lifetime

ModSecurity collections have the default value of 3600 seconds, but that's too short for sessions, which may remain active for hours under normal circumstances. Some faulty applications might even not impose a limit on session duration. To be able to monitor sessions throughout their life, you need to choose a timeout value that is at least as long as the duration of the longest possible application session. In most cases, however, you should aim the SESSION collection to remain alive for several times the maximum duration of the application session, because that will allow you to perform reliable session blocking. For the examples in this section, I will use 48 hours (172,800 seconds) as the SESSION collection timeout value.

To initialize a session from a cookie, you first need to identify the correct cookie. Have a look at one request that contains session information:

```
GET /index.php HTTP/1.1
Host: 192.168.3.100:8080
User-Agent: Mozilla/5.0 (Windows; U; Windows NT 5.1; en-GB; rv:1.9.1.7) ↵
Gecko/20091221 Firefox/3.5.7 (.NET CLR 3.5.30729)
Accept: text/html,application/xhtml+xml,application/xml;q=0.9,*/*;q=0.8
Accept-Language: en-us,en;q=0.5
Accept-Encoding: gzip,deflate
Accept-Charset: ISO-8859-1,utf-8;q=0.7,*;q=0.7
Keep-Alive: 300
Connection: keep-alive
Cookie: PHPSESSID=64c24d4e35dc753cd085ca574def4131
Pragma: no-cache
Cache-Control: no-cache
```

I've emphasized the session cookie, and you can see that it is very easy to identify the session token. In the effort to extract the session token, you won't have to deal with the request header directly. Because ModSecurity parses inbound cookies, you'll be able to retrieve it by name using the REQUEST_COOKIES variable. Session initialization is thus as simple as:

```
# Initialize SESSION from PHP session token
SecRule REQUEST_COOKIES:PHPSESSID !^$ \
    "phase:2,nolog,pass,\
    setsid:%{REQUEST_COOKIES.PHPSESSID},\
    setvar:SESSION.TIMEOUT=172800"
```

It is advisable, however, to verify session tokens before you use them as collection keys. Anything user-supplied should be validated first, because you never know what you will get. For all you know, an attacker may try to bypass your session defences by submitting multiple session cookies. Also, if the token is invalid, then it will probably not be recognized by the application, in which case you probably don't have any reason to use it either.

In the following example, we first perform the necessary checks (and block if something suspicious is discovered), then use the value of the session token to initialize the SESSION collection:

```
# Check that we have at most one session token
SecRule &REQUEST_COOKIES:PHPSESSID "@gt 1" \
    "phase:2,log,block,msg:'More than one session token'"

# Catch invalid PHP session tokens
SecRule REQUEST_COOKIES:PHPSESSID !^[0-9a-z]{32}$ \
    "phase:2,log,block,msg:'Invalid session token'"

# Initialize SESSION from PHP session token
SecRule REQUEST_COOKIES:PHPSESSID ^[0-9a-z]{32}$ \
    "phase:2,nolog,pass,\
    setsid:%{REQUEST_COOKIES.PHPSESSID}"

# Set the default timeout value for new SESSION records
SecRule SESSION:IS_NEW "@eq 1" \
```

```
"phase:1,nolog,pass,\
setvar:SESSION.TIMEOUT=172800"
```

If your application uses URI-based session tokens, head to the section called "Capturing Data" in Chapter 6, where I give a complete example showing how to use the data capture facility to extract session tokens from URIs.

Blocking Sessions

After the SESSION collection is initialized, blocking a session is a matter of setting a flag (with the correct expiry time) and checking for it on all requests. You have seen this technique earlier in this chapter. I describe the flag method, as well as several variations and other blocking methods in the section called "Advanced Blocking" in Chapter 9.

In addition to blocking sessions with ModSecurity rules, you should consider communicating with the application so that it too blocks the session or signs the user out. Signing out the user can be as simple as proxying the current request to the sign-out page:

```
SecAction "log,proxy:/sign-out.php,msg:'Logging out current user'"
```

An alternative to using the proxy action is to write a Lua script that can then communicate with an external system to achieve a similar effect. Some information on this approach is available in the section called "External Blocking" in Chapter 9.

If you couple the signing-out with a block on the user account (described later in this chapter), the potentially rogue user may be banned from the application until an investigation can be carried out.

Forcing Session Regeneration

Blocking sessions might work well for security, but isn't very user-friendly. If you use session blocking alone, you may leave your users confused, because they won't be able to continue to use the application and won't know how to obtain a new session (close all browser windows and start using the application again). The solution to that problem is to generate a new session for the user. There are two ways to achieve session regeneration, and I will demonstrate both here.

Both approaches use header manipulation, which means that you will need to use ModSecurity in tandem with mod_headers. (At this point, you should probably first go to read the section called "Integration with Other Apache Modules" in Chapter 9, where I explain how to get ModSecurity to collaborate with other Apache modules.)

The following code contains two mod_headers rules, each activated by setting an environment variable:

```
# Neutralize the cookies containing disabled session IDs
```

```
RequestHeader edit Cookie "(?i)^(PHPSESSID)=(.+)$" "DISABLED_$1=$2" \
    env=DISABLE_INBOUND_SESSION

# Instruct browser to delete session cookie
Header always set Set-Cookie "PHPSESSID=;expires=Fri, 31-Dec-1999 00:00:00 GMT" \
    env=DISABLE_OUTBOUND_SESSION
```

The first rule is activated by the DISABLE_INBOUND_SESSION environment variable, after which it renames inbound session cookies. When a session cookie is renamed, it is no longer a session cookie, but some cookie whose value will be ignored. As a result, the application will likely generate a brand new session cookie.

The second rule is activated by the DISABLE_OUTBOUND_SESSION environment variable, and sends a command to the user's browser to delete the session cookie (by using the same name as the session cookie, with an expiry time in the past).

To maximize both security and usability, use both mechanisms in your rules: delete the session cookie of a session you are deciding to block (by executing setenv:DISABLE_OUTBOUND_SESSION in any phase except phase 5), and suppress inbound session cookies of the sessions that have previously been blocked (by executing setenv:DISABLE_INBOUND_SESSION in phase 1 or in phase 2).

Restricting Session Lifetime

Because sessions in today's web applications function as temporary passwords, it is important to cancel them as soon as they are not needed. Two mechanisms are typically used to do that:

Inactivity timeout

When a session is not used for a period of time, it is reasonable to assume that it had been abandoned. Allowing such sessions to remain only increases the danger of them being reused by someone other than the original user.

Session duration timeout

You should also put an absolute limit on session duration. Very long session life span is very unusual and may be an indication of automated activity, or of a bad guy trying to extract as much information as possible from a hijacked session.

Here's what we need to do to implement the two limits:

1. Record the last time a session is used. As you may recall from earlier sections, whenever a collection record is persisted, its LAST_UPDATE_TIME variable is updated. We need that value. So, in order to force session records to be persisted, we'll use the same approach as the one used with the IP collection: increment an arbitrary variable on every request.

2. Now that we have access to LAST_UPDATE_TIME, we can check it upon every request to ensure that it hasn't been too long since the previous request.

---

3. All collections have the `CREATE_TIME` variable, which we'll use to enforce maximum session duration.

We'll use the following Lua rule (placed in the file `check_session.lua`) to check those two conditions:

```lua
function main()
    -- Retrieve session key
    local key = m.getvar("SESSION.KEY");

    -- If there's no key there's no session,
    -- so return without a match.
    if (key == nil) then
        return nil;
    end

    -- Retrieve CREATE_TIME
    local createTime = m.getvar("SESSION.CREATE_TIME");

    -- If the session was created more than 8
    -- hours ago, trigger a match
    if (os.time() - createTime > 28800) then
        -- Match
        return "Session older than 8 hours: " .. key;
    end

    -- Retrieve LAST_UPDATE_TIME
    local lastUpdateTime = m.getvar("SESSION.LAST_UPDATE_TIME");

    -- Check for a period of inactivity
    if (os.time() - lastUpdateTime > 600) then
        -- Match
        return "Session inactive for more than 10 minutes ("
            .. (os.time() - lastUpdateTime) .. "s):" .. key;
    end

    -- No match
    return nil;
end
```

Because this particular feature is more complex than your average rule, I am going to put all the required rules together in a self-contained example, which combines everything we've discussed about session initialization, collection timeouts, session inactivity detection (the Lua rule), session blocking, and header manipulation:

```
# Check that we have at most one session token
SecRule &REQUEST_COOKIES:PHPSESSID "@gt 1" \
    "phase:2,log,block,msg:'More than one session token'"
```

```
# Catch invalid PHP session tokens
SecRule REQUEST_COOKIES:PHPSESSID !^[0-9a-z]{32}$ \
    "phase:2,log,block,msg:'Invalid session token'"

# Initialize SESSION from PHP session token
SecRule REQUEST_COOKIES:PHPSESSID ^[0-9a-z]{32}$ \
    "phase:2,nolog,pass,\
    setsid:%{REQUEST_COOKIES.PHPSESSID}"

# Set the default timeout value for new SESSION records
SecRule SESSION:IS_NEW "@eq 1" \
    "phase:1,nolog,pass,\
    setvar:SESSION.TIMEOUT=172800"

# Check for expired session
SecRule SESSION:expired "@eq 1" \
    "phase:2,log,redirect:/session-timeout.html\
    setenv:DISABLE_INBOUND_SESSION,\
    setenv:DISABLE_OUTBOUND_SESSION"

# Check session inactivity and duration
SecRuleScript check_session.lua \
    "phase:2,log,redirect:/session-timeout.html,\
    setvar:SESSION.expired\
    setenv:DISABLE_INBOUND_SESSION,\
    setenv:DISABLE_OUTBOUND_SESSION"

# Increment the session counter
SecRule REQUEST_FILENAME "!\.(jpg|png|gif|js|css|ico)$" \
    phase:1,nolog,pass,setvar:SESSION.counter=+1

# Neutralize the cookies containing disabled session IDs
RequestHeader edit Cookie "(?i)^(PHPSESSID)=(.+)$" "DISABLED_$1=$2" \
    env=DISABLE_INBOUND_SESSION

# Instruct browser to delete the session cookie
Header always set Set-Cookie "PHPSESSID=;expires=Fri, 31-Dec-1999 00:00:00 GMT" \
    env=DISABLE_OUTBOUND_SESSION
```

Detecting Session Hijacking

Session hijacking is a potentially devastating attack, often executed as the next step after a successful XSS attack. Once the attacker obtains a session token, he or she can assume the identity of the original user. Although it is not possible to detect and prevent session hijacking 100% reliably, there are a few defenses that can prove to be very effective. Before you resort to stateful session monitoring as a measure against session hijacking, however, you should verify that you have done everything you can to secure the session cookies—if you make them safe from compromise, then session hijacking is not possible. I discuss the necessary session cookie rewriting in the section called "Integration with Other Apache Modules" in Chapter 9.

Our session hijacking detection measures are going to focus on two pieces of information:

Session IP address

Sessions are not attached to IP addresses. Anyone with knowledge of the session token is allowed to participate in a session. Having said that, the IP address to which the session was initially assigned (on the first request) will in many situations remain the same throughout a session. For example, a user accessing an application from his or her workstation attached to the internal network is not likely to change his or her IP address. That's probably the best-case scenario.

When it comes to Internet users and roaming users, the change of IP address is possible and you can never be quite sure whether a hijacking is taking place. For example, AOL is famous for having their proxies using a number of completely different addresses. The rumor is that AOL users can have a different IP address on every subsequent request. Roaming users can start a session while they are in one place, put their laptop in standby, and resume the session from a completely different place.

It should also be said that it is possible for the attacker and the victim to have the same IP address as far as you are concerned. That could happen, for example, if they are behind the same proxy or a network address translation (NAT) system.

Ultimately, the value of this detection mechanism will depend on your user base. My advice is to try the mechanism out as a warning system initially, and see if it produces false positives.

Session user-agent

Whereas it's possible that the session IP address will change, it's far less likely that the user agent identification will. If you start a session in one browser, it's very unlikely that you will finish it in another—unless you hijack someone's session, that is. Research carried out by the Electronic Frontier Foundation [https://www.eff.org/deeplinks/2010/01/tracking-by-user-agent] indicated that one in about 1500 users have the same User-Agent request field. Checking that the user agent identification remains the same across all session requests is thus a decent detection mechanism. It is also a mechanism that can be easily defeated by a determined attacker who knows that it exists and who can somehow uncover the victim's own identification string (with a bit of social engineering, for example).

Putting that lengthy discussion aside, here's how to store the original IP address and User-Agent values and check them on subsequent requests:

```
# Generate a readable hash out of the User-Agent
# request header and store it in TX.uahash
SecRule REQUEST_HEADERS:User-Agent ^(.+)$ \
```

```
    "phase:2,nolog,pass,t:none,t:sha1,t:hexEncode,capture,\
    setvar:TX.uahash=%{TX.0}"

# Initialize SESSION, storing a hash of the User-Agent
# value, as well as the originating IP address.
SecRule SESSION:IS_NEW "@eq 1" \
    "phase:2,nolog,pass,\
    skipAfter:999,\
    setvar:SESSION.uahash=%{TX.uahash},\
    setvar:SESSION.ip=%{REMOTE_ADDR}"

SecRule SESSION:ip "!@streq %{REMOTE_ADDR}" \
    "phase:2,pass,msg:'Possible session hijacking: Expected session address ↵
%{SESSION.ip} but got %{REMOTE_ADDR}'"

SecRule SESSION:uahash "!@streq %{TX.uahash}" \
    "phase:2,pass,msg:'Possible session hijacking: Expected session U-A hash ↵
%{SESSION.uahash} but got %{TX.uahash}'"

SecMarker 999
```

There's nothing in these rules that you haven't already seen—they are just a combination of the techniques already covered in this chapter.

User Management

When it comes to persistent state, user management is the final piece of the puzzle. By following individual users, you come as close as possible to using the same data model the applications do. I have already used the USER collection in this chapter to keep track of authentication attempts. Now we're going to see if it is possible to detect users as they sign in and out. (Of course it is.) If we manage to detect those two events, we might be able to associate each session with a user account and use that information to initialize the USER collection.

One thing to have in mind is that tracking users in ModSecurity is not going to be an exact science. You have to work with the information you have available, which means that you are going to have to rely on many assumptions—some of which may not be true. That's going to be just fine, as long as you use the user management facilities with that unreliability in mind.

Detecting User Sign-In

The work we'll need to perform to detect a sign-in event is just the opposite of what we did to detect brute force attacks against authentication. I will base the examples in this section on the assumption that we're dealing with an application whose sign-in form is located at /login.php, and that the application redirects back to the home page (/index.php) when authentication is successful. (If you recall, in the case of failed authentication the redirection was back to the same /login.php page.)

The following example assumes that the SESSION collection was initialized by an earlier rule:

```
# Initialize the USER collection based on
# the user information we keep in the session store
SecRule SESSION:user !^$ \
    "phase:2,nolog,pass,\
    setuid:%{SESSION.user},\
    setvar:USER.TIMEOUT=2592000"

<Location /login.php>
    # Check for successful authentication
    SecRule REQUEST_METHOD "@streq POST" \
        "phase:5,chain,t:none,nolog,pass"
    SecRule RESPONSE_HEADERS:Location ^/index.php \
        setvar:SESSION.user=%{ARGS.username}
</Location>
```

The first of the two rules simply looks in the SESSION.user variable to see if we had previously established who the user behind the session is. If the information is available, the rule uses it to initialize the USER collection. The second rule detects the sign-in event, as previously discussed.

> **Warning**
>
> Look at the previous example carefully and try to answer what will happen if the sign-in function receives two (different) username parameters. Do you think that it's possible that the application chooses one of those parameters, while the rules choose the other? If that happens, the rules may end up associating the session with a wrong user account. Best practice is to use a positive security model to verify every aspect of the entire sign-in operation, as discussed in the section called "Virtual Patching" in Chapter 9.

Detecting User Sign-Out

Detecting the sign-out function is much easier, as the action is rarely conditional. In the following example, I assume an application in which it is enough to visit the /signout.php page in order to sign out of the application:

```
<Location /signout.php>
    # Disassociate user from session
    SecAction phase:5,nolog,pass,setvar:!SESSION.user
</Location>
```

When we're on the sign-out page, we need just to remove the user information from the SESSION collection and we're done.

Summary

Now that we've concluded the persistence chapter, I hope that you understand why I was so excited about this aspect of ModSecurity. The persistent storage facility is the feature that quite literally adds a complete new dimension to ModSecurity—that of time. With the ability to track external parties over time and correlate events, you gain a far more useful tool in ModSecurity.

In the next chapter, aptly named *Practical Rule Writing*, we tie together everything you've learned so far by discussing a number of practical issues that you will encounter in your everyday life with ModSecurity.

9 Practical Rule Writing

This chapter is dedicated to the many practical aspects and requirements of rule writing. We go beyond looking at features in isolation to discuss what we can achieve when multiple features are used together. This is the chapter where, finally, everything comes together.

Whitelisting

Rule sets are usually written to single out unusual requests, but it turns out that most networks contain one or more sources of requests that are not only unusual but also desired. The more complex the network, the more likely it is that you'll need to use whitelisting. In most cases, there will be at least one crude monitoring script that is practically indistinguishable from some other Perl script that will be attacking it. In others, you might have outsourced security testing to a third party, and you don't want your rules to interfere with their work. Finally, even if you don't have any of that, you won't be able to avoid the unexpected—Apache sending requests to itself.

Whitelisting Theory

You have to be very careful when writing whitelisting rules, because each such addition to your rule set creates a bond of trust. If you make a mistake, you can end up with a hole in your rule set that can be used by your adversaries. You should be asking yourself three questions:

How do I know the request is from the person or device I want to whitelist?
In the ideal case, the remote client will authenticate itself in some way, ideally with a password (embedded, for example, in the User-Agent request header). The drawback of this approach is that you will probably have to make some configuration changes on the remote end to support authentication, and sometimes that might not even be possible. As an alternative to authentication, you can choose to look at the IP address or range from which the request is coming. If you do, take a moment to consider whether it is possible (and likely) that something else could send you (potentially malicious) requests from the same IP address range.

Is there anything specific about the requests I want to whitelist?

You may have established that the requests are coming from a source you can reasonably trust, but it's still a good idea to narrow down the attack vector as much as possible. Observe, over time, the requests you want to whitelist: is there a recurring pattern? For example, most monitoring requests are identical. In other cases, the requests will be restricted to a part of your web site and will have predictable parameters.

What changes do I want to make to the default configuration?

This last question pertains to the action you wish to take after you definitely decide that you want to go through with whitelisting. The easiest thing to do is to simply use the allow action to let the remote party continue unconditionally, but are you really comfortable with giving them unrestricted access? A better solution might to be to switch the rule engine to detection mode. You will not regret this, as long as you get false positives only occasionally.

In the next section, I will discuss the placement of whitelisting rules, followed by several simple examples and finishing with the rule that you will need to silence the Apache web server itself.

Whitelisting Mechanics

Whitelisting rules need to be executed before all your other detection rules, which means that they should always follow your configuration and system rules. It is a good idea to have a special file for this category of rule alone. That will make them easy to find, after a simple glance at the list of your configuration files.

Most whitelisting rules look at the remote address first, so let's do just that. Let's assume that there is a trusted employee to whom you want to give unrestricted access to your web site. The IP address of his workstation is 192.168.1.1. The whitelisting rule is as follows:

```
SecRule REMOTE_ADDR "@streq 192.168.1.1" \
    phase:1,t:none,nolog,allow
```

Because you need to work with only one IP address, use the @streq operator. Upon detecting a request from the employee's IP address, the allow action will interrupt the operation of the rule engine, skipping all phases except phase 5.

ModSecurity does not have an operator designed specifically to work with IP addresses, so you'll need to be creative if you are given several IP addresses to whitelist. Suppose that you are given three IP addresses. You could write three separate rules, which is not only inelegant, but inefficient as well. In most such cases, the @rx operator will do the job. For example:

```
SecRule REMOTE_ADDR "@rx ^192\.168\.1\.(1|5|10)$" \
    phase:1,t:none,nolog,allow
```

This example whitelists three IP addresses: 192.168.1.1, 192.168.1.5, and 192.168.1.10.

Chapter 9: Practical Rule Writing

As previously discussed, you should avoid using the allow action whenever you can. Switching the rule engine to detection-only instead is recommended:

```
SecRule REMOTE_ADDR "@streq 192.168.1.1" \
    phase:1,t:none,nolog,pass,ctl:ruleEngine=DetectionOnly
```

In this rule, I replaced allow with pass (which won't do anything else but move to the next rule once the current rule is done), and added an invocation of the ctl action with the instruction to change the operating mode of the rule engine.

If you take my advice and require some form of authentication in order to activate your whitelisting rules, consider the following example, in which I also require a correct password to be placed in the User-Agent request header:

```
SecRule REMOTE_ADDR "@streq 192.168.1.1" \
    phase:1,t:none,nolog,pass,ctl:ruleEngine=DetectionOnly,chain
SecRule REQUEST_HEADERS:User-Agent "@contains SECRET_PASSWORD"
```

Granular Whitelisting

Although every invocation of the allow action interrupts the phase in which it runs, you are able to choose whether and how other phases in the same transaction are affected. The allow action has an optional parameter, and the following rules apply:

Interrupt current phase and skip all other inspection phases
If you invoke allow without a parameter then, regardless of the current phase, all inspection phases will be skipped.

Interrupt current phase only
When allow is invoked with phase as a parameter (allow:phase), it restricts the effect of this action to the current phase.

Interrupt current phase and any remaining request phase
When allow is invoked in phase 1 with request as a parameter (allow:request), the processing of phase 1 will be interrupted and phase 2 will be skipped completely. The processing will continue with the first response phase (phase 3).

Complete Whitelisting Example

Earlier in this section, I mentioned how Apache talks to itself. Because it's a case that every ModSecurity administrator will have to deal with, I will use that example to demonstrate how to implement whitelisting.

First, let's look at the complete request we need to ignore:

```
::1 - - [26/Oct/2009:16:01:06 +0000] "OPTIONS * HTTP/1.0" 200 - ↩
"-" "Apache (internal dummy connection)"
```

> **Note**
>
> If you are using an older version of Apache, you may see variations of this request. Initially, the wake-up request used just GET /, but it was improved over the years, because very few system administrators knew what that meant. On a similar note, if your Apache ever gets a HTTP client that speaks plain-text on an SSL-enabled port, Apache will log such a request as GET / in the access log.

What can we deduce from the example log line?

1. The first thing that you will notice about this request is that it always arrives from the server itself. In the example, the remote address is ::1 (IPv6 localhost). In other cases, you will see 127.0.0.1 there. We can use this information to restrict the source of requests that our rule will take into account.

2. The request is always the same and involves the OPTIONS request method. This is even more helpful, because it allows us to write a rule that only matches that specific usage.

3. The user agent identification is the same for all requests.

Using the obtained information, we write a robust and safe rule:

```
SecRule REQUEST_LINE "@streq OPTIONS * HTTP/1.0" \
    "phase:1,chain,t:none,nolog,allow,\
    msg:'Allowing wake-up request from Apache itself'"
SecRule REMOTE_ADDR "^(::1|127\.0\.0\.1)$" t:none
```

I used only the first two facts for my rule, because I felt that they allow me to uniquely identify a request and that no more narrowing is needed. Besides, the User-Agent request header is trivial to subvert.

Can the example rule be improved? It sure can:

1. We restrict the remote address and the request line, but there's no mention of request headers. In theory, someone could place an exploit payload into one of the request headers, and send it using the OPTIONS request method. As an exercise, record one Apache request to the audit log, examine the request headers it sends, and modify the example rule to nail every header down.

2. The really paranoid could look in the Apache source code to change the default user agent identification and thus allow for reliable identification of Apache access.

Virtual Patching

In the ideal world, when you identify a flaw in an application, you get the developers to fix the problem. You then get the developers to examine the entire code base for similar problems, fixing other flaws that they discover. In the real world, however, there are many obstacles to fixing the problems in this way:

No access to source code

When you are running third-party applications or using third-party libraries, you don't have a choice. You are at the mercy of the vendors to deal with the issues. Many vendors won't have the same sense of urgency; in some cases, months and even years may pass before an issue is fixed.

No legal right to change source code

When you outsource your development, you may have access to the source code, but you may not be able to do anything with it until the contract with the developer expires. At best, you can identify the location of the problem and assist the developer.

Changing source code prohibitively expensive

Let's say that there are no legal issues in fixing the problem in an application for which you have the source code. If you are currently using the stock version (e.g., the one that comes with the operating system), to fix a flaw requires an additional packaging and distribution of the new package. You would also need to continue to produce new application versions until the original flaw is fixed upstream.

Lack of expertise to fix flaw

All the source code in the world won't mean a thing if you lack the expertise needed to devise a fix. Employing a random developer is not going to cut it; you have to have access to a senior developer with security expertise who already understands the application. If you don't, you risk the danger of making a bigger problem. Lack of expertise can especially be a problem when the flaw is in a legacy application that has been long forgotten. How on earth are you going to find someone to not only fix the problem but also build a complete development, staging, and deployment environment from scratch?

In the best-case scenario for fixing problems in the source code, the flaw will be in a critical internal application developed by an agile experienced team with security expertise. But even in that case, there may be issues with the timings and the cost:

- Should you disrupt a development cycle halfway?

- How will that affect the quality of the release?

- Will subsequent releases (and features) be affected?

- How will the changes have an impact on the business?

- Are you able to roll out an update to the application?

- Is the production version a freeze during the critical time of the year?

- Is the key developer out sick or away on a vacation?

- Do you dare make changes without him or her?

- Are there any bigger fires to deal with?

Virtual patching presents a way to deal with a known problem in a web application—almost any application—without actually touching the application itself. Because most web application traffic uses standard data transport protocols, it is relatively easy to reroute information flow and install a policy capable of preventing the exploitation. This technique is also sometimes referred to as *just-in-time patching*, or *dynamic patching*.

The principal advantage of virtual patching is that it is very effective and quick to deploy. Assuming you've laid the foundation for virtual patching in advance, it can take literally minutes to mitigate a problem. Compare that to the days, weeks, and months that it might take to fix the same problem in the source code. In addition, if you neutralize a problem in this way, you relieve the pressure on your developers, giving them enough time to fix the problem properly and roll out the fix in the next scheduled software update.

Some application security practitioners are concerned that the use of virtual patching, as effective as it can be, contributes to the culture of not caring about security flaws and leaving them to linger in the source code. That's a legitimate concern, but ultimately, the culture in an organization is going to be exactly what the people in charge want it to be. The truth is that virtual patching is an operational tool, which shouldn't affect how problems are treated on the development level.

Vulnerability vs. Exploit Patching

There are two ways in which virtual patches can be written: vulnerability-oriented and exploit-oriented. Vulnerability-oriented virtual patches are designed to address the core issue; you work to understand the problem and write a policy that essentially does the work that the vulnerable application should have done—typically, adding the required input validation. This approach is also known as *positive security model* or *whitelisting*. You make no attempts to determine whether something is unsafe. Instead, you just figure out what is safe (which is much easier), and you then write the policy to implement just that.

Exploit-oriented patches focus on the known exploits instead. No attempts are made to understand the root cause; the focus is on trying to catch the attacks instead. This approach is also known as the *negative security model*, or *blacklisting*. Exploit-oriented patches are not as effective as vulnerability-oriented patches, because they will fail if someone is able to rework an existing exploit to be different yet remain effective. Similarly, such defense measures will fail if someone discovers another way to exploit the underlying problem.

I prefer to use the term "virtual patching" only for the policies that employ the whitelisting approach.

Failings of Exploit Detection

Let's assume that we are dealing with a web application that is vulnerable to SQL injection. We'll say that the vulnerable page has a parameter called `articleid`, which is supposed to be just an integer, but that no checks are made on what the supplied value actually contains. Normally, you'd use the page with an URL such as this one:

```
http://www.example.com/showArticle.jsp?articleid=4545789
```

However, there's nothing preventing you from adding a bit of SQL to the parameter, and getting it to execute in the site's database:

```
http://www.example.com/showArticle.jsp?articleid=4545789;drop%20table%20articles
```

If you were to circulate this "exploit," someone might write a rule that focuses on detecting the SQL keywords used in it:

```
SecRule ARGS:articleid "(drop|table)" \
    phase:2,log,block,t:none,t:lowercase,t:compressWhitespace
```

This rule is not the worst written, but it creates an imperfect net that catches some attacks, but not necessarily all of them. Someone with enough time on his or her hands could perform many tests and work methodically to reverse-engineer your rule just by sending varying requests. In the end, what he or she will do is find a way to bypass the rule.

If you want to be safe, write positive security patches, allowing only what you know to be safe. So let's try to do that:

```
SecRule ARGS:articleid "^[0-9]{1,10}$"
```

This rule, being vulnerability-based, is a great improvement over the previous attempts. The key difference is that now the attacker can try to use every SQL injection technique available, but they will fail unless he or she can make the exploit payload be an integer. The attacker won't be able to do that, and you'll be safe. Or will you?

Impedance Mismatch

When you use the whitelisting approach to virtual patch creation, the attacker should no longer be able to successfully attack the application. What he or she can do, however, is attack the web application firewall, or, in our case, ModSecurity. If you look at the previous rule very carefully, you may realize that it depends entirely on the ability to correctly inspect the articleid parameter.

A common attack technique is to use multiple parameters with the same name, with some using a correct value and some containing exploit payloads, and hoping that the inspection device will allow the request after seeing one of the correct values. This technique does not work against ModSecurity, because when you use the named parameter syntax (e.g., ARGS:articleid), it inspects all parameters with that name.

But what if the attacker changes the name of the parameter in some way to make ModSecurity see it as a different name, while the target application sees it as the original name? Strictly speaking, that shouldn't be possible. After all, we have standards that define how parameter names are specified. In reality, however, it's quite easy with some application servers, because they will handle input in nonstandard ways.

PHP, for example, is quite liberal as to how it handles parameter names. It's trying to be helpful, actually, correcting the things it thinks are wrong, but is ultimately causing problems, from the security perspective. One thing it will do is ignore the whitespace at the beginning of parameter names. Take the following request, for example:

```
http://www.example.com/showArticle.jsp?%20articleid=4545789;drop%20table%20articles
```

You might be surprised to learn that the application would process the request as if you used the parameter `articleid` without the space as the first character. Meanwhile, ModSecurity will see the parameter for what it is, as `articleid` (with the space), causing the virtual patch to fail. Back to the drawing board.

Using the negative security mentality, you might want to detect the parameters that have spaces in them:

```
SecRule ARGS_NAMES "\s+" \
    "phase:2,log,block,msg:'Whitespace in parameter name'"
```

You don't want to only look for the whitespace at the beginning of parameter names, because PHP will also convert whitespace inside parameter names, replacing it with underscores. Anyway, the approach in the previous rule would probably be good enough, assuming you are not running any applications that actually have whitespace in the parameter names. However, you shouldn't rely on that approach, because you don't really know all the weird ways in which PHP will change parameter names. A positive-security approach would be to define what you consider to be normal. Like the following rule, for example, which allows only the characters you would normally expect in a parameter name:

```
SecRule ARGS_NAMES "!^[-0-9a-zA-Z_.]+$" \
    "phase:2,log,block,msg:'Invalid parameter name'"
```

That's an improvement, because now, if we accept a parameter name, we'll know exactly what it can be.

Preferred Virtual Patching Approach

The preferred virtual patching approach is actually to cast a wider net, and lock down the entire script that exhibits the vulnerability you are patching. With the previously described vulnerability in mind, consider the following group of rules:

```
<Location /index.php>
    SecDefaultAction phase:2,t:none,log,deny
```

```
    # Validate parameter names
    SecRule ARGS_NAMES "!^(articleid)$" \
        "msg:'Unknown parameter name: %{MATCHED_VAR_NAME}'"

    # Validate each parameter's cardinality
    SecRule &ARGS:articleid "!@eq 1" \
        "msg:'Invalid parameter: articleid'"

    # Validate parameter 'articleid'
    SecRule ARGS:articleid "!^[0-9]{1,10}$" \
        "msg:'Invalid parameter: articleid'"
</Location>
```

The preferred virtual patching approach is to use the following methodology:

1. Use the `<Location>` or `<Directory>` (preferred, but only works in embedded mode) configuration containers to focus on only a single script or page

2. Allow only known parameter names

3. Check that each parameter appears only once, or as many times as needed

4. Check that the value provided in each parameter matches what is desired

Although my example demonstrates the concept on a script with only one parameter, the same approach can be used with any number of parameters.

IP Address Reputation and Blacklisting

There are only two things that are guaranteed for every HTTP request you get: you will have an IP address and port to work with. Even when everything else is wrong or broken, the two pieces of information can be retrieved from the TCP network level. At first you might think that an IP address is not worth much, but it is surprising how much you can actually do with it:

- Using geolocation, you can determine a client's geographic location.

- You can ban an IP address from your site forever.

- You can keep long-term information on an IP address in a local database and use it to influence your policies.

- You can ask a remote fraud detection service whether it believes the IP address is "bad."

IP Address Blocking

Conceptually, blacklisting is done in the same way as whitelisting, which I've covered earlier in this chapter. You keep a list of IP addresses you don't want to do business with, and you refuse the requests that arrive from them. There's often a difference in the number of IP addresses that are used. Blacklists often contain hundreds and often thousands of IP addresses, which means that you need to work harder to maintain good inspection performance.

Parallel matching offers best matching performance, but because it wasn't designed for the matching of IP addresses, you'll need to do some extra work to implement it correctly. The problem is that the @pm operator does not understand pattern boundaries. If you ask it to match "192.168.1.1", it will match it no matter where in the string pattern it sits, which means that it will match "192.168.1.10" and "192.168.1.100", to list just a couple of the possible false positives.

The extra work I mentioned is needed to create artificial boundaries where they are needed. First, you need to create a new variable to keep the remote IP address, adding something in front of the IP address and something at the end. I'll use a forward slash character:

```
SecAction phase:1,nolog,pass,\
    setvar:TX.REMOTE_ADDR=/%{REMOTE_ADDR}/
```

The actual blacklisting is just a normal use of the @pmFromFile operator, but you use TX:REMOTE_ADDR instead of REMOTE_ADDR:

```
SecRule TX:REMOTE_ADDR "@pmFromFile blacklist.dat" \
    "phase:1,log,block,msg:'IP address on blacklist'"
```

The file blacklist.dat contains one IP address per line, with a forward slash character at the beginning and end of every line:

```
/192.168.1.1/
/192.168.1.2/
/192.168.1.3/
```

> **Warning**
>
> Older versions of ModSecurity supported only LF line endings in the parallel matching pattern file. A CR character before LF would be considered to be part of the pattern, not part of the line terminator. If you edited your files on Windows, for example, and used them on Unix, the patterns would mysteriously fail. In addition, any whitespace at the beginning of each line and at the end, would become part of the pattern. Starting with ModSecurity 2.5.12, the CRLF line endings are processed correctly and whitespace trimmed.

Because we have the forward slash characters in both places (in the rule and in the file), the matching will work as it should, without the previously described false positives. As a matter of fact, now you can take advantage of the side effect, making the blacklisting of entire segments easier. For example, if you want to match an entire class C address space (256 IP addresses), you could have the following line in the file:

```
/192.168.1.
```

Geolocation

Geolocation is the identification of the geographic location of a HTTP client by means of an IP address. The identification is done by performing a lookup against a database that "knows" where every IP address belongs. The process is not 100% accurate and may not work at all for some addresses.

ModSecurity supports geolocation through the integration with the free Geo-Lite Country [http://www.maxmind.com/app/geolitecountry] or GeoLite City [http://www.maxmind.com/app/geolitecity] databases. To start using this feature, first download the database and put it somewhere on the local filesystem where ModSecurity can get to it.

To obtain the geographic location of someone whose IP address you have, you'll need one configuration directive and one rule:

```
# Initialize GeoIP database
SecGeoLookupDb /path/to/GeoIP.dat

# Perform geolocation
SecRule REMOTE_ADDR "@geoLookup" "phase:1,t:none,nolog,pass"
```

You can afford to perform a lookup on every request because the database is available locally. It is unlikely that the performance is going to be an issue.

From this point on, you can use the geographic information in your rules. For example, to detect access from Great Britain, write this:

```
# Detect access from Great Britain
SecRule GEO:COUNTRY_CODE3 "@eq GBR" \
    phase:1,log,pass,msg:'Access from Great Britain'
```

Of course, this example is silly, because it was designed only to show how the geolocation features are used. In practice, you will want to add the geographic information to the list of variables that influence your rules and your policies. Let me give you a couple of ideas:

Assign a risk score to each country

Then, when deciding whether a request is an attack, or whether to block, use the risk score to sway your decision one way or another.

Know where your users are

Keep track of where your users are. If a user session changes country, or if a user "travels" a great distance in a short period of time, that may be an indication that his or her account was compromised.

Implement defense conditions

The majority of your users may be in one or a few countries, but you normally don't want to restrict access because some users are often travelling. However, in extraordinary circumstances (e.g., when you're under attack), you may want to lock down your systems and allow access only from a small number of countries.

Real-Time Block Lists

A real-time block list (RBL) is an IP address reputation tool that is able to tell you whether an IP address or domain name is bad. Real-time block lists are most commonly used to fight email spam, but they can be quite useful for web applications. After all, if you know that there's a spammer behind an IP address, do you really want him or her in your application? In recent years, we have seen the rise of RBLs that are designed to work with application security in mind.

Unlike geolocation, real-time block lists are usually accessed over the network. The upside is that there's usually zero maintenance. The downside is that there can be a significant performance hit, depending on where the servers that power the RBL are located (relative to your own servers). When I recently experimented with a RBL, I discovered that I had introduced additional latency of about 400 ms. Because RBL lookups are performed over the DNS infrastructure, there's limited caching support, which means that not all requests will take the latency hit. If you are planning on using RBLs in production, best practice is to install a local caching DNS server (rbldnsd [http://www.corpit.ru/mjt/rbldnsd.html], for example). Because some lists are available for download, with a local DNS server you solve the latency problem.

In ModSecurity, a lookup of an address against a RBL is done using the @rbl operator:

```
# Only allow the IP addresses cleared by sc.surbl.org
SecRule REMOTE_ADDR "@rbl sc.surbl.org" \
    "phase:1,log,block,msg:'IP address denied by sc.surbl.org'"
```

If you get a match, it means that the IP address is listed in the real-time block list. You don't have to block immediately, but if you don't, store the information in a TX variable so that you can refer to it later. I have found the following RBLs to be widely used:

- The Spamhaus Project [http://www.spamhaus.org/]
- SURBL [http://www.surbl.org]

Local Reputation Management

Every time you create a whitelist or a blacklist, you practice local reputation management. Similarly, the various persistent storage techniques that are used to track IP addresses and application sessions are part of the same concept:

Static network access control
> Keep track of the IP addresses that require special treatment, be it whitelisting or blacklisting. If the number of addresses is small, any approach will do. If you are dealing with

a large number of IP addresses, use parallel matching for performance. The disadvantage of the static approach is that every change to the list requires a restart of Apache (even when the IP addresses are kept in an external file and used with @pmFromFile).

Local (internal) geographic and organizational information

For the sites whose users are strongly clustered (e.g., internal applications used by different departments and company groups), consider creating a local database for geographic and organization lookups. Again, you can write the rules in any way, but use parallel matching if there are too many IP addresses on the list.

Dynamic network, session, and user access control

Write rules to keep track of the behavior of the individual system elements (IP addresses, sessions, users, and so on, as discussed in Chapter 8, *Persistent Storage*), denying access to those elements that cross thresholds. The rules from this category should ideally require little or no maintenance and use only temporary bans that do not require manual interventions. For example, if you keep an anomaly score per IP address, you want to ensure the score will go up as well as down as appropriate.

Integration with Other Apache Modules

One of the biggest advantages of Apache is its modular nature. When you put modularity and popularity together, it sometimes seems that whatever need you can think of, there's already a module to fulfill it. In most cases, modules are used on their own, but multiple modules can sometimes communicate one with another. ModSecurity generally tries to avoid reimplementing the features available in other modules, even for the functionality that could come under the security label. Thus there will be times when you will need to send or receive instructions to and from other modules.

There are two mechanisms in Apache that allow for the communication among modules:

Environment variables

Inter-module communication using environment variable is the common approach to having modules exchange information and influence one another. Whenever two modules need to communicate, the receiving module will be configured to watch for the presence (and possibly the value) of a particular environment variable, and act on it. Many modules are built with environment variables in mind, so whenever you discover that a particular module supports them, you can use them to talk to the module from ModSecurity using the setenv action. Because in ModSecurity you can use the ENV collection to retrieve the value of a named variable, you can write rules that use the information prepared by other modules. The only limitation is that the module you want to utilize must run after the ModSecurity phase in which you're setting the environment variables.

Optional functions

Optional functions make possible for a module to export one or more named functions for other modules to consume. This mechanism is intended for module developers to use—chances are you won't be using it very often. ModSecurity builds its extension APIs on top of optional functions. The extension APIs are described in Chapter 14, *Extending Rule Language*.

The modules you may find yourself integrating with are:

- mod_deflate
- mod_headers
- mod_log_config
- mod_proxy
- mod_rewrite
- mod_setenvif

Conditional Logging

Normally, an access log will record every transaction processed by Apache, but sometimes you will want to record only some transactions. That is called *conditional logging*. Apache's logging facilities support it, enabling use of environment variables to decide what to log.

- Log by default, but do not log if an environment variable is set
- Do not log by default, but log if an environment variable is set

In the following example, I create a custom access log that logs only the transactions from a specific IP address:

```
# Detect the condition that require logging
SecRule REMOTE_ADDR "@streq 192.168.1.1" \
    phase:1,nolog,pass,setenv:SPECIAL_ACCESS_LOG

# Create a special access log file, which reacts to
# the SPECIAL_ACCESS_LOG environment variable.
CustomLog logs/special_access.log combined env=SPECIAL_ACCESS_LOG
```

> **Note**
>
> With ModSecurity 2.5.x, it is not possible to control logging from a phase 5 rule, because this phase executes only after Apache has completed writing to its log files. This is expected to change in the next major release of ModSecurity. In fact, phase 5 already runs before Apache's logging in the current development version in the trunk.

Header Manipulation

In Apache, the `mod_headers` module is used for header manipulation. Its `Header` and `Request-Header` directives know how to look up an environment variable, as I described in the previous section, which means that you can use them to conditionally change request and response headers. As before, the idea is to check for a condition using ModSecurity and set an environment variable if the condition is met.

In the following example, I use ModSecurity to instruct `mod_headers` to delete the session cookie:

```
# Simulate a condition that would want us
# to force the user to use another session
SecRule ARGS attackPattern \
    "phase:2,t:none,log,pass,setenv:DISABLE_OUTBOUND_SESSION"

# Expire session cookies when instructed
Header set Set-Cookie "PHPSESSID=;expires=Fri, 31-Dec-1999 00:00:00 GMT" \
    env=DISABLE_OUTBOUND_SESSION
```

Securing Session Cookies

In web applications that support user authentication, session cookies function as temporary passwords. Users provide their credentials only once and, assuming they are correct, their sessions are marked as authenticated. From that point on, whoever knows a session's ID can exercise full control over it. Great care needs to be taken when constructing session cookies to ensure that they are secure. In many applications, the security of session cookies can be improved by changing two aspects of how they are constructed:

Use of the httpOnly flag

> The httpOnly flag is an Internet Explorer innovation that aims to prevent access to session cookies from JavaScript (which is the most common way to steal a session ID after a successful XSS attack). The idea is that session cookies are needed only by the server-side code, and that we lose nothing by forbidding access from JavaScript. With the httpOnly flag in place, session hijacking becomes significantly more difficult.

Use of the secure flag

> When a site uses SSL, there is no way for an attacker to gain access to the data that is being exchanged between the site and the users. A frequent omission, when using SSL, is to omit marking the session cookies as secure. The omission can lead to a compromise of users' session cookies, giving the attacker complete access to the corresponding sessions.

If you are using Apache 2.2.4 or better, you can fix these problems quickly, using just two `mod_headers` instructions. The following example improves the security of the session cookies used by PHP:

```
# Add missing httpOnly flag
Header edit Set-Cookie "(?i)^(PHPSESSID=(?:(?!httponly).)+)$" "$1; httpOnly"

# Add missing secure flag
Header edit Set-Cookie "(?i)^(PHPSESSID=(?:(?!secure).)+)$" "$1; secure"
```

The general idea is that we look at the Set-Cookie header, which is used to create new cookies, and look for the session cookies that do not have the desired flags set. If such incorrectly set cookies are found, we modify the headers to append the missing flags. The example uses several rarely used, but very useful features:

- The regular expression patterns both begin with (?i), which ensures that matching is case-insensitive.

- In the second part, there is a *negative lookahead assertion*, causing the entire pattern to match only if the bits in the assertion do not appear anywhere in the header.

- The fourth parameter, which contains the value that will replace an existing Set-Cookie value, makes use of backreferences ($1), which are replaced by the existing header value.

It's interesting how much information can be contained on a single line of text, isn't it?

Advanced Blocking

Chapter 8, *Persistent Storage*, already introduced many advanced blocking techniques, but that was only half of the story. This section is the second half, discussing a few practical details, as well as introducing the concept that blocking does not need to be a purely black and white affair. In fact, as you will soon see, the wealth of facilities provided in ModSecurity allows you to do what you want, when you want, and how you want.

Immediate Blocking

When we talk about blocking, we tend to have in mind the straightforward approach, in which you detect a problem and block immediately:

```
SecRule ARGS attack \
    "phase:2,log,deny,status:403,msg:'Attack detected'"
```

When you use the deny action, which is the primary blocking mechanism, ModSecurity will instruct Apache to cut short transaction processing and respond with a HTTP status code of your choice. By default, the status code 403 (Forbidden) is used, but you can specify any other status code using the status action. Responding with the 403 status code is probably the best choice if you don't have a desire to hide your actions from a potential attacker.

Having said that, there's a case to be made for laying low and keeping the attacker guessing. I often use the 500 status code (Internal Server Error), because that's how a malfunctioning site would respond. On the other hand, if you have a false positive with a 500, you create an impression to your user base that your web site is crashing.

To some errors you can respond with a meaningful status code, such as 405 (Method Not Allowed) and 501 (Not Implemented). Responding with an inappropriate status code (e.g., blocking with 504 or 501) is not recommended, because it may confuse many HTTP clients, and also makes it easy for others to fingerprint your rules.

Not all phases are created equal when it comes to blocking. You are able to reliably block from some, but not from others. The full details are presented in Table 9.1, "Phase blocking suitability".

Table 9.1. Phase blocking suitability

Phase	Blocking notes
REQUEST_HEADERS (1)	Request and response always possible.
REQUEST_BODY (2)	Request and response always possible.
RESPONSE_HEADERS (3)	Response blocking always possible. Request already processed.
RESPONSE_BODY (4)	Response blocking possible, but only when response buffering is enabled. Request already processed. Response headers might have been sent. Conflicts with mod_deflate are possible (blank output with status 200, or duplicated response headers).
LOGGING (5)	Never possible. Request already processed. Response already sent.

Keeping Detection and Blocking Separate

Although ModSecurity rules have the ability to be very specific about blocking, specifying whether to block and how to block, I take a view that those decisions are none of the rules' business. The rules should focus on detecting issues and raising flags, and generally leave it to the system administrator to decide what to do. There's a facility in ModSecurity that enables the rule writers to do just that—the block action.

When a rule uses the block action, it essentially gives the system a hint that it believes blocking should take place. The administrator is free to specify what really happens. In the following example, the rules rely on the blocking policy specified at the beginning of the block:

```
# Define how blocking takes place
SecDefaultAction phase:2,log,deny,status:403

# Detect attacks
SecRule ARGS attack1 phase:2,block
SecRule ARGS attack2 phase:2,block
```

The advantage of this approach is that there is now only one location where you change the blocking policy. You don't have to make extensive changes in the rules. More importantly, the blocking policy defined in this way will work with third-party rule sets (but only assuming they were correctly implemented, avoiding the use of any specific blocking instructions):

```
# Define how blocking takes place
SecDefaultAction log,deny,status:403

# Include Acme Rule Set
Include conf/acme/*.conf
```

It is even possible to avoid blocking, if the default action list uses pass:

```
# No blocking by default
SecDefaultAction phase:2,log,pass
```

User-Friendly Blocking

Whenever you use blocking, you need to be aware that you'll probably catch a few innocent users over time. The security of your system may be your primary concern (otherwise, you wouldn't be blocking, right?), but the innocent users that get caught as collateral damage won't be very happy. In fact, the experience is likely to frustrate them and lose you money.

To lessen the users' frustration, you need to set up a user-friendly response page where you explain to the users why they were blocked. Depending on the nature of the block, you may even be able to give them some practical advice (e.g., "try again in a few minutes").

Simple blocking response page can be set up if you use a redirection for blocking:

```
# Respond to attacks with a user-friendly response
SecRule ARGS attack \
    phase:2,redirect:/security-error.html
```

A disadvantage of this approach is that the action of redirection makes users move away from the original transaction that may have caused a problem. If they contact support, you'll only have their account name to work with, but not much else. Apache has a built-in response redirection mechanism whereby the information about the original requests is preserved. It also works on a per-response code basis.

In your rules, you need to ensure only that you use the correct status code. The magic is in the additional ErrorDocument directive:

```
SecRule ARGS attack \
    phase:2,deny,status:509

ErrorDocument 509 /security-error.php
```

The redirection will still take place, but it will be handled internally by Apache. In the script you use to handle the problem, you will have access to the REDIRECT_UNIQUE_ID environment variable, which contains the unique identifier of the original request. You should consider displaying that information to your users, thus enabling them to pass it on to your support personnel.

> **Note**
>
> If you set an environment variable from ModSecurity, it will be available to the script that's handling the error, but with the REDIRECT_ prefix. For example, if you execute setvar:x=y in a rule somewhere (before the block takes place), the environment variable REDIRECT_x will be available in the error script.

The following example uses PHP for the dynamic functionality:

```
<? header("HTTP/1.0 403 Forbidden"); ?>
<html>
<head>
<title>Security Error</title>
<meta http-equiv="Content-Type" content="text/html;charset=utf-8" />
</head>

<body>
<h1>Security Error</h1>

<pre>
Your request has been blocked for security reasons. Please try again
in a few minutes. Should the problem persist and you need to call
support, please write down the following problem information:

<? echo htmlspecialchars($_SERVER["REDIRECT_UNIQUE_ID"], ENT_QUOTES, 'UTF-8'); ?>


We apologize for any inconvenience.

<!--
This comment is here to increase the page size and prevent Internet
Explorer from masking the message. More information is available at
the following address:

    http://support.microsoft.com/default.aspx?scid=kb;en-us;Q294807
 -->

</body>
</html>
```

You will note that I used the 509 status code for blocking. This is to avoid a conflict between the security responses and the responses to a particular status code. It would be misleading to respond with the security page on a genuine 500 error, for example. The 509 response code is one of the rare status codes Apache will accept in ErrorDocument that are not in any RFC. We don't really want to propagate that status code back to the client, so it's fortunate that Apache allows the final status code to be overridden from the error handling script. You will notice that the first thing the script does is change the status code to something more meaningful.

External Blocking

In some cases, such as when you are under a denial of service attack, friendly blocking is not exactly going to be a priority—but efficient blocking will. Discussing the defense against DoS attacks in Chapter 8, *Persistent Storage*, I mentioned that defending against this type of attack on the web server level is not the most efficient approach. If you move your blocking (of some attack types) to the network level, you will be able to simply block all traffic from the offending IP address, taking the load off your web server.

ModSecurity cannot perform network-level blocking, but there are several ways in which you can pass the required information to an external system that can:

External scripts
> By using the exec action on a rule match, you are able to invoke a system program that may initiate external blocking. The external script will have access to the offending IP address through the REDIRECT_REMOTE_ADDR environment variable.

Lua scripts
> Using Lua along with the Curl bindings (liblua5.1-curl0 package on my Debian server), you can perform a HTTP request, passing on the offending IP address to some remote system. From Lua, you have full access to transaction data, so you are able to send anything you need.

Honeypot Diversion

If you have a lot of extra time on your hands, an interesting possibility is to block without the attacker being aware of it happening. You can implement this type of blocking by using the proxy action to redirect attacker's requests to a separate system. Such a system is usually called a *honeypot*. The idea behind honeypots is that you want to be able to observe attackers' actions for as long as possible, because each additional request may tell you more about the problems you have in your system. Honeypots have a potential to unearth the information your rules never could.

Honeypot diversion is not very practical implemented on a per-transaction level. Your honeypot system may see only some transactions, and the transactions that happen after an attack will again go to the main production system, which defies the purpose of the honeypot. However, activating your honeypot in persistent manner can work reasonably well. Working on a per-session or per-user basis is a good choice. A per-IP address honeypot could catch many innocent users.

Delayed Blocking

Immediate blocking is the easiest approach to use, but it prevents the remaining phase rules from running. You have blocked the transaction, but the messages associated with it may not tell you the whole story. For example, your block could have been for a generic problem, but a very specific attack could be hiding in the request data somewhere. In my experience, rule sets tend to order their rules from generic to more specific, and that adds to the problem of information loss.

Delayed blocking, in which you wait until the end of each phase to decide whether to block, solves the information loss problem. With it, all rules in a phase run, which means that you get all the messages you can in the audit log.

To implement delayed blocking, use one transaction variable (TX.block, for example) as an indicator of whether blocking is needed. In your rules you no longer block, but set the indicator instead. Then you add a rule to check the indicator at the end of each phase.

The following example demonstrates the concept:

```
# Detect attack X
SecRule ARGS attackX \
    "phase:2,msg:'Detected attack X',\
    setvar:TX.block"

# Detect attack Y
SecRule ARGS attackY \
    "phase:2,msg:'Detected attack Y',\
    setvar:TX.block"

# Delayed blocking
SecRule TX:block "@eq 1" \
    "phase:2,log,deny,msg:'Phase block due to an earlier match'\
    setvar:!TX.block"
```

In addition to blocking, the last rule unsets the blocking indicator, which prevents it from "leaking" into subsequent phases when the engine is running in detection-only mode.

Score-Based Blocking

Score-based blocking is a variation on the delayed-blocking approach. Instead of using an indicator, you use a score, and decide whether to block depending on the resulting phase score. For example:

```
# Detect attack X
SecRule ARGS attackX \
    "phase:2,msg:'Detected attack X',\
    setvar:TX.score=+1"
```

```
# Detect attack Y
SecRule ARGS attackY \
    "phase:2,msg:'Detected attack Y',\
    setvar:TX.score=+5"

# Delayed blocking
SecRule TX:score "@gt 5" \
    "phase:2,log,deny,msg:'Phase block due to high score'\
    setvar:!TX.score"
```

The interesting thing about scoring is that you are not restricted to using only one score; you can have a score for any transaction characteristic you choose. Consider the following approaches:

Phase scores

Keep a separate score for every phase. This enables you to implement delayed per-phase blocking, but if blocking does not take place, the scores remain available for use in subsequent phases.

Attack class score

Each attack class could have a score of its own, which would allow for a really fine-grained approach to detection. The Core Rule Set uses this approach (as well as a few others) starting with version 2.

Transaction score

Keep a combined transaction score, possibly combining the individual phase scores.

Request and response scores

Keep one score for the first two phases, and another for the second two phases. This approach allows for the correlation between attack detection and attack results detection. For example, suppose the request score reflects your suspicion that an SQL injection attack is taking place. If the response score indicates a trace of the attack (e.g., a database error message), you can decide to block.

Persistent scores

Once persistent collections are initialized, the concept of scoring can be applied to higher-level elements such as IP addresses, sessions, and users. The only difference is that transactions always start afresh, with a score of zero, whereas the persistent elements keep their scores until they expire. Persistent score thus needs to involve a depreciating element so that it effectively maintains itself. I discussed persistent scoring at length in Chapter 8, *Persistent Storage*.

Score-based blocking is very neat, but it can be difficult to implement. The burden is on the rule writer to come up with a meaningful way to combine rule scores into combined values, which is necessary for that final threshold check to work. For example, you can't have several rules match for the same underlying problem, because that could artificially push the score over the threshold.

Chapter 9: Practical Rule Writing

Making the Most of Regular Expressions

Although ModSecurity supports many operators, regular expressions are so powerful and versatile that they remain the most often seen choice in rules. ModSecurity uses the Perl Compatible Regular Expressions library [http://www.pcre.org], better known as PCRE. This is a well-known and widely used regular expression library, and it is also used by Apache. Because they are so powerful, regular expressions will often surprise you, and you'll realize that they are more capable than you thought. This section will highlight the most important aspects of PCRE and the way this library is used in ModSecurity, but it is only the tip of the iceberg. I highly recommend that you familiarize yourself with the PCRE documentation [http://www.pcre.org/pcre.txt], which contains everything you need to know.

How ModSecurity Compiles Patterns

Regular expression patterns are compiled (converted into an efficient internal representation) before they are used. The compilation step helps the library improve performance, doing as much work as possible only once, at configure time. The compilation flags affect how patterns are used and you need to be aware about them. In the most important place where regular expressions are used, the @rx operator, ModSecurity uses two compilation flags:

PCRE_DOLLAR_ENDONLY

> Also by default, a dollar metacharacter will match a newline at the end of a string. Users often do not expect this, and it messes with the rules that want to have complete control over what is allowed in certain places. By using PCRE_DOLLAR_ENDONLY to compile patterns, the dollar character is made to match only at the end of the input.

PCRE_DOTALL

> By default, a dot metacharacter in a pattern matches all characters except those indicating newlines. In a security context, that opens a potential weakness where an attacker is able to use a newline to break up the attack payload and prevent a pattern from matching. With PCRE_DOTALL set, a dot metacharacter will genuinely match any character.

Now that you know which compilation flags are used, it is important to learn about two that are *not* used:

PCRE_CASELESS

> Enabled case-insensitive matching. Because this flag is absent when the @rx patterns are compiled, all patterns are case-sensitive. (Use the t:lowercase transformation function to achieve case-insensitive matching, or read the next section, which shows another way.)

PCRE_MULTILINE

> This flag changes the behavior of the ^ and $ metacharacters to force them to match at a beginning of a line and at an end of a line, respectively. Without it, PCRE will treat

the entire input string as a single line. The PCRE default is used for the @rx operator. That means that a ^ metacharacter will *always* match at the beginning of the string, and $ will *always* match at the end.

There are several other places where regular expressions are used, and although they are not as security-sensitive as the @rx operator, you should still be aware of how they are compiled. Table 9.2, "Pattern compilation flags" gives a complete picture.

Table 9.2. Pattern compilation flags

Usage	Compilation flags used
@rx	PCRE_DOLLAR_ENDONLY, PCRE_DOTALL
@verifyCC	PCRE_DOTALL, PCRE_MULTILINE
SecAuditLogRelevantStatus	PCRE_DOTALL
SecRuleRemoveByMsg	No flags used
Variable selection (e.g., ARGS)	PCRE_CASELESS, PCRE_DOLLAR_ENDONLY, PCRE_DOTALL

Changing How Patterns Are Compiled

If you are not happy with how ModSecurity compiles patterns, you'll be glad to hear that PCRE allows you to override the compile flags from within the pattern itself. For example, the following rule, which does not use any transformation functions, will match the word attack no matter what case is used:

```
SecRule ARGS "(?i)attack" phase:2,t:none
```

The (?i) part, placed at the beginning of the pattern, activates the PCRE_CASELESS flag for the entire pattern. It is also possible to change a setting for only a part of a pattern, by placing the modifier within.

```
SecRule ARGS "attack (?i)keyword" phase:2,t:none
```

The previous expression will match attack keyword and attack KeYWORD, but not ATTACK keyword. If you place the modifier in a subpattern, then only the remainder of the subpattern will be modified:

```
SecRule ARGS "(key(?i)word) attack" phase:2,t:none
```

The previous expression will match keyWORD attack, but not keyWORD ATTACK nor KeYWORD attack.

To remove a flag, use a dash in front of the letter. The following pattern unsets the PCRE_DOTALL flag that is used by ModSecurity by default:

```
SecRule ARGS "(?-s)keyword" phase:2,t:none
```

The complete list of the modifiers you can use in this way is in Table 9.3, "Pattern modifiers". For complete meanings, look the modifiers up in the PCRE documentation.

Table 9.3. Pattern modifiers

Modifier	Meaning
i	PCRE_CASELESS
J	PCRE_DUPNAMES
m	PCRE_MULTILINE
s	PCRE_DOTALL
U	PCRE_UNGREEDY
x	PCRE_EXTENDED
X	PCRE_EXTRA

Common Pattern Problems

Mistakes in regular expression patterns are common, but two are seen more often than others:

Forgetting to escape the metacharacters

The most frequently unescaped metacharacter is the dot. It most commonly happens when you're writing patterns to match IP addresses, which have many dots in them. An unescaped dot will match any character, matching against unintended characters if it was not meant to be used as a metacharacter. Problems with the + and ? characters are frequent as well.

Not using the ^ and $ anchors when matching entire input

The use of the ^ and $ anchors is required when you want your patterns to match complete input strings. If you omit one or the other, you allow the attacker to send anything before your pattern (when you don't have the ^ at the beginning) and anything after your pattern (when you don't have the $ at the end). Without the anchors, a pattern may match a substring in the middle, ignoring anything else.

Regular Expression Denial of Service

Regular Expression Denial of Service (or ReDoS) is a relatively obscure problem that affects every regular expression writer. Some regular expression constructs are known to suffer from very bad (exponential) performance when certain edge cases are encountered. If you are not careful, you can write a pattern that can be manipulated from the outside by an attacker to consume most or all of your server's resources.

Here are some examples of vulnerable patterns borrowed from Alex and Adar (reference follows):

- (a+)+
- ([a-zA-Z]+)*
- (a|aa)+
- (a|a?)+
- (.*a){x}, for x > 10

For more information on this subject, look for the following presentations:

- *Regular Expression Denial of Service* (2003), by Scott A. Crosby
- *Regular Expression Denial of Service* (2009), by Alex Roichman and Adar Weidman

> **Note**
>
> Starting with ModSecurity 2.5.12, the regular expressions use conservative limits (the PCRE defaults were previously used), allowing only up to 1,500 matches and up to 1,500 internal recursions. This change makes the rules less prone to denial of service problems.

Resources

Don't be surprised if you sometimes get overwhelmed working with regular expressions. That's entirely normal and will go away in time. You don't have to buy a book in order to become proficient in regular expressions, but it will certainly help if you do. My only issue with the available books is that they all cover many regular expression flavors, and I am interested only in PCRE. There are at least two books you should look at:

- *Mastering Regular Expressions*, by Jeffrey Friedl (O'Reilly, 2006), is widely considered to be a classic work on regular expressions.
- *Regular Expressions Cookbook*, by Jan Goyvaerts and Steven Levithan (O'Reilly, 2009), is a recent addition to the regular expression work, and adopts a more practical style of learning.

You should also look at one of these tools, as they will enable you to interactively design and analyze regular expressions:

- RegexBuddy [http://www.regexbuddy.com], a commercial tool written by *Regular Expressions Cookbook* co-author Jan Goyvaerts, is often recommended as the ultimate regular expression assistant.
- The Regex Coach [http://weitz.de/regex-coach/] is a free tool written by Edi Weitz.
- Expresso [http://www.ultrapico.com/Expresso.htm] is a free tool (requires registration) from Ultrapico.

Working with Rule Sets

Rule sets are packaged collections of rules designed to address a particular problem. In this section I will discuss them first from a user's point of view, and then from a rule set writer's point of view. You should read both sections no matter which group you belong to, because they are just different aspects of the same story.

Deploying Rule Sets

If a rule set is well-written, deploying it is a matter of deciding how to react to its alerts and adding the rule set to your configuration. In other words:

```
# Configure default blocking policy
SecDefaultAction "phase:1,log,auditlog,pass"

# Activate Ultimate rules
Include conf/ultimate-rules-9.99/*.conf
```

You shouldn't use blocking when you deploy a rule set for the first time, because you don't know if it will produce many false positives. Warnings will be sufficient for the first couple of days, or weeks. Once you gain confidence that the rule set will not ruin you financially, you can switch to blocking if you wish.

There are only two maintenance activities you should ever do when it comes to rule sets: dealing with false positives and updating to new releases.

Dealing with False Positives

It's all right for a rule set to have false positives, as long as it doesn't have too many. You can deal with them in the following ways:

- Ignore occasional false positives.
- Use `SecRuleRemoveById` or `SecRuleRemoveByMsg` to deactivate the rule that is producing too many false positives.
- Use `SecRuleUpdateActionById` to change how a rule reacts.
- Deactivate the original rule, copy it to your local configuration (don't forget to change the ID in the process), then modify it to work better in your environment.

No matter which option you choose, you should strive not to change the original rule set files. Doing so will prevent you from upgrading the rules with a simple file copy.

Upgrading to New Releases

Updating to a new version should involve downloading the new files, going through the documentation to understand the changes, and possibly using `diff` to see exactly what changed.

Some people prefer to switch back to detection-only for a while, just to make sure there won't be any nasty surprises. Others, who have adequate budgets, will first try the new rules in a staging environment. It is advisable to keep the previous version of the rule around, just in case you don't find the new version satisfactory.

If you've copied and modified any of the rules, when upgrading to a new release don't forget to check if the rule has been improved in the meantime.

Writing Rules for Distribution

When you're writing rules for yourself, you are often able to make design shortcuts because you do things in certain ways, and there is little sense in allowing for different behavior. When writing for others, however, about the only certain thing is that they will want things done differently. When someone downloads a rule set, they basically expect to be able to plug it into their web site and use it with little fuss. What they don't expect is to have their site overtaken by the newly installed rules. Thus the key to writing rules for distribution is to give your users options and let them decide what to do:

Avoid mixing rules with configuration
Your users will have spent significant time deciding exactly how they wish to run Mod-Security, and you don't want to surprise them by overriding their configuration with something else. Besides, your configuration choices may not be adequate for their circumstances.

Detect problems, but do not react to them
Your job, as a rule set writer, is to detect problems, not react to them. Leave the reacting to your users. If you are writing straightforward blocking rules, you only need to remember to use block as your disruptive action. If you're writing advanced rules that produce attack scores, don't take any action, but document what the outcome of your rules is going to be and leave to your users to do the rest.

Split rules into modules
Splitting complex rule sets into modules is always a good idea, especially if you can make the modules differ in terms of precision and performance. The split into modules is a recipe for user satisfaction when coupled with good documentation that explains the characteristics of each module.

Document your rules
Everything is game provided you tell your users in advance what to expect. Include such items as installation instructions, performance, the update mechanism, and so on. The more you tell them, the happier they'll be. On the rule level, make sure that every rule contains every little bit of meta-data you can think of.

If you want practical advice, consider the following:

- Always specify id, rev (unless 1), msg and severity.
- IDs must be allocated from the pool assigned to the publisher.
- Once allocated, the rule IDs must not be reused for other rules.
- Rule revision number must be incremented with every change to the rule.
- List all desired transformation functions, starting with t:none.
- Use only pass and block as the disruptive action.
- Never use nolog in combination with block.
- Use logdata:%{TX.0} with complex rules, which will help your users understand exactly what matched.

Use only the following directives:

- SecAction
- SecComponentSignature
- SecMarker
- SecRule
- SecRuleScript

Never use the following actions:

- allow
- append
- ctl
- drop
- exec
- initcol
- pause
- prepend
- proxy
- redirect
- setuid
- setsid
- status

Resources for Rule Writers

First of all, you are off to a good start, because this book will tell you most of what you need to know about ModSecurity and rule writing. You are already in a much better position than anyone who's used ModSecurity in the past several years.

Your next step should be to get up to speed with application security. Good books on application security are hard to find, but there are a few that you can't afford to miss:

- *The Web Application Hacker's Handbook*, by Dafydd Stuttard and Marcus Pinto (Wiley, 2007)
- *SQL Injection Attacks and Defense*, by Justin Clarke et. al (Syngress, 2009)

With the books, you will be able to cover a lot of ground quickly, but you will pick up the majority of your skills by observing the application security mailing lists and reading new research papers as they are published.

In addition, consider the following resources:

- XSS Cheat Sheet [http://ha.ckers.org/xss.html], assembled by Robert Hansen (also known as RSnake)
- The Spanner [http://www.thespanner.co.uk], blog written by Gareth Heyes
- PHPIDS [http://php-ids.org], an IDS for PHP applications (but the signatures are universal)

Rule writing is mostly about trial and error. You start with a known attack and try to write rules to detect it. Then you go back and try to modify the attack to still work but evade the rules. Detecting attacks actually isn't that difficult, but doing the same while avoiding innocent traffic can be a real challenge.

To help you get started with rule writing, I have added a rule writing workshop to this book's online companion. The workshop combines rule writing and application security in a way that extends beyond the scope of this book. It contains many practical examples that show how to write rules to detect attacks such as cross-site scripting, SQL injection, remote file inclusion, and many more.

Similarly, you shouldn't forget to download and examine the publicly available rule sets, which contain numerous examples of rule writing:

- Core Rule Set 2.x is currently included with ModSecurity
- Core Rule Set 1.6.1 used to be included with ModSecurity and you can get it from the 2.5.9 tarball
- Gotroot [http://www.gotroot.com] rules
- Emerging Threats [http://www.emergingthreats.net] deal with Snort, but their rules contain a wealth of information that can be reused

You shouldn't expect those rule sets to be perfect, but you will learn a lot by studying how they approach inspection and detection.

Summary

In this chapter, I touched on a number of practical tasks, most of which are needed by every single ModSecurity user. Whitelisting, blacklisting, and virtual patching constitute the core of what ModSecurity was designed to do. In the section on regular expressions, I gave you a good introduction to the topic, but you really need to buy another book or two and learn everything there is to know about it. It's the single most powerful tool for inspection, and, to this day, I am sometimes amazed with what can be done with it.

Our next step is everyone's favorite topic—performance. I will give you the information you need to understand performance, which is important for your ability to write efficient rules, as well as measure performance, which is important so that you can know how your ModSecurity installations perform.

10 Performance

In this chapter, I present a detailed analysis of the performance of ModSecurity. Performance is everybody's favorite topic, but, judging on evidence alone (i.e., the lack of the users complaining), ModSecurity runs fast enough. That said, there is no reason for it to run slower than it could, and this chapter will both measure the performance and tell you how to get ModSecurity to run efficiently.

Understanding Performance

Our first task is to understand where ModSecurity spends its time. Or, rather, where it can spend its time. Different sites have different usage profiles, and when you consider the fact that the rules will be different, too, one performance aspect that is not important to you may be very important to someone else.

With three key resources in mind (CPU, RAM, and I/O), I present you with a detailed list of the performance hot spots in ModSecurity:

Parsing

ModSecurity reuses the work performed by Apache, but, because it goes deeper, it needs to do more parsing of its own. It's not much work, however. On a simple GET request, only the parameters in the query string will be parsed. On POST requests, the parameters placed in a request body will be parsed. Unless you're parsing XML (disabled by default), the overhead of parsing will not be a cause of concern.

Buffering

I guess you could say that ModSecurity uses a lot of RAM, which is necessary in order to allow for reliable blocking. Even without the buffering requirement, the additional data processed by ModSecurity has to be stored somewhere. The difficult thing with RAM is that the added consumption is difficult to measure, and can be measured only indirectly, by observing the differences in behavior with and without ModSecurity.

File upload interception

Handling file uploads can slow things down, for two reasons. First, to avoid using too much RAM, request bodies will typically be stored on disk, which adds to I/O requirements. There'll be two passes: one to store a request body and another to read it (so that it can be forwarded for processing). The I/O overhead is further increased if you choose to use file upload interception, because ModSecurity will also need to extract individual files from the stream of request body data in order to store them separately.

Rule processing

The rule processing CPU requirements constitute the bulk of the ModSecurity overhead. The good news is that you are in full control: the fewer rules you have in your configuration, the better the performance. If you read this book and follow my advice, I don't expect you'll have any performance trouble. Watch it with third-party rule sets, though. Do not assume that they will perform well and always test them before using them in production.

Persistent storage operations

By definition, a persistent storage mechanism is going to cost more than just storing data in RAM, because you need to ensure that the data you put in survives application restarts. ModSecurity's persistent storage is disk-based, which means that it is not as fast as it could be (if it used shared memory, for example). Modern operating systems are very good at buffering filesystem operations, so the performance should be decent. It's not something to be concerned about, but it's something that should be monitored.

External operations

External operations are not going to cost you anything unless you use them, which means that this entry is here to remind you of the potential cost. Things such as the @rbl operator (which performs a DNS request) and the exec action (which executes an external binary) are outside the control of ModSecurity and should be watched for.

Logging

Assuming you don't make any configuration mistakes (like enabling debug logging in production), logging is not going to cost you much. Most of the cost will go toward performing audit logging, which should take place only once in a while, after all. If you are keen to use full audit logging, you should consider using a separate disk array for that purpose alone.

Top 10 Performance Rules

If there's one thing that people love more than talking about performance, it's top 10 lists. So what better way to discuss performance but with its own top 10 list! If you have just 10 minutes to spend thinking about this problem, give the following list a go. In no particular order:

Avoid debug logging in production

The debug log is very verbose, especially at higher levels. At best, the debug log level in production should be kept at 3, in which case it will contain only the essential messages. A copy of the essential messages will be recorded in the error log, so it is even possible to completely turn debug logging off. If your web server installation uses an error log per virtual host, however, you may benefit from keeping the debug log level at 3, because you will then have a record of all ModSecurity actions on the server, for all virtual hosts.

Understand performance

Hopefully, you have already read the previous section, which gives an overview of where the performance issues may appear. When you know that, and you also know what affects the performance of the rules, you've made it halfway to achieving the desired performance levels.

Enforce limits

The role of runtime limits is to put a cap on the unknown. You can never control the external factors, but you can (and should) refuse to process a request that would negatively affect your system. For more information on what to configure and how, refer to the detailed configuration instructions in Chapter 3, *Configuration*.

Minimize false positives

Eliminating false positives will not only make it easier to spot real problems, but will also eliminate the unnecessary I/O operation required to perform audit logging.

Be reasonable in what you expect

Extensive content inspection can be costly. That usually isn't a problem on a dedicated reverse proxy (especially one designed to work as a web application firewall), but if you are dealing with a web server that's already running at the limit of its capacity, you can't expect to add ModSecurity and get away with it.

Use adequate matching techniques

If you're writing your own rules, the best way to make them run efficiently is to use the pattern matching techniques that match the requirements. You'll find a detailed analysis of the differences among the available options later in this chapter.

Know your sites and your rules

Knowing what your sites do and what your rules do (even if you didn't design either yourself) will give you a rough idea what to expect. The more you know about the system, the better.

Keep track of performance

Always keep a performance log. It will give you a peace of mind when you are doing fine, and help you spot performance issues early when you aren't. Having a performance log is also essential to deal with the usually unsubstantiated "your site is slow" accusations.

Test response content types before buffering

Another configuration mistake that's easy to make is to use response body buffering on all requests, which would increase RAM consumption and waste the time used on the response inspection.

Test your limits
> You should know what your system is capable of before you post that link to Slashdot. Finding out afterwards is usually not good. It is also a good idea to have a plan for what you'll do when your system becomes overloaded.

Performance Tracking

If performance is a concern, your first step should always be to measure it. In that area, I have some good news and some bad news. The bad news is that ModSecurity 2.5.x does not provide much when it comes to performance measurement. There is some limited support in the Stopwatch header in the audit logs, but the information contained there is a relic of ModSecurity 1.x, and inadequate for ModSecurity 2.x.

The good news is that this area was greatly improved in the development trunk, which means that you'll be able to accurately track ModSecurity performance, starting with the next major version. In this section, I will focus on what's possible to do with that future version, because there's really little you can do with a stable version at the moment.

Performance Metrics

The new implementation of performance tracking in ModSecurity always keeps track of a number of performance metrics. Partial access to that data is available in real time, using any of the variables from the PERF_ family. You can, for example, retrieve the duration of a previously completed phase, but you can't get any information for the phase that is currently being processed.

All the metrics, apart from the duration of the audit logging phase, are recorded in the audit log entry of a transaction, for which the new Stopwatch2 header is used:

```
Stopwatch2: 1264256494438648 5131; combined=3917, p1=11, p2=3653, p3=3, p4=29, ↵
p5=221, sr=0, sw=0, l=0, gc=0
```

The first two values are the same as in the original Stopwatch header (request start time and duration). The performance metrics follow after the semicolon:

- combined: combined processing time
- p1–p5: time spent in each of the rule phases
- sr and sw: time spent reading from and writing to persistent storage, respectively
- l: time spent on audit logging
- gc: time spent on garbage collection

All the values are given in microseconds.

Performance Logging

Performance logging must be performed when all work ModSecurity does on a transaction is complete. That means that you'll have to use Apache's logging facilities (mod_log_config). You can choose to add the additional information to your existing access log, or create a separate log file. Using a feature that was added as part of the performance tracking improvements, it is possible to log any ModSecurity variable from within mod_log_config, using the special %{VARNAME}M format string (only the uppercase M works; the case is not important in variable names). That improvement, along with the move of phase 5 to happen prior to Apache doing its logging, makes the final performance logging possible.

Use the CustomLog directive (of mod_log_config) to create a special log to track ModSecurity performance:

```
CustomLog logs/modsec_performance.log "%V %h %l %u %t \"%r\" %>s %b | ↲
%{UNIQUE_ID}e %D | %{PERF_ALL}M"
```

We are taking advantage of the special PERF_ALL variable, which was designed to include all the combined performance metrics in the same format as in the Stopwatch2 header. What other information you include is up to you, but I suggest that you always record the UNIQUE_ID value, which will enable you to cross-reference an entry in this log to other information you might have (a complete audit log entry, for example).

If you don't want to keep a separate performance log, you should at least add %{PERF_COMBINED}M to your existing access log.

Real-Time Performance Monitoring

Because you are able to access the performance counters from within ModSecurity itself, you can write a rule to track the performance in real time. Assuming that you want to be warned about the requests on which ModSecurity spends more than 2.5 milliseconds working, you write:

```
SecRule PERF_COMBINED "@gt 2500" \
    "phase:5,log,pass,msg:'Slow ModSecurity rules detected'"
```

Load Testing

The only way to truly measure the performance of a rule set is in production, or with a staging platform from which the production traffic can be faithfully replicated. Web performance testing is difficult on its own, even when ModSecurity is not involved. Because rule sets do many things, using anything but real traffic will mean that you are testing only one aspect of the rule set, which may or may not be important for you.

Still, having some idea about what the performance will be like is advisable. In this section, I will test the performance of the free ModSecurity rule sets that are currently available:

- ModSecurity Core Rule Set 2.0.4, which is the latest version at the time of writing. The Core Rule Set 2.x is distributed with ModSecurity as of version 2.5.10.

- ModSecurity Core Rule Set 1.6.1, which is the final version from the 1.x branch (and you can get it from the ModSecurity 2.5.9 tarball).

- The free version of the Gotroot rules, dated October 2009 (the most recent version available at the time of this writing).

For the test, I used the complete rule sets (with minor alterations to remove a false positive or two), with the exception of the CRS 2.0.4, where I also removed the rules derived from the PHPIDS project.

In addition to the rule set tests, I made two baseline tests: one without ModSecurity and the other with ModSecurity, but without any rules.

In preparing for the test, I opted for a simple approach that will test the rule sets with a non-trivial request. It's not the best-case scenario, but not the worst-case scenario, either:

1. I wrote a PHP script that simulates an application doing some work. I tweaked the script until I got it to spend about 30 ms "working."

2. I performed some initial tests without ModSecurity to determine the limits of the installation. The hardware used was a quad-core 2 GHz Xeon processor, with 4 GB RAM. Based on the results, I settled on testing using between 10 and 150 requests per second. I also made sure that neither the Apache configuration nor network bandwidth was going to create a performance bottleneck. For the performance tests, you want the CPU to be the bottleneck.

3. For the test, I picked up a GET request with 12 parameters, with the size just under 300 bytes.

For the testing I used the autobench tool, with the following command line:

```
$ autobench --single_host --host1 IPADDRESS --uri1 /index.php\?firstname=John\
\&lastname=Smith\&username=john.smith\&password=12345678\&password_repeat=\
12345678\&addressline1=First%20line%20of%20address\&addressline2=Second%20\
line%20of%20address\&postcode=WXXXX\&city=London\&country=United%20Kingdom\
\&phone=+447766XXXXXX\&param=john.smith@example.com --low_rate 1 \
--high_rate 15 --rate_step 1 --num_call 10 --num_conn 100 \
--timeout 5 --file results.tsv
```

I extracted two sets of data from the tests results: response rate and response time. I then used gnuplot to create the graphs:

```
set terminal postscript eps mono dashed
set output "response_rate.ps"
```

```
set key inside left
set key box
set data style linespoints
set ylabel "Response rate [req/s]"
set xlabel "Request rate [req/s]"
set grid
set xrange [10:150]
set yrange [0:400]

plot "response_rate.tsv" using 1:2 title "Baseline", \
  "response_rate.tsv" using 1:3 title "No Rules", \
  "response_rate.tsv" using 1:4 title "CRS 2.0.4", \
  "response_rate.tsv" using 1:5 title "CRS 1.6.1", \
  "response_rate.tsv" using 1:6 title "Gotroot Oct 20"
```

The resulting graphs are shown in Figures 10.1 and 10.2.

Figure 10-1. Response time test

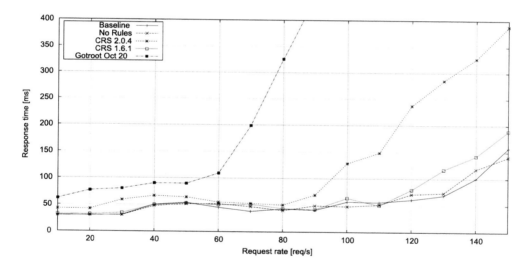

The response time graph is the more informative one:

1. Without ModSecurity, the server response time is roughly 30 ms when the load is low. It stays the same until about 30 requests per second, after which it begins to hover around 50 ms. Performance deteriorates after 100 requests per second.

2. There is virtually no difference in performance when ModSecurity is added without any rules.

3. The three rule sets vary greatly in performance:

   • The CRS 1.6.1 is very fast, adding only a couple of milliseconds of latency.

- The CRS 2.0.4 adds about 12 milliseconds of latency.
- The free Gotroot rules add about 30 milliseconds of latency, doubling the request processing time.

4. Each rule set has a different point at which the performance is significantly degraded. With CRS 2.0.4, you can get up to 80 requests per second; with the free Gotroot rules, about 50. You can see these points better in Figure 10.2. With CRS 1.6.1, the point remains pretty much where it was when the rules weren't there.

Figure 10-2. Response rate test

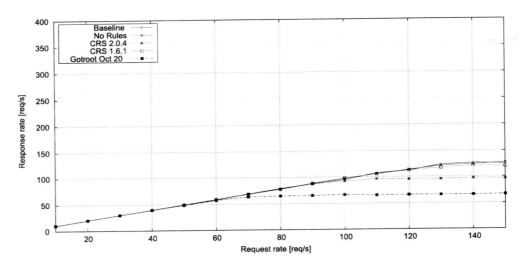

During the tests, I used vmstat to keep my eye on the overall state of the test system. I noticed a rough correlation between the speed of a rule set and its RAM consumption. None of the rule sets made a significant dent to the free RAM on the 4 GB server, but there were variations of about 100 MB (CRS 2.0.4) and 200 MB (Gotroot).

> **Note**
>
> Keeping a historical record of the vital system information of production systems is very important in case you ever need to troubleshoot a problem after the fact. On Debian systems, install the sysstat package; for others, consult the vendor documentation.

The test results show us that not all rule sets are created equal: some are focused on performance more than others. Whenever possible, you should test the rule set you are evaluating under circumstances that are as close as possible to the ones in production. Also, the rule sets consist of many parts—you don't necessarily have to run all of them. If you invest some time

Chapter 10: Performance

into understanding what a rule set does, you'll probably be able to remove some parts you don't need and achieve better performance.

Rule Benchmarking

Accurately measuring the performance of individual rules in not possible using the same version of ModSecurity that you use in production. Because the rules run for a very short period of time, not only would any attempts to measure the individual performance be inaccurate, but because the measurements themselves take time too, the overall execution speed would be noticeably reduced.

To allow for fine-grained performance measurement, ModSecurity has a compile-time option called `--enable-performance-measurement`, which activates the normally inactive performance measurement code. The version of ModSecurity you produce this way is not usable in production, because it will be 1,000 times slower than a normal one. That is so because in the performance measurement mode, each rule is run 1,000 times in a loop!

In this section, I will guide you through the steps to accurately measure the performance of your rules.

Preparation

For your rule performance tests, you will need to prepare a specially-compiled version of ModSecurity. This is how to prepare one:

1. Choose a computer that is not used for anything else, which will enable you to get consistent performance numbers. This computer will be used as a test server. You will not need a client computer, because the nature of the tests is that virtually no resources are consumed on the client side.

2. Install Apache on the test server.

3. Run ModSecurity `configure` with `--enable-performance-measurement` and any other configure-time option that you need.

4. Install and configure ModSecurity, performing some basic tests to ensure that everything works as expected.

5. Make sure to disable audit logging and set the debug log level to 0. This is very important to prevent the logging with interfering with the tests.

At this point, you may wish to perform a request or two to understand how performance measurement works. Add a couple of rules to your configuration and send one request to the web server. In your error log, you will get output similar to this one (I've removed a bunch of nonessential stuff to make it easier to read):

```
ModSecurity: Phase 1
```

```
ModSecurity: Phase 2
ModSecurity: Rule 9341350 [id "-"][file "/home/ivanr/apache/conf/httpd.conf"]↲
[line "464"]: 1 usec
ModSecurity: Phase 3
ModSecurity: Phase 4
ModSecurity: Phase 5
```

In performance mode, ModSecurity will quietly run all the rules it has in the configuration (looping 1,000 times around each rule) and print the results at the end of transaction processing. The results will contain a measurement taken for every rule. In my example, I had only one rule in my configuration. This particular rule ran very fast, because it wanted to look at request parameters, but my request didn't have any. If you wish to experiment for a while before moving on to more complex tests, add the following rule to your configuration:

```
SecRule ARGS test phase:2,t:none,nolog,pass
```

After you restart Apache, start sending requests with a varying number of parameters, and observe the differences in rule performance.

The way you write your rules—every little difference—will affect the performance, just as it would in real life. To get consistent results, you need to watch for two things:

Your rules shouldn't block

> If a rule blocks, the rules that follow will not get a chance to run. You can easily fix this problem by using the detection-only mode of deployment.

Your rules shouldn't log

> If you can't avoid the matching, use the nolog action to suppress logging.

Test Data Selection

Not all transactions are equal when it comes to rule testing. For example, most rules focus on request parameters, which means that a request that has no parameters will complete very quickly (as our first performance test earlier shows). For your tests, you should select several transactions that are representative of the workload on the target system. You can construct the test data based on what you know about the production system, or you can simply guess. If you have the time, the best approach is to record the key characteristics and build the tests based on that data.

The key characteristics are the following:

- Timestamp
- Duration
- Request method
- Query string length

- Request content type
- Request body length
- Combined size of all parameters, with file data excluded
- Number of parameters
- Response status
- Response content type
- Response body size

To record these characteristics, you will need a few ModSecurity rules and one `CustomLog` directive. The rules are used to collect the required information and transform it into the form that can be logged by Apache:

```
# How many parameters are there? We have to do this because
# variable expansion does not currently support counting
SecRule &ARGS ^.+$ \
    "phase:5,nolog,pass,t:none,capture,\
    setvar:TX.ARGS_COUNT=%{TX.0}"

# Find out the length of the query string
SecRule QUERY_STRING ^.+$ \
    "phase:5,nolog,pass,t:none,t:length,capture,\
    setvar:TX.QUERY_STRING_LENGTH=%{TX.0}"

# Record per-transaction statistics
CustomLog logs/stats.log "%V %h %t %D \"%r\" | %{TX.QUERY_STRING_LENGTH}M \
\"%{REQUEST_CONTENT_TYPE}M\" %{REQUEST_BODY_LENGTH}M %{ARGS_COMBINED_SIZE}M \
%{TX.ARGS_COUNT}M %>s \"%{RESPONSE_CONTENT_TYPE}M\" %B"
```

If you collect a representative sample of your site's traffic over a period of time, you should be able to build an accurate profile for testing.

> ### Note
>
> Most of the variables that you will be logging depend on ModSecurity having access to request body data, which means that the `SecRequestBodyBuffering` directive must be enabled for the statistics to be accurate.

Having described this thorough approach to performance testing, I will admit that I often use a much simpler approach. I have three requests that I used:

1. A simple `GET` request, representative of the requests used to retrieve static resources. No parameters.

2. A short `POST` request that simulates a registration form, or a feedback form. It has 12 parameters with about 300 bytes of data. This request is designed to see how the performance changes as the number of parameters grows.

3. A long POST request with a single very long parameter (about 15 KB), aimed at determining how rules handle large amounts of data.

I will use those three requests for testing in the remainder of this section.

Performance Baseline

Without further ado, I present the rules that I use to establish the baseline performance of the ModSecurity rule engine. Each test is designed to exercise one aspect of the rule engine performance while minimizing all others. Examine the comments that precede the rules to understand what each rule does.

```
# A rule that uses a non-existent variable.
SecRule XML @noMatch phase:1,nolog,pass

# A rule that always has one target variable,
# but which never matches (and there's no operator cost).
SecRule REMOTE_ADDR @noMatch phase:1,nolog,pass

# A rule that always matches, designed to assess the cost
# of the tasks performed on a match. (Also no operator cost.)
SecRule REMOTE_ADDR @unconditionalMatch phase:1,nolog,pass

# Unconditional action that doesn't do anything.
SecAction phase:1,nolog,pass

# Unconditional action that sets a variable.
SecAction phase:1,nolog,pass,setvar:tx.x=1

# A rule that applies a no-cost operator to every parameter,
# which was designed to see how the cost rises with the
# number of parameters present.
SecRule ARGS @noMatch phase:2,nolog,pass

# A rule designed to test the cost
# of the lowercase transformation function.
SecRule ARGS:param @noMatch phase:2,nolog,pass,t:none

# A rule designed to test the cost
# of the lowercase transformation function.
SecRule ARGS:param @noMatch phase:2,nolog,pass,t:lowercase

# One complete, reasonably complex rule, with
# no transformation functions.
SecRule ARGS "\bon(abort|blur|change|click|dblclick|dragdrop|end|error|\
focus|keydown|keypress|keyup|load|mousedown|mousemove|mouseout\
mouseover|mouseup|move|readystatechange|reset|resize|select|submit|\
unload)\b\W*?=" \
```

```
phase:2,nolog,pass,t:none
```

The baseline performance testing results (of ModSecurity 2.5.x) can be seen in Table 10.1, "Baseline performance results". The results are given in microseconds.

Table 10.1. Baseline performance results

Rule	GET	POST	Long POST
No variable cost	1	1	1
One variable, no match, no operator cost	6	6	6
One variable, match, no operator cost	9	9	9
Unconditional match, but no actions	9	9	9
Unconditional match, set variable	10	10	10
All arguments, no match, no operator cost	1	66	7
One argument, no match	1	7	7
One argument with t:lowercase, no match	1	7	114
Nontrivial regular expression	1	68	62

We draw the following conclusions:

- There seems to be a fixed per-variable handling cost (engine overhead) of about 5 microseconds. This does not seem like much, but it adds up. Running a rule against one variable took 6 microseconds, but running it against 12 variables took 66 microseconds. This cost is significant, because that's what most rules will do: iterate through all available parameters.

- There's a per-match cost of about 3 microseconds. Because matches are relatively rare, it's not something we need to be concerned about.

- Rules without any parameters are processed very quickly.

- The cost of transformation is substantial when used with long parameters. With the one 15 KB parameter, the lowercase transformation used in excess of 100 microseconds. You should thus use case-insensitive regular pattern matching, which will give you better performance. Use the transformation functions when there's no other option.

Optimizing Pattern Matching

Using the performance measurement mode of ModSecurity, we established that there's an inherent cost to every rule. We are now going to explore several optimization techniques that increase the overall performance of pattern matching, especially when dealing with a large number of patterns.

The basis for our tests will be 114 SQL injection keywords, which I have retrieved from the Core Rule Set v2.0.4. Here's a few of them, just to give you an idea of what they look like:

```
sys.user_objects
sys.user_triggers
@@spid
msysaces
instr
sys.user_views
sys.tab
charindex
locate
sys.user_catalog
constraint_type
msysobjects
attnotnull
select
delete
... 99 more keywords
```

As you can see, some of them are likely to result with many false positives (locate, select, delete, ...); however, the goal of those keywords is not necessarily to detect an SQL injection, but rather to give you an indication based on which you could decide to perform further tests.

Rule per Keyword Approach

We'll start with the naïve approach to implementing the keyword detection, using one rule per keyword and arriving at exactly 114 rules. The performance of this approach will be the baseline against which we will compare all other tests:

```
SecRule ARGS "@rx sys.user_objects"
SecRule ARGS "@rx sys.user_triggers"
SecRule ARGS "@rx @@spid"
... 111 more rules
```

Although this approach is not likely to result in great performance, it's straightforward and allows us to deal with each keyword individually. For example, if you determine that a keyword is causing too many false positives in a particular location, you can use SecRuleRemoveById to remove the entire rule. The ability to deal with false positives in this way is especially important for third-party rules, where the ability to easily update from one release to another is very important. You want to be able to tweak third-party rules without modifying the actual files.

Combined Regular Expression Pattern

To eliminate the per-rule overhead, we can combine all the keywords in a single regular expression pattern using alternation:

```
SecRule ARGS "(?i)(sys.user_objects|sys.user_triggers|@@spid|msysaces|instr|↵
sys.user_views|sys.tab|charindex|locate|sys.user_catalog|constraint_type|↵
```

```
msysobjects|attnotnull|select|sys.user_tables|sys.user_constraints|↵
...15 lines of text omitted from the middle
dbms_java|benchmark|xp_regread|xp_regwrite)"
```

The single-rule approach is likely to give us a significant speed boost, but we've lost the ability to suppress individual keywords. On the positive side, it's fairly easy to locate a keyword in the entire regular express pattern and remove it manually.

Optimized Regular Expression Pattern

Regular expression patterns are compiled into state machines. Our crude attempt at combining keywords is easy to understand and do, but it does not produce very efficient results. The more keywords you have the more likely it is that they have a lot in common. If you can figure out what it is that they have in common, you can write a regular expression pattern that is very efficient. I did just that, and here's the resulting regular expression:

```
SecRule ARGS "(?i-xsm:(?:s(?:ys(?:.(?:user_(?:(?:t(?:ab(?:_column|le)|rigger)|↵
object|view)s|c(?:onstraints|atalog))|all_tables|tab)|(?:(?:process|tabl)e|↵
... 13 lines of text omitted from the middle
[fs]null)|'(?:s(?:qloledb|a)|msdasql|dbo)'|p(?:g_(?:attribute|class)|rint)|↵
(?:n?varcha|waitfo)r|@@(?:version|spid)|benchmark|having|locate|rownum))"
```

The result is almost an incomprehensible mess. You can probably make out the original keywords in the text, but they've all been "melted" together. You'll notice that alternation is still used, but with deep nesting, combining the shared keyword bits. In addition, data capture is disabled.

The increased pattern matching performance comes at a further maintenance cost. In addition to not being able to work with individual keywords directly (the same problem as with our earlier attempt at optimization), now it is not even possible to modify the one resulting regular expression by hand.

> **Note**
>
> Although the combined regular expressions cannot be maintained by hand, nothing says that manual maintenance is the only way. You can easily put together a script or two to generate optimized regular expressions from a simple list of individual ones. By doing that, you get the best of both worlds!

Of course, I didn't manually construct the heavily optimized regular expression. I used a clever Perl module called Regexp::Assemble [http://search.cpan.org/~dland/Regexp-Assemble-0.30/Assemble.pm], and followed the instructions written by Ofer Shezaf in a blog post on the ModSecurity blog [http://blog.modsecurity.org/2007/06/optimizing-regu.html]. Ofer pioneered the use of heavily optimized regular expressions in the first generation of the Core Rules.

I used `apt-get install libregexp-assemble-perl` to install `Regexp::Assemble` on my Debian box. In the blog post, Ofer provides the instructions for the installation on Windows, and there's even a Windows binary available for download.

A trivial script is needed to operate `Regexp::Assemble`:

```perl
#!/usr/bin/perl

use strict;
use Regexp::Assemble;

my $ra = Regexp::Assemble->new;

while (<>) {
  $ra->add($_);
}

print $ra->re . "\n";
```

You feed the script a list of keywords (one per line), and it spits back the optimized regular expression:

```
$ ./optimize-regex.pl < sqli_keywords.dat
(?-xism:(?:s(?:ys(?:.(?:user_(?:(?:t(?:ab(?:_column|le)|rigger)
...and so on
```

> **Note**
>
> If you examine the beginning of the resulting pattern, you will notice that it disables case-sensitive matching. (If you are not familiar with pattern compilation options, head to the section called "Changing How Patterns Are Compiled", in this chapter.) The optimizing tool does not know whether your keywords are case-sensitive. If they are not, you'll need to manually enable case-insensitive matching, as I've done for this same pattern in an earlier rule.

Parallel Pattern Matching

An alternative optimization technique is to use the parallel matching facilities of ModSecurity, which use the Aho-Corasick algorithm to match all supplied keywords at once. I will use the `@pmFromFile` operator, which allows me to refer to the file in which the keywords are stored (which is nice, because it keeps the configuration file neat and tidy):

```
SecRule ARGS "@pmFromFile sqli_keywords.dat"
```

Test Results

The testing results of the four pattern matching techniques can be seen in Table 10.2, "Performance comparison of pattern-matching approaches". The results are given in microseconds.

We got pretty much what we had expected, but there are some surprises. We draw the following conclusions:

- The multi-rule approach carries a nonnegligible cost, even with requests with no parameter. It may take 1 microsecond to process a rule, but those microseconds add up.

- Parallel matching is very fast. You should therefor aim to use it whenever you can, which in practice means whenever you have a large number of keywords and the expressiveness of regular expressions is not required.

- If you must use regular expressions, using optimized combinations may increase the speed several-fold.

- Using a large number of regular expressions against large amounts of data (e.g., response bodies) is not recommended. It will consume significant amounts of CPU power.

- Somewhat surprisingly, the one-rule-per-keyword approach produced better results with a large amount of data than the optimized versions. That indicates that optimized regular expressions are better for smaller amounts of data.

Table 10.2. Performance comparison of pattern-matching approaches

Approach	GET	POST	Long POST
Rule (@rx) per keyword	114	7,752	7,895
Combined regular expression (@rx)	1	473	45,812
Optimized regular expression (@rx)	1	178	13,114
Parallel matching (@pm)	1	73	671

Summary

In the course of writing this chapter, I learned more about ModSecurity than ever before. You see, I too was happy with the performance of ModSecurity and rarely had a need to look deeper into the topic. But I always wondered what the situation was, and now we know.

The chapter that follows looks at content injection, which is a very interesting and innovative feature that enables you to extend your inspection capabilities from the server side into your users' browsers.

11 Content Injection

Content injection is an innovative security technique that allows you to inject arbitrary content into HTTP response bodies. The technique was designed to address the attacks that take place in the browser itself, which is outside the reach of most server-side defenses.

With content injection, a server can reach out to inject dynamic content and code (JavaScript) into responses, gaining in-browser inspection capabilities. The idea is that you first perform your normal server-side inspection, after which you inject JavaScript into the HTTP response to continue the inspection with full access to the browser's internal state. This section will give you a good overview of several useful and easy-to-use techniques based on content injection.

> **Note**
>
> There is nothing to say that content injection has to be used only for defense. There is a school of thought that says that offense is the best defense. If you subscribe to that view, you could use content injection to attack the attackers, injecting malware directly into their browsers. Just make sure that you understand your legal position before you do anything that might be crossing the line.

Writing Content Injection Rules

Content injection allows you to inject content, possibly on a per-response basis, either at the beginning of a response or at the end. Injecting at the beginning is useful if you want to attempt to prevent attacks. Injecting at the end is useful if you want to inspect the content of the page and the internal browser state after all other JavaScript code has already been run.

To start, enable the injection feature using the SecContentInjection directive:

```
# Enable content injection
SecContentInjection On
```

> **Note**
>
> Content injection does not require that you have SecResponseBodyAccess enabled. It works equally well with this setting disabled.

In the next step, determine whether injection would make sense. Web servers process many types of requests, and only some responses can be injected. You wouldn't, for example, want to inject anything into an image—it would end up being corrupted. To find out whether a response is injectable, check its content type, which you will find in the RESPONSE_CONTENT_TYPE variable, in phase 3. (You shouldn't try to use RESPONSE_HEADERS:Content-Type, which may not always contain the necessary information.)

I suggest that you use the following framework for all of your content injection rules:

```
SecContentInjection On

# First check if we should inject anything
SecRule RESPONSE_CONTENT_TYPE !^text/html \
    phase:3,nolog,pass,skipAfter:999

# ... your content injection rules here

SecMarker 999
```

First, you check for the correct content type, jumping over all your content injection rules if an incorrect type is used in a response. If you are going to inject into more than one type of document (e.g., text/plain and text/html), then you are probably going to need different rules, with different content for each type. In that case, just repeat the previous example fragment, making sure to choose the content type correctly and to use a unique SecMarker value in each group.

Finally, to inject content, use the append and prepend actions. The following example injects a header and a footer into an HTML response:

```
SecAction phase:3,nolog,pass,prepend:'Header<hr>'
SecAction phase:3,nolog,pass,append:'<hr>Footer'
```

Note

The content injection facilities will not perform any output encoding, which means that you must manually encode everything that you want injected. The prepend and append actions do support variable expansion (as of ModSecurity 2.5.9) and make it possible to inject dynamically generated content, but you *must* take care to *never* inject any user-controlled content. Doing so would create a XSS vulnerability, right there in your web application firewall! Inject only what you have 100% control over.

For testing purposes, you can also try this simple JavaScript code, which will write the URL of the current page on the screen:

```
SecAction phase:3,nolog,pass,prepend:↵
'<script>document.write(document.location)</script>'
```

So we've established that you can have your JavaScript code inside the browser. But what can you do with this ability? Here are some ideas.

- Inspect request parameters, including the fragment identifier, which is normally not sent to servers.

- Inspect browser state. For example, a popular technique used to assist in XSS attacks is to store the payload in window names (property `window.name`). That field is out of bounds to a server, but not to the injected JavaScript code.

- Inspect browser configuration; for example, look for vulnerable plug-ins.

- Inspect page state and structure (DOM) at the end of page execution.

- Redefine the built-in JavaScript functions to detect unusual activity patterns.

JavaScript is a fascinating language that is endlessly tweakable. Describing advanced JavaScript attacks is out of the scope of this book, but if you want to go there, simply pick up the most advanced JavaScript book you can find and use it as a starting point.

CRSF Defense Using Content Injection

A very imaginative use of the content injection feature is that devised by Ryan C. Barnett, the ModSecurity Community Manager and author of the Core Rule Set. He established a way to use content injection to defend vulnerable applications against cross-site request forgery (CSRF) attacks, otherwise possible only through the modification of the source code of the vulnerable applications. (If you are not familiar with CSRF, I suggest that you read through the CSRF entry on Wikipedia [http://en.wikipedia.org/wiki/Cross-site_request_forgery].)

The usual way to defend against CSRF is to embed special tokens into application forms, and accept only submits that contain the correct token values. CSRF requests faced with such defenses always fail, because they have no way to "know" the correct token value.

Ryan's approach is to use content injection to inject JavaScript, which is then used to modify all page forms to add tokens where they wouldn't normally exist. In the second part of the trick, he would have ModSecurity rules inspect all POST requests to verify that they contain the correct values. Brilliant!

For more information, look up Ryan's Black Hat DC 2009 whitepaper *WAF Virtual Patching Challenge: Securing WebGoat with ModSecurity*. The 26-page document contains many other interesting techniques.

Communicating Back to the Server

When you detect a problem using JavaScript, you need to somehow communicate that fact back to the server. The best way to do that is to get the browser to send a special request. The simplest way to do that is by writing some HTML into the response:

```
document.write("<script src=/security-error.js><" + "/script>");
```

To the special request, add a rule that detects it and raises an alert in ModSecurity. While you're there, you might want to consider doing other things, such as cancelling the victim's application session. You might want to consider including an error code in the request (e.g., as a parameter), which will help you in establishing exactly where the problem was. You should also be prepared that this communication mechanism can be discovered and subverted by the attacker. In that light, don't use any information obtained from such requests for anything apart from logging.

Interrupting Page Rendering

Perhaps you'll decide that detection is not enough and will want to prevent in-browser attacks. JavaScript does not offer a way to stop page rendering, but you can do the next best thing—redirect the user someplace else using `location.replace()`. In my tests, the invocation has the effect of effectively stopping rendering and moving elsewhere. For example:

```
location.replace("http://www.example.com/security-error.html");
```

The stopping of page rendering when `location.replace()` is invoked is a side effect and you should generally not expect it to work across all browsers, or to continue to work in the browsers it works in today. For example, some browsers may continue to process JavaScript while another page is being loaded. You should assume that some attacks may get through.

If you choose to implement prevention in this way, don't forget to put some user-friendly explanation for the sudden redirection to another page. Your users will appreciate it. The advantage of using prevention like this is that it also notifies you of the problem—whenever someone accesses that special page, you will know that they have been attacked.

Using External JavaScript Code

In the current implementation of content injection, you are limited to the content you can put in a parameter to the append and prepend actions. In particular, you won't be able to inject any non-printable characters. You can escape a single quote with a backslash, but that's the only escape option ModSecurity supports at present. If you do run into trouble, you can always store the JavaScript code in a separate file and just inject a link to it.

If you can place a file onto the root of the web site that is being protected, use this:

```
SecAction "phase:3,nolog,pass,prepend:'<script src=/ids.js></script>'"
```

If you have several web sites and you'd like to use one file for all of them, use an absolute address:

```
SecAction "phase:3,nolog,pass,prepend:↩
'<script src=https://www.example.com/ids.js></script>'"
```

Finally, if you need to construct the address dynamically, you can do that by injecting JavaScript that will generate the HTML code that is needed to include the external JavaScript:

```
SecAction "phase:3,nolog,pass,prepend:↩
'<script>document.write(unescape(\"<script src=\'\" + document.location.protocol ↩
+ \"//www.example.com/ids.js\'%3c/script>\"));</script>'"
```

Several aspects of this rule need explaining:

1. Use `document.write()` to output HTML to the document body.

2. Make sure to escape all single and double quotes in the code.

3. In the previous example, I used URL encoding (converting the opening angle bracket to `%3c`) in combination with `unescape()` to deactivate the closing script tag. This approach can also be used if you need special characters in JavaScript (and you cannot write them directly because of ModSecurity's poor escape syntax).

4. The code uses the `document.location.protocol` property, which will be `http:` for plain-text connections and `https:` for encrypted connections, to construct an URL that will correspond to the security level of the including document. That will help with the performance on non-SSL sites.

Communicating with Users

Another interesting application of content injection is "talking" to the application users. Ages ago I wrote some code, practically as a party trick, that would detect access using vulnerability scanners (e.g., Paros Proxy) and send a message back that we don't like being probed.

Such a rule can be as simple as this example:

```
SecRule REQUEST_HEADERS:User-Agent Paros \
    "phase:3,pass,prepend:'Use of Paros Proxy is strictly forbidden'"
```

If your site uses sessions and you've configured ModSecurity to track them, you can send per-session messages that expire after a period of time. I will show you how to do that, using an example that detects the word `attack` anywhere in request parameters (let's pretend that we are detecting an SQL injection attack), then sets a message that will be displayed to the same session for 60 seconds (even in the requests that do not contain the attack). The example consists of only two rules.

The first rule is used to trigger the message:

```
# The following rule triggers a message. Session must have been
# established (using setsid) beforehand, otherwise the execution
# of this rule will cause an error.
SecRule ARGS attack "nolog,pass,msg:'Detected SQL Injection',\
    setvar:SESSION.message_flag=1,\
    expirevar:SESSION.message_flag=60,\
    setvar:'SESSION.message=SQL Injection is lame'"
```

The detection itself is trivial, but the rest needs an explanation:

1. The first setvar action (setvar:SESSION.message_flag=1) creates a per-session flag that is used to indicate that a message exists.

2. The expirevar action (expirevar:SESSION.message_flag=60) is used to delete the SESSION.message_flag variable after 60 seconds.

3. The second setvar action (setvar:'SESSION.message=SQL Injection is lame') defines the message.

Another rule is used to detect the presence of SESSION.message_flag and display the message stored in SESSION.message:

```
# The following rule displays the message. As before, the prepend action
# must be executed only if the response content type is right.
SecRule SESSION.message_flag "@eq 1" \
    phase:3,nolog,pass,prepend:%{SESSION.message}
```

When, after 60 seconds, the expirevar statement from the first rule kicks in, the SESSION.message_flag variable will be deleted and the message will go away.

Summary

To me, content injection is a fascinating ability of ModSecurity, because you get to move into the ever-complex world of JavaScript. You get to extend your virtual hand into every single user's browser, and have a look at what they know. It's all right to look, by the way, because you will have access to only the pages that come from your own sites. Everything else will be off-limits.

In the next chapter, I'll cover a topic that's possibly even more interesting than the one covered here—the ability to write rules in Lua, a proper programming language.

12 Writing Rules in Lua

The ModSecurity Rule Language is relatively easy to use, but it is fairly limited. After all, the directives have to obey the Apache configuration syntax, so there is only so much we can do within those boundaries. I like to think that you can use the rule language to get 80% of your tasks done, and quickly too: common things are simple to do, complex things are possible. At some point, however, the rule language stops being an appropriate tool for the task, and you need to look elsewhere. Starting with ModSecurity 2.5 you can write rules in Lua [http://www.lua.org], a fast and memory-efficient scripting language. These attributes made it very popular with game programmers, who are always trying to get that extra ounce of performance.

The advantage of Lua is that it is a proper programming language, which means that you are limited only by your programming skills. The disadvantage, as you might expect, is a performance penalty. Some of that penalty comes from the fact that Lua scripts need to be interpreted at runtime, and some because the current implementation in ModSecurity (version 2.5.x) is not as efficient as it could be. Having said that, I think the performance is adequate—provided that you run only a small number of Lua rules per transaction.

> **Note**
>
> The support for Lua in ModSecurity is experimental. The code itself is stable and production-ready, but the APIs may change. A future version of ModSecurity may make changes to the way things are implemented and then you may need to update your rules to make them compatible. Other than that, there is no reason not to use Lua rules.

There are two ways in which Lua can be used to enhance your rule sets. First, you can write detection rules in it. Second, you can write scripts that are executed on a rule match. The remainder of this section explains both of these features.

Rule Language Integration

Although the previous section made it sound like Lua rules are separate from the rule language, that's not actually true. In ModSecurity, Lua is implemented as an rule language extension, via the SecRuleScript directive. For example, this is how you run a Lua script:

```
SecRuleScript /path/to/script.lua phase:2,log,deny
```

Comparing to the SecRule directive, the variables and the operators are gone. They are replaced with a single parameter, which is the location of the Lua script you wish to run. That means that the script will choose which variables it wishes to inspect and in which order. The action list is still there, though. You can see that the rule in the previous example runs in phase 2, and that it logs and blocks on a match.

Lua Rules Skeleton

Every Lua rule needs to have an entry point that ModSecurity can find—the main function. This is what the simplest Lua rule looks like:

```
function main()
    -- Never match
    return nil;
end
```

As you suspect, the previous rule does not do much. It only returns nil, which means that there is no match. For a Lua rule to match, it needs to return a message:

```
function main()
    -- Always match
    return "Error message";
end
```

The beauty of the way Lua is integrated with ModSecurity is that once you return an error message, the rule language takes over and processes the action list. Thus, with Lua rules, you still get to use what you already know. For example, you provide all the metadata information for Lua rules in the exact same way as you do for normal rules:

```
SecRuleScript /path/to/script.lua \
    phase:2,log,deny,id:1001,rev:1,severity:3
```

Whatever you can do with a SecRule directive, you can do with SecRuleScript. There's no limit to what is possible, including using Lua in rule chains.

Accessing Variables

Once inside a Lua rule, the first thing you will need to do is access some variables. The following example retrieves two variables from ModSecurity:

```
function main()
    -- Retrieve remote IP address
    local remote_addr = m.getvar("REMOTE_ADDR");

    -- Retrieve username
    local username = m.getvar("ARGS.username", {"lowercase"});

    if ((username == "admin") and (remote_addr ~= "192.168.1.1")) then
        return "Admin sign-in not allowed from IP address: " .. remote_addr;
    end

    -- No match
    return nil;
end
```

A call to the m.getvar() function will retrieve the variable named in the first parameter. In the example, the value of REMOTE_ADDR is retrieved and placed into the Lua variable remote_addr.

The function has an optional second parameter. If used, it must contain a list of transformation functions that will be applied to the variable before it is returned to Lua. In the example, the value of ARGS.username is retrieved from ModSecurity, passed through the lowercase transformation function, and placed into the Lua variable username.

It is also possible to retrieve more than one variable at once, but for that you use the m.getvars() function (note the additional s in the name). The following example retrieves all request parameters, then examines them one at a time.

```
function main()
    -- Retrieve all parameters
    local vars = m.getvars("ARGS", {"lowercase", "htmlEntityDecode"});

    -- Examine all variables
    for i = 1, #d do
        -- Examine one value
        if (string.find(d[i].value, "<script>")) then
            return ("Suspected XSS in variable: " .. d[i].name .. ".");
        end
    end

    -- Nothing wrong found.
    return nil;
end
```

The m.getvars() function works differently. It does not return just the value of the requested variable. Instead, it returns an object with two members: name, which contains the name of the variable, and value, which contains the corresponding value. The previous example demonstrates how both are used.

Logging

Sometimes a Lua rule will not be working as you expect, but you won't have any clues as to why. You can troubleshoot your scripts by emitting debug log messages, using the m.log() function.

```
function main()
    -- Log something
    m.log(4, "Hello World from Lua!");

    -- Never match
    return nil;
end
```

The m.log() function takes two parameters, the first of which is the desired log level (1–9) and the second is the desired message.

Lua Actions

With the addition of Lua, the exec action was extended to support Lua natively. Normally, you supply the exec action with a path to an external script and ModSecurity executes that script in a separate process. If the script path ends with .lua, however, ModSecurity will process the script using the embedded Lua interpreter. This approach not only achieves better performance (no need to start a new process), but also gives the Lua script access to the current transaction context.

```
SecRule ARGS test phase:2,log,pass,exec:/path/to/script.lua
```

A Lua script called from exec must define the same entry point as all other Lua scripts. There is no need to return anything from the main() function.

```
function main()
    -- Log something
    m.log(4, "Lua executed in exec!");
end
```

Now, the example looks deceptively simple—so much that you may wonder what use could Lua possibly have. The answer is that you can do from Lua pretty much anything you want. You not only get the programming language and the standard Lua libraries, but you also get access to a number of extensions that take care of filesystem access, sockets, database access, and so on. And, because Lua scripts executed in this way have access to the transaction context and the persistent storage, what you have is a seamless scripting extension of ModSecurity.

Summary

This chapter is very short, but the topic is important enough to warrant its own chapter. Lua is what you will turn to when implementing a particular functionality using just the rule language fails, or when the resulting rules are too difficult to maintain. The way in which Lua is currently used in ModSecurity just scratches the surface of what can be done, so let's hope that future versions will continue to extend in this direction.

In the next chapter, we will focus on XML processing. The XML features of ModSecurity are not used by all installations, but those that do use them find the capabilities crucial.

13 Handling XML

ModSecurity has very good XML support, which is made possible by a tight integration with libxml2 [http://xmlsoft.org]. Libxml2 is one of the fastest XML libraries available, making it very suitable for the performance-sensitive work in ModSecurity. The integration is seamless, effectively making XML payloads just another source of data to which you can apply your usual rule-writing techniques. The following functionality is supported:

- XML parsing
- DTD validation
- XML Schema validation
- XPath expressions

Once upon a time it was possible to leave out XML functionality when compiling ModSecurity, but newer versions do not support that any more. You should reasonably expect for the XML processing features to be available in ModSecurity.

> **Note**
>
> You don't want to use ModSecurity as an XML testing tool, because the entire cycle (write rules, then send payload, then analyze debug log) is very slow. You should instead use an XML validation tool. Probably the best option is xmllint, because it is based on the same library used by ModSecurity.

The examples used in this section were adapted from the sample written by Steve Traut for the XMLBeans project [http://xmlbeans.apache.org].

XML Parsing

Although ModSecurity is capable of parsing XML, it won't attempt any parsing by default. XML parsing is very resource-intensive and many installations do not need it. Even when they do, recognizing that XML parsing is needed is not something that can be done in a way that works for everyone. Other request body processors (URLENCODED and MULTIPART) rely on using a standardized content type for detection when they are needed, but there is no such thing for XML.

To enable XML parsing, you'll have to go through the manual request body processor activation. There are two things you will need to do:

1. Analyze request to determine whether XML parsing is needed. Most requests won't need XML parsing enabled. Figuring out which do will depend on the exact content type used by your application. In many cases, the Content-Type header will contain text/xml, and that is what I will assume in my examples.

2. Instruct ModSecurity to use the XML request body processor for the requests that do need it.

For example:

```
# Detect XML payloads and activate XML parsing
SecRule REQUEST_HEADERS:Content-Type ^text/xml$ \
    phase:1,t:none,t:lowercase,nolog,pass,ctl:requestBodyProcessor=XML
```

The example uses the @rx operator, but a straightforward @streq would have worked as well. Notice how I used t:lowercase to ensure that the comparison is case-insensitive (which is always appropriate when working with Content-Type).

It is important to always use phase 1 (REQUEST_HEADERS) when determining request body processors. Request body parsing is done right after phase 1 completes and the processor choice must be made before then.

When you're writing ModSecurity rules, you usually have to test a lot, and when you're working with XML, you will have to test even more. For my testing, I use the little utility script that was distributed with ModSecurity 1.x, called run-test.pl. Although this script isn't distributed with ModSecurity 2.x., you can still get it directly from the repository:

```
http://mod-security.svn.sourceforge.net/viewvc/mod-security/m1/trunk/util/↩
run-test.pl?revision=6
```

With this script in hand, you can construct and send raw HTTP requests to your web server to test your rules. For example, I used the following file (which I named xml.t) to test XML parsing:

```
POST / HTTP/1.0
Content-Type: text/xml
Content-Length: 633

<employees>
    <employee>
        <name>Fred Jones</name>
        <address location="home">
```

```
        <street>999 Aurora Ave.</street>
        <city>Seattle</city>
        <state>WA</state>
        <zip>98115</zip>
    </address>
    <address location="work">
        <street>2022 152nd Avenue NE</street>
        <city>Redmond</city>
        <state>WA</state>
        <zip>98052</zip>
    </address>
    <phone location="work">(425)555-0100</phone>
    <phone location="home">(206)555-0101</phone>
    <phone location="mobile">(206)555-0102</phone>
    </employee>
</employees>
```

To send a file to a web server, you specify the server information (in the following example, both the IP address and the port) and the file you wish to send. I also often use the debug switch (-d), which makes the tool output all traffic to standard output:

```
./run-test 192.168.3.100:8080 -d xml.t
```

Let's see how ModSecurity processed this test request. Following is the debug log output at level 8 (which is shorter than the level 9 output, but equally meaningful in this case).

First, the rule ran in phase 1 to check the value of the Content-Type request header. It matched, causing the ctl action to set the request body processor to XML:

```
[4] Recipe: Invoking rule 8de36c8; [file "/home/ivanr/apache/conf/httpd.conf"] ↵
[line "518"].
[5] Rule 8de36c8: SecRule "REQUEST_HEADERS:Content-Type" "@rx ^text/xml$" ↵
"phase:1,auditlog,t:none,t:lowercase,nolog,pass,ctl:requestBodyProcessor=XML"
[4] Transformation completed in 24 usec.
[4] Executing operator "rx" with param "^text/xml$" against ↵
REQUEST_HEADERS:Content-Type.
[4] Operator completed in 54 usec.
[4] Ctl: Set requestBodyProcessor to XML.
[4] Warning. Pattern match "^text/xml$" at REQUEST_HEADERS:Content-Type. ↵
[file "/home/ivanr/apache/conf/httpd.conf"] [line "518"]
[4] Rule returned 1.
```

Then we see the second phase starting and ModSecurity reading the request body and forwarding it to the XML parser:

```
[4] Second phase starting (dcfg 8dfee38).
[4] Input filter: Reading request body.
[4] XML: Initialising parser.
[4] XML: Parsing complete (well_formed 1).
```

The last line indicates the completion of XML parsing. It also indicates that the XML was well formed. It it weren't, the message would display a 0 instead of the 1. This message makes a good point, actually: you need to not only enable XML parsing, but also verify that it was successful.

To verify how XML parsing went in a rule, use the REQBODY_PROCESSOR_ERROR variable, as you do with all request body processors. I covered this topic in detail in the section called "Handling Processing Errors" in Chapter 3. If you follow my advice from that section and use the rule to check for request body processors errors (also reproduced here), you will be covered for XML parsing errors, too:

```
# Verify that we've correctly processed the request body.
# As a rule of thumb, when failing to process a request body
# you should reject the request (when deployed in blocking mode)
# or log a high-severity alert (when deployed in detection-only mode).
SecRule REQBODY_PROCESSOR_ERROR "!@eq 0" \
    "phase:2,t:none,log,block,msg:'Failed to parse request body: ↵
%{REQBODY_PROCESSOR_ERROR_MSG}'"
```

We can easily check whether that is correct. Make a copy of xml.t, calling the new file xml-invalid.t, then replace one of the angle brackets with a space. (Replacing a character will ensure that the payload length remains the same. If you add or remove a character, you will need to update the Content-Length request header to reflect the change.) When you send such modified file to the server, the debug log will report the problem:

```
[4] Second phase starting (dcfg 8df6e68).
[4] Input filter: Reading request body.
[4] XML: Initialising parser.
[4] XML: Parsing complete (well_formed 0).
[2] XML parser error: XML: Failed parsing document.
```

Then, a few lines down in the log file, you will see the second rule triggering:

```
[4] Recipe: Invoking rule 8e5e538; [file "/home/ivanr/apache/conf/httpd.conf"] ↵
[line "522"].
[5] Rule 8e5e538: SecRule "REQBODY_PROCESSOR_ERROR" "!@eq 0" ↵
"phase:2,status:500,t:none,log,block,msg:'Failed to parse request body: ↵
%{REQBODY_PROCESSOR_ERROR_MSG}'"
[4] Transformation completed in 3 usec.
[4] Executing operator "!eq" with param "0" against ↵
REQBODY_PROCESSOR_ERROR.
[4] Operator completed in 8 usec.
[4] Rule returned 1.
[1] Access denied with code 500 (phase 2). Match of "eq 0" against ↵
"REQBODY_PROCESSOR_ERROR" required.  [file "/home/ivanr/apache/conf/httpd.conf"] ↵
[line "522"] [msg "Failed to parse request body: XML parser error: XML: Failed ↵
parsing document."]
```

> **Note**
>
> Just because an XML payload is not well-formed does not mean that your subsequent rules are not going to run. They will run, but they will have access to only a partial XML tree, created until the parsing error was encountered. What this tree will contain depends on the nature of the error. If you choose not to block on a request body processor failure, then you need to at least ensure that you don't rely on the results of your subsequent XML rules. For example, you could evaluate REQBODY_PROCESSOR_ERROR again and skip over them. If you don't mind working with a partial XML payload, or even if that's desired, then you don't need to do anything.

DTD Validation

Sometimes you will be happy to work with a partial (invalid) XML payload, but some other times you will want to perform further validation. The validation requires one further rule, in which you specify the type of validation and the file that contains the rules:

```
SecRule XML "@validateDTD /path/to/apache2/conf/xml.dtd" \
    "phase:2,log,block,msg:'Failed to validate XML payload against DTD'"
```

The file `xml.dtd`, which contains a DTD for the XML payload used earlier in this section, contains the following:

```
<!ELEMENT phone (#PCDATA)>
<!ATTLIST phone location CDATA #REQUIRED>
<!ELEMENT street (#PCDATA)>
<!ELEMENT city (#PCDATA)>
<!ELEMENT state (#PCDATA)>
<!ELEMENT zip (#PCDATA)>
<!ELEMENT address (street, city, state, zip)>
<!ATTLIST address location CDATA #REQUIRED>
<!ELEMENT name (#PCDATA)>
<!ELEMENT employee (name, address+, phone+)>
<!ELEMENT employees (employee)>
```

When you submit the same XML payload as before, you get:

```
[4] Recipe: Invoking rule 8265d30; [file "/home/ivanr/apache/conf/httpd.conf"]
[line "525"].
[5] Rule 8265d30: SecRule "XML" "@validateDTD /home/ivanr/apache/conf/xml.dtd"
"phase:2,status:500,log,block,msg:'Failed to validate
XML payload against DTD'"
[4] Transformation completed in 1 usec.
[4] Executing operator "validateDTD" with param "/home/ivanr/apache/conf/xml.dtd"
against XML.
[9] Target value: "[XML document tree]"
[4] XML: Successfully validated payload against DTD: /home/ivanr/apache/conf/xml.dtd
```

```
[4] Operator completed in 612 usec.
[4] Rule returned 0.
```

> **Note**
>
> The @validateDTD operator returns a match if it fails to validate, and no match if everything is all right.

When validation fails, the error messages from libxml2 will be recorded as notices (level 3), which means that they will appear in the debug log, the audit log, and the Apache error log. For example, when I changed the payload to transmit the employee name with the first name and the last name separately:

```
<firstname>Fred</firstname>
<lastname>Jones</lastname>
```

I got three libxml2 errors in return:

```
[3] Element employee content does not follow the DTD, expecting (name , ↩
address+ , phone+), got (firstname lastname address address phone phone phone )
[3] No declaration for element firstname
[3] No declaration for element lastname
```

And there was also one fatal error from the validation rule itself:

```
[1] Access denied with code 500 (phase 2). XML: DTD validation failed. [file ↩
"/home/ivanr/apache/conf/httpd.conf"] [line "525"] [msg "Failed to ↩
validate XML payload against DTD"]
```

> **Note**
>
> You must ensure that you enter the correct path to the DTD that you need for validation. If the path is incorrect, validation will fail silently, without a match. This is a flaw in ModSecurity, which is scheduled to be fixed in the next major release (ticket MODSEC-12 in the Tracker).

XML Schema Validation

The XML Schema validation rule is functionally identical to that used for DTD validation:

```
SecRule XML "@validateSchema /path/to/apache2/conf/xml.xsd" \
    "phase:2,log,block,msg:'Failed to validate XML payload against schema'"
```

XML Schemas allow for much stricter validation, but the rule files are much more complicated. Here is the XML Schema equivalent of the DTD used in the previous section:

```
<?xml version="1.0" encoding="UTF-8"?>
<xs:schema xmlns:xs="http://www.w3.org/2001/XMLSchema"
```

```
elementFormDefault="qualified"
targetNamespace="http://xmlbeans.apache.org/samples/xquery/employees"
xmlns="http://xmlbeans.apache.org/samples/xquery/employees">
<xs:element name="employees">
  <xs:complexType>
    <xs:sequence>
      <xs:element name="employee" type="employeeType" maxOccurs="unbounded"/>
    </xs:sequence>
  </xs:complexType>
</xs:element>
<xs:complexType name="employeeType">
  <xs:sequence>
    <xs:element name="name" type="xs:string"/>
    <xs:element name="address" type="addressType" maxOccurs="unbounded"/>
    <xs:element name="phone" type="phoneType" maxOccurs="unbounded"/>
  </xs:sequence>
</xs:complexType>
<xs:complexType name="addressType">
  <xs:sequence>
    <xs:element name="street" type="xs:string"/>
    <xs:element name="city" type="xs:NCName"/>
    <xs:element name="state" type="xs:NCName"/>
    <xs:element name="zip" type="xs:integer"/>
  </xs:sequence>
  <xs:attribute name="location" type="xs:NCName" use="required"/>
</xs:complexType>
<xs:complexType name="phoneType">
  <xs:simpleContent>
    <xs:extension base="xs:string">
      <xs:attribute name="location" type="xs:NCName" use="required"/>
    </xs:extension>
  </xs:simpleContent>
</xs:complexType>
</xs:schema>
```

Libxml2, the underlying XML library used by ModSecurity, is known to not fully implement the XML Schema standards. You may encounter validation problems that are not a result of a problem in a request, but a result of the incomplete XML Schema implementation in libxml2. In that case, your best bet is to try to upgrade the library to a newer version (ModSecurity will use the same library version as used by your operating system). If that does not help, try seeking help on the libxml2 users mailing list.

XML Namespaces

Initially, XML was simple and easy to understand, like the one example I've used many times in this chapter. As it gained in popularity, however, people decided that they wanted to combine XML documents of different types and needed a way to distinguish which elements belong to which types. Thus XML namespaces were born. You've already seen a namespace in the one XML Schema we used so far, but that document used only one namespace.

To demonstrate how namespaces work, I have reworked the original example to split it into two namespaces—one for the employees element and the other for the address element:

```
<employees xmlns="http://www.example.org/employees">
    <employee>
        <name>Fred Jones</name>
        <a:address location="home" xmlns:a="http://www.example.org/address">
            <a:street>999 Aurora Ave.</a:street>
            <a:city>Seattle</a:city>
            <a:state>WA</a:state>
            <a:zip>98115</a:zip>
        </a:address>
        <a:address location="work" xmlns:a="http://www.example.org/address">
            <a:street>2022 152nd Avenue NE</a:street>
            <a:city>Redmond</a:city>
            <a:state>WA</a:state>
            <a:zip>98052</a:zip>
        </a:address>
        <phone location="work">(425)555-0100</phone>
        <phone location="home">(206)555-0101</phone>
        <phone location="mobile">(206)555-0102</phone>
    </employee>
</employees>
```

To use a namespace, choose a prefix (it can be anything) and associate it with a namespace URI. In the previous example, the prefix is a (nice and short) and the URI is http://www.example.org/address (it's not necessary for the URI to work; its role is just to serve as a unique identifier). Once a namespace has been introduced, you need to rewrite all the tags that belong to it to use the prefix.

Of course, the original XML Schema we used for validation won't work any more. The assumption, with the new XML payload, is that two schemas are needed. The address schema (xml-address.xsd) defines the rules only for addresses:

```
<?xml version="1.0" encoding="UTF-8"?>
<xs:schema xmlns:xs="http://www.w3.org/2001/XMLSchema"
  elementFormDefault="qualified"
  targetNamespace="http://www.example.org/address"
  xmlns="http://www.example.org/address">

<xs:element name="address" type="addressType"/>

<xs:complexType name="addressType">
  <xs:sequence>
    <xs:element name="street" type="xs:string"/>
    <xs:element name="city" type="xs:NCName"/>
```

```
        <xs:element name="state" type="xs:NCName"/>
        <xs:element name="zip" type="xs:integer"/>
      </xs:sequence>
      <xs:attribute name="location" type="xs:NCName" use="required"/>
    </xs:complexType>

    <xs:complexType name="phoneType">
      <xs:simpleContent>
        <xs:extension base="xs:string">
          <xs:attribute name="location" type="xs:NCName" use="required"/>
        </xs:extension>
      </xs:simpleContent>
    </xs:complexType>

  </xs:schema>
```

The employees schema (xml-employees.xsd), defines the rules for everything else:

```
<?xml version="1.0" encoding="UTF-8"?>
<xs:schema xmlns:xs="http://www.w3.org/2001/XMLSchema"
  elementFormDefault="qualified"
  targetNamespace="http://xmlbeans.apache.org/samples/xquery/employees"
  xmlns="http://xmlbeans.apache.org/samples/xquery/employees"
  xmlns:a="http://www.example.org/address">

  <xs:import namespace="http://www.example.org/address"
  schemaLocation="xml-address.xsd"/>

  <xs:element name="employees">
    <xs:complexType>
      <xs:sequence>
        <xs:element name="employee" type="employeeType" maxOccurs="unbounded"/>
      </xs:sequence>
    </xs:complexType>
  </xs:element>
  <xs:complexType name="employeeType">
    <xs:sequence>
      <xs:element name="name" type="xs:string"/>
      <xs:element ref="a:address" maxOccurs="unbounded"/>
      <xs:element name="phone" type="phoneType" maxOccurs="unbounded"/>
    </xs:sequence>
  </xs:complexType>
  <xs:complexType name="phoneType">
    <xs:simpleContent>
      <xs:extension base="xs:string">
        <xs:attribute name="location" type="xs:NCName" use="required"/>
      </xs:extension>
    </xs:simpleContent>
  </xs:complexType>
</xs:schema>
```

Notice how this second schema uses the XML Schema import facility to refer to xml-address.xsd, and then uses the address element by reference.

When you need to validate a document that uses multiple schemas, like in the previous example, the parameter that you supply to @validateSchema must be the path to the main schema. You should also place all dependent schemas in the same directory as the main one, which will enable libxml2 to find them.

The validation rule is the same as before:

```
SecRule XML "@validateSchema /path/to/apache2/conf/xml-employees.xsd" \
    "phase:2,log,block,msg:'Failed to validate XML payload against schema'"
```

If the validation fails, you'll get the following information in your debug log:

```
[4] Element '{http://www.w3.org/2001/XMLSchema}import': Failed to locate a schema ↵
at location '/path/to/apache2/conf/xml-address.xsd'. Skipping the import.
[3] Element '{http://www.w3.org/2001/XMLSchema}element', attribute 'ref': The ↵
QName value '{http://www.example.org/address}address' does not resolve to a(n) ↵
element declaration.
[4] Operator completed in 940 usec.
[4] Operator error: XML: Failed to load Schema: /path/to/apache2/conf/↵
xml-address.xsd
[4] Rule returned -1.
[1] Rule processing failed.
```

XPath Expressions

XML Path Language (XPath) is a language for addressing parts of an XML document. The addressing is done by writing XPath expressions, which are very powerful and very easy to use. I've compiled several examples in Table 13.1, "XPath expression examples", but if you have never worked with XPath expressions before, I recommend that you go through this very nice tutorial on zvon.org [http://www.zvon.org/xxl/XPathTutorial/].

Table 13.1. XPath expression examples

XPath expression	Description
/	Root element
/employees/employee	All employees
//address	An address, under any parent element
//*	All elements in payload
/employees/employee/address[2]	The second employee address
//phone[@location='work']	All work phone numbers

XPath expressions can be used only against the XML collection, and in phase 2 (REQUEST_BODY) and later. For example:

```
SecRule XML:/employees/employee/name/text() "!^[a-zA-Z ]{3,33}$" \
    "phase:2,deny,msg:'Invalid employee name'"
```

Unless you've worked with XPath expressions before, the results may not always be what you expect. Some XPath expressions will give you tidy results. For example, the one used in the previous example will return Fred Jones. But that happens only when you select a simple element (one that does not have any children). If the element you select has children, you get back everything they contain too, excluding the markup.

Try this, for example:

```
# Get the complete second employee address
SecRule XML:/employees/employee/address[2] TEST \
    "phase:2,deny"
```

The address fragment in the XML payload contains the following text (notice the whitespace, which I left the same as in the original payload):

```
<address location="work">
    <street>2022 152nd Avenue NE</street>
    <city>Redmond</city>
    <state>WA</state>
    <zip>98052</zip>
</address>
```

The debug log reveals what was used for matching:

```
[4] Recipe: Invoking rule 978d260; [file "/home/ivanr/apache/conf/httpd.conf"] ↵
[line "565"].
[5] Rule 978d260: SecRule "XML:/employees/employee/address[2]" "@rx TEST" ↵
"phase:2,log,auditlog,deny"
[4] Expanded "XML:/employees/employee/address[2]" to "XML|XML".
[4] Transformation completed in 2 usec.
[4] Executing operator "rx" with param "TEST" against ↵
XML:/employees/employee/address[2].
[9] Target value: "\n                2022 152nd Avenue NE\n          Redmond\n ↵
        WA\n            98052\n         "
```

You can see that the whitespace is all there, including the newline characters.

As a rule of thumb, when working with XML, you should restrict yourself to the analysis of specific fields. Bulk analysis (for example, using //*, which returns all elements in an XML payload) is just not going to be very effective, because even smaller payloads will be broken into dozens, and larger ones will be broken into possibly hundreds and thousands of small pieces. The performance of bulk XML matching is likely to be very bad. When the //* expression is used with our short XML example, it creates 16 variables.

XPath and Namespaces

Once you move away from simple XML documents to those using namespaces, your XPath expressions might stop working. For example, we could have used this "clean" XPath expression to validate ZIP codes in the first XML example:

```
SecRule XML://address/zip !^\d+$ \
    "phase:2,deny,msg:'Invalid ZIP code'"
```

To get the rule working with an XML document that uses prefixes, like the second XML example, you could try to modify the XPath the expression to include the prefixes, but that will just cause XPath evaluation to fail, because libxml2 will try to match the prefix to a namespace, but won't know how. You will get `XML: Unable to evaluate xpath expression` in the debug log. Even if libxml2 didn't complain, this approach wouldn't work, because the choice of prefix is in the hands of the request sender. You don't get to control it on the server.

The solution is to use prefixes in XPath expressions, but also tell libxml2 about the namespace, using the xmlns action:

```
SecRule XML://a:address/a:zip !^\d+$ \
    "phase:2,deny,msg:'Invalid ZIP code',xmlns:a=http://www.example.org/address"
```

This example will work as it would in the original example, returning two ZIP codes. It will even work if the sender chooses an entirely different prefix.

XML Inspection Framework

The validation examples so far all assumed one validation per request, but an average application will have many entry points, with a different set of rules needed for each. In this section, I sketch a framework that you can use whenever you need to deal with XML in ModSecurity.

```
# Establish the baseline for all XML entry points
<Location /api/>
    # Is the Content-Type correct?
    SecRule REQUEST_HEADERS:Content-Type !^text/xml$ \
        "phase:1,t:lowercase,deny,msg:'Invalid Content-Type for XML API'"

    # Activate XML parsing
    SecAction phase:1,t:lowercase,nolog,pass,ctl:requestBodyProcessor=XML

    # Was the payload successfully parsed?
    SecRule REQBODY_PROCESSOR_ERROR "!@eq 0" \
        "phase:2,t:none,log,block,msg:'Failed to parse request body: ↵
%{REQBODY_PROCESSOR_ERROR_MSG}'"

    # By default, we assume that XML validation did not take place
```

```
    SecAction phase:2,nolog,pass,setvar:TX.xml_validated=0
</Location>

# Entry point One
<Location /api/entryPointOne.php>
    # Validate payload first
    SecRule XML "@validateDTD /path/to/conf/entryPointOne.dtd" \
        "phase:2,deny,msg:'Failed to validate XML against entryPointOne.dtd'"

    # Restrict employee name to known good characters only
    SecRule XML:/employees/employee/name/text() !^[a-zA-Z ]{3,33}$ \
        "phase:2,deny,msg:'Invalid employee name'"

    # Validation was successful
    SecAction phase:2,nolog,pass,setvar:TX.xml_validated
</Location>

# Entry point Two
<Location /api/entryPointTwo.php>
    # Validate payload first
    SecRule XML "@validateDTD /path/to/conf/entryPointTwo.dtd" \
        "phase:2,deny,msg:'Failed to validate XML against entryPointTwo.dtd'"

    # Implement additional restrictions
    # ...

    # Validation was successful
    SecAction phase:2,nolog,pass,setvar:TX.xml_validated
</Location>

# Finally, verify that the entry point was valid
<Location /api/>
    # The xml_validated flag will only be set after a
    # successful validation
    SecRule TX:xml_validated "!@eq 1" \
        "phase:2,deny,msg:'Invalid API entry point'"
</Location>
```

With this example framework, we achieve the following:

1. There is first one <Location> section where we establish the baseline for all XML entry points. It is here that we activate XML parsing, but also reject all requests that are not XML. The assumption is that the /api/ folder contains only XML entry points. This assumption is usually valid, as API calls do not need any accompanying files (such as embedded images, stylesheet files, and so on).

2. With a further one <Location> section per entry point, we ensure that we apply the correct validation rules to each entry point, followed by the per-entry point rules.

3. We finalize the XML rules by adding another global `<Location>` section, where we use one rule that checks whether validation was successfully completed. This final check is needed in case a request specifies an unlisted entry point, in which case the `xml_validated` flag will be 0 (set in the first global section).

> **Note**
>
> Remember that configuration merging for the `<Location>` directive works in the same order in which the sections appear in the configuration file. Thus, the rules will be processed in the way they appear in the configuration too. If you are not familiar with Apache's configuration merging, there's a refresher available in the section called "Apache Configuration Syntax" in Chapter 7.

With XML rules, as with all other rules, the best approach is to use whitelisting, or positive security. In this approach you look at every single bit of data you accept and check that it is correct. You don't try to discover "bad" characters (that would be negative security, or blacklisting). DTD validation is generally not powerful enough, but you may be able to use XML Schemas as a pretty good validation mechanism. Then, if there are parts that you cannot cover with schemas, you should use custom XPath expression as the last line of validation.

Summary

Being able to properly process XML is always important, especially now that so many web applications are adopting XML-based APIs. In ModSecurity, you will generally find everything you need to parse, validate, and inspect XML in a meaningful way. If you find certain parts of the XML support difficult to work with, that's probably not because of ModSecurity, but because the XML world continues to increase in complexity. No effort on part of ModSecurity developers can make that go away.

There is only one chapter left in this book, and it will teach you how to extend ModSecurity by writing native code, which is something that you may need to do when you reach the edges of ModSecurity's capabilities. You need not worry; it's easy to do. I promise.

14 Extending Rule Language

The ModSecurity Rule Language is pretty good at meeting users' requirements—especially now that it's entering maturity—but sometimes you'll need it to do something that it cannot. In ModSecurity, there is an easy way to extend the rule language if you can program in C. There are three extension points, enabling you to add custom variables, operators, and transformation functions.

Because ModSecurity is part of Apache, it does not have to implement its own extension infrastructure: you extend ModSecurity by writing Apache modules. It's a great time-saver if you have previous Apache programming experience. But, even if you don't, finding people who do will be generally easy. After all, Apache is one of the most popular programs ever.

For years, the common way to learn how to write Apache modules was to study existing modules, especially the ones bundled with Apache itself. (My favorite always has been `mod_rewrite`.) These days, however, we have proper documentation, thanks to Nick Kew, who wrote *The Apache Modules Book* (Prentice Hall, 2007). If you are planning to do some serious work, you should definitely get Nick's book. For simple efforts, what's in this section should be sufficient.

With or without the book, you should familiarize yourself with the Apache Portable Runtime [http://apr.apache.org] (APR) and the Apache Portable Runtime Utility [http://apr.apache.org] (APR-Util) libraries, which make the infrastructure on top of which Apache is built. Whenever you program an Apache module, you have full access to the APR and APR-Util libraries. That's quite handy, because they contain tons of useful functionality.

The remainder of this section will introduce a template module, which you can use as a starting point for your ModSecurity extensions, and then implement three modules, one for each extension point. For the examples, I will use the sample code included with ModSecurity and stored in the `apache2/api` subfolder.

Extension Template

I am first going to show you how to create a template module that only establishes the infrastructure on top of which we will build later.

> **Note**
>
> Before you begin, ensure that you have the ability to compile custom Apache modules. This is the same process as the one where you custom-compile ModSecurity itself. In addition, you will need the source code for the exact version of ModSecurity you are writing extensions for.

The template module is a complete Apache module, which you should be able to compile and install. You can practice with it to ensure that your environment has all the right components for custom Apache module development.

Here is the complete module source code:

```c
#include "httpd.h"
#include "http_core.h"
#include "http_config.h"
#include "http_log.h"
#include "http_protocol.h"
#include "ap_config.h"
#include "apr_optional.h"

#include "modsecurity.h"

/**
 * This function is just a placeholder in this template.
 */
static int hook_pre_config(apr_pool_t *mp, apr_pool_t *mp_log, apr_pool_t ↵
*mp_temp) {
    /* Empty for now, but will be used later. */
    return OK;
}

/**
 * Register to be invoked before configuration begins.
 */
static void register_hooks(apr_pool_t *p) {
    ap_hook_pre_config(hook_pre_config, NULL, NULL, APR_HOOK_LAST);
}

/**
 * This structure is used by Apache to determine that a dynamic
 * library it is loading is a genuine module.
 */
```

```
static module AP_MODULE_DECLARE_DATA security_template_module = {
    STANDARD20_MODULE_STUFF,
    NULL,
    NULL,
    NULL,
    NULL,
    NULL,
    register_hooks
};
```

There are three points of interest in the module:

1. The `security_template_module` is a structure used by Apache to verify that the dynamic library is indeed a module. The name is important and should be unique. You will use the same name when you instruct Apache to load the module, later on.

2. The initialization structure `security_template_module` points to the `register_hook` callback, which is going to be the module's main initialization entry point.

3. The `register_hook` callback registers another callback, `hook_pre_config`, which is invoked every time Apache is reconfigured. This callback doesn't do anything in the template module, but we will add to it later.

You will be compiling the template module using the `apxs` Apache tool. If it is not in your path, it will be in the `bin/` subfolder of your Apache installation. Assuming you placed the source code in the file called `mod_security_template.c`, to compile the template module, invoke:

```
$ apxs -cia -I/path/to/modsecurity/source_code -I/usr/include/libxml2 ↵
mod_security_template.c
```

> **Note**
>
> On Linux, processes are known to crash when the dynamic libraries they are using change. It is best practice to shut down Apache before adding or removing any of its modules.

The `apxs` command line in the example uses 5 switches, which perform the following functions:

1. Compile the module (switch -c).

2. Copy the compiled module to the directory where all other Apache modules are stored (switch -i).

3. Activate the module by adding the correct `LoadModule` directive to the configuration (switch -a).

4. Point to the location of the ModSecurity include files (switch -I/path/to/modsecurity/source_code).

5. Point to the location of the libxml2 include files (switch -I/usr/include/libxml2).

The activation step will work if you have at least one existing `LoadModule` directive in your configuration. The last line will say something similar to the following:

```
[activating module 'security_template' in /path/to/apache/conf/httpd.conf].
```

If you have a more elaborate configuration layout and the `apxs` tool cannot find at least one existing `LoadModule` directive in your `httpd.conf`, you will have to activate the module manually by adding the following line to the configuration:

```
LoadModule security_template_module modules/mod_security_template.so
```

The first parameter must match the module name used in the source code. You should always place a ModSecurity extension module after the `LoadModule` line that activates ModSecurity itself. If you don't, ModSecurity might not be able to recognize the newly added function.

If Apache starts with the new `LoadModule` line in the configuration, you've successfully completed this step.

Adding a Transformation Function

Starting from the template module, implementing a new transformation function requires two steps. First you need to implement a single function, which will be called by ModSecurity every time a transformation is needed. All transformation functions (in C) use the following signature:

```
static int reverse(apr_pool_t *mptmp, unsigned char *input,
    long int input_len, char **rval, long int *rval_len)
{
    /* Transformation code here. */

    /* Return 1 if you change the input, 0 if you don't/ */
    return 1;
}
```

To examine the implementation of the built-in transformation functions, refer to the file `re_tfns.c` in the ModSecurity source code.

You should generally use the same name for the C function as the name you intend to use for the transformation function in ModSecurity. The 5 parameters in the signature are the following:

1. `apr_pool_t *mptp`: APR memory pool you can use to allocate memory from

2. `unsigned char *input`: pointer to the input string you need to transform

3. `long int input_len`: length of the input string

4. `char **rval`: pointer in which to return the output string

5. `long int rval_len`: length of the output string

> **Note**
>
> Remember that ModSecurity does not use NUL-terminated strings. Always use the `input_len` parameter, which contains the input length.

If your transformation always results with an output string that is equal to or shorter than the input string, you should make your changes in place, overwriting the input string. By doing so, you save on memory allocation, thus speeding up your transformation function. In this case, the `rval` pointer should point to the input string on return.

If the output can be longer, use the `mptmp` memory pool to allocate from, then point `rval` to the newly allocated memory chunk. The memory you allocate will be deallocated automatically, when ModSecurity clears the temporary memory pool. With any other memory allocation method, you would create a memory leak, because deallocation is always manual and you won't have an opportunity to invoke it.

Here's the complete source code of the transformation function example included with Mod-Security:

```
/**
 * This function will be invoked by
 * ModSecurity to transform input.
 */
static int reverse(apr_pool_t *mptmp, unsigned char *input,
    long int input_len, char **rval, long int *rval_len)
{
    /* Transformation functions can choose to do their
     * thing in-place, overwriting the existing content. This
     * is normally possible only if the transformed content
     * is of equal length or shorter.
     *
     * If you need to expand the content use the temporary
     * memory pool mptmp to allocate the space.
     */

    /* Reverse the string in place, but only if it's long enough. */
    if (input_len > 1) {
        long int i = 0;
        long int j = input_len - 1;
        while(i < j) {
            char c = input[i];
            input[i] = input[j];
            input[j] = c;
            i++;
            j--;
```

```
        }
    }

    /* Tell ModSecurity about the content
     * we have generated. In this case we
     * merely point back to the input buffer.
     */
    *rval = (char *)input;
    *rval_len = input_len;

    /* Must return 1 if the content was
     * changed, or 0 otherwise.
     */
    return 1;
}
```

The return value from a transformation function should always be 1 if the content you are returning is different from the content you received on input, and 0 otherwise. Even if you placed the output in a newly allocated memory chunk, if it is the same, the return code should be 0. Returning the correct response code will allow ModSecurity to optimize certain things when there are no changes, but you shouldn't worry to much about it. If keeping track of whether you made a change is difficult or expensive, just return 1.

Now that you have the function, you need to register it with ModSecurity. For that, use the Apache mechanism called *optional functions*. It's a two-step process:

1. Ask Apache to find you the registration function, which will have been exported by ModSecurity beforehand.

2. Register the new transformation function.

```
/**
 * Register transformation function with ModSecurity.
 */
static int pre_config(apr_pool_t *mp, apr_pool_t *mp_log, apr_pool_t *mp_temp) {
    void (*fn)(const char *name, void *fn);

    /* Look for the registration function
     * exported by ModSecurity.
     */
    fn = APR_RETRIEVE_OPTIONAL_FN(modsec_register_tfn);
    if (fn) {
        /* Use it to register our new
         * transformation function under the
         * name "reverse".
         */
        fn("reverse", (void *)reverse);
    } else {
        ap_log_error(APLOG_MARK, APLOG_ERR | APLOG_NOERRNO, 0, NULL,
```

```
                    "mod_tfn_reverse: Unable to find modsec_register_tfn.");
    }

    return OK;
}
```

Once you restart Apache, the new transformation function will be equal to the ones that come with ModSecurity. You should always test your new functionality. For example, add the following rule to the configuration:

```
SecRule ARGS test phase:1,log,deny,t:none,t:reverse
```

Then, if you send a request with parameter p whose value is set to tset (the opposite of test), you should get a 403 response in return. The debug log excerpt shows the new reverse transformation function working as expected:

```
[4] Recipe: Invoking rule 9d77ed8; [file "/home/ivanr/apache/conf/httpd.conf"] ⏎
[line "509"].
[5] Rule 9d77ed8: SecRule "ARGS" "@rx test" "phase:1,auditlog,t:none,t:reverse,⏎
log,deny"
[9] T (0) reverse: "test"
[4] Transformation completed in 56 usec.
[4] Executing operator "rx" with param "test" against ARGS:p.
[9] Target value: "test"
[4] Operator completed in 59 usec.
[4] Rule returned 1.
[9] Match, intercepted -> returning.
[1] Access denied with code 403 (phase 1). Pattern match "test" at ARGS:p. [file ⏎
"/home/ivanr/apache/conf/httpd.conf"] [line "509"]
```

> **Note**
>
> Another example of a transformation function implemented as an extension is t:cmdLine [http://www.approach.be/security-modsecurity.html], written by Marc Stern. Even if you are not interested in the code, the transformation function is a good addition to ModSecurity.

Adding an Operator

Creating new operators is slightly more difficult, because two functions are needed: there's an additional (and optional) initialization step, which allows your code to do some work at configure-time and reuse it at runtime. The split of the work sometimes allows for significant performance improvements. In ModSecurity, the source code for the built-in operators is in the file re_operators.c.

The new operator example adds a new string matching function based on the Boyer-Moore-Horspool algorithm [http://en.wikipedia.org/wiki/Boyer%E2%80%93Moore

%E2%80%93Horspool_algorithm]. I will not show here the code for the algorithm itself, assuming that the following two functions are already implemented:

```
static void initBoyerMooreHorspool(const char *pattern, int patlength,
    int *bm_badcharacter_array);

static int BoyerMooreHorspool(const char *pattern, int patlength,
    const char *text, int textlen, int *bm_badcharacter_array);
```

If you are curious, of course, you can always look at the implementation at the end of the mod_op_strstr.c file (included with ModSecurity). The string matching algorithm does require initialization, so we will be using both steps.

The initialization code is as follows:

```
/**
 * Operator parameter initialisation entry point.
 */
static int op_strstr_init(msre_rule *rule, char **error_msg) {
    /* Operator initialisation function will be called once per
     * statement where operator is used. It is meant to be used
     * to check the parameters to see whether they are present
     * and if they are in the correct format.
     */

    /* In this example we just look for a simple non-empty parameter. */
    if ((rule->op_param == NULL)||(strlen(rule->op_param) == 0)) {
        *error_msg = apr_psprintf(rule->ruleset->mp, "Missing parameter ↵
for operator 'strstr'.");
        return 0; /* ERROR */
    }

    /* If you need to transform the data in the parameter into something
     * else you should do that here. Simply create a new structure to hold
     * the transformed data and place the pointer to it into rule->op_param_data.
     * You will have access to this pointer later on.
     */
    rule->op_param_data = apr_pcalloc(rule->ruleset->mp, ↵
ALPHABET_SIZE * sizeof(int));
    initBoyerMooreHorspool(rule->op_param, strlen(rule->op_param), ↵
(int *)rule->op_param_data);

    /* OK */
    return 1;
}
```

Unlike with the transformation function example, here we get to work with ModSecurity structures directly. The first parameter of the operator initialization is a pointer to the msre_rule structure (full definition in re.h). There are two fields in this structure that you will want to use:

- op_param: a NUL-terminated string that may contain a parameter for your operator.
- op_param_data: a generic pointer for your operators' use.

The idea is that you will check the parameter available in op_param and do something with it, then perform the initialization work and store a pointer to the results in op_param_data. When your operator is invoked at runtime, it will have access to the same msre_rule structure, and thus to op_param_data. Should you need an example, the code for the @rx and @pm operators demonstrates how parameter preparation is done.

- If you need to allocate memory, use the memory pool in rule->ruleset->mp, as in the example.
- If your initialization fails, generate an error string, store it in error_msg (the second function parameter), and return a zero.

The operator execution code is equally simple:

```
/**
 * Operator execution entry point.
 */
static int op_strstr_exec(modsec_rec *msr, msre_rule *rule, msre_var *var, ↵
char **error_msg) {
    /* Here we need to inspect the contents of the supplied variable. */

    /* In a general case it is possible for the value
     * to be NULL. What you need to do in this case
     * depends on your operator. In this example we return
     * a "no match" response.
     */
    if (var->value == NULL) return 0; /* No match. */

    /* Another thing to note is that variables are not C strings,
     * meaning the NULL byte is not used to determine the end
     * of the string. Variable length var->value_len should be
     * used for this purpose.
     */

    if (BoyerMooreHorspool(rule->op_param, strlen(rule->op_param),
        var->value, var->value_len, (int *)rule->op_param_data) >= 0)
    {
        return 1; /* Match. */
    }

    return 0; /* No match. */
}
```

This time, you will receive 4 parameters:

1. `modsec_rec *msr`: the structure where all transaction data is stored

2. `msre_rule *rule`: the same rule structure you received in the initialization phase

3. `msre_var *var`: the variable structure, which holds the data the operators needs to inspect

4. `char **error_msg`: an error message pointer, which needs to contain an error message on error

The data you need to inspect is stored in a `msre_var` instance, which has the following layout:

```
struct msre_var {
    const char          *name;
    const char          *value;
    unsigned int         value_len;
    const char          *param;
    const void          *param_data;
    msre_var_metadata   *metadata;
    msc_regex_t         *param_regex;
    unsigned int         is_negated;
    unsigned int         is_counting;
};
```

Although it looks complex, you need be concerned with only two fields:

• `const char *value`: pointer to the variable the operator needs to inspect

• `unsigned int value_len`: the length of the variable

After you inspect the variable, return 0 if there is no match and 1 if there is.

The operator registration step is conceptually identical to that used for transformation functions, except that you use the `modsec_register_operator` optional function:

```
static int hook_pre_config(apr_pool_t *mp, apr_pool_t *mp_log, ↵
apr_pool_t *mp_temp) {
    void (*fn)(const char *name, void *fn_init, void *fn_exec);

    /* Look for the registration function
     * exported by ModSecurity.
     */
    fn = APR_RETRIEVE_OPTIONAL_FN(modsec_register_operator);
    if (fn) {
        /* Use it to register our new
         * transformation function under the
         * name "reverse".
         */
        fn("strstr", (void *)op_strstr_init, (void *)op_strstr_exec);
    } else {
        ap_log_error(APLOG_MARK, APLOG_ERR | APLOG_NOERRNO, 0, NULL,
            "mod_op_strstr: Unable to find modsec_register_operator.");
```

```
    }

    return OK;
}
```

Adding a Variable

To generate new variables, you typically need to implement one function call. The example that comes with ModSecurity is actually split across three functions, but that's done for code reuse. Here's the simplified code:

```
static int var_remote_addr_port_generate(modsec_rec *msr, msre_var *var,
    msre_rule *rule, apr_table_t *vartab, apr_pool_t *mptmp)
{
    msre_var *rvar = NULL;

    if (value == NULL) return 0;

    /* Generate new variable. */
    rvar = apr_pmemdup(mptmp, var, sizeof(msre_var));
    rvar->value = apr_psprintf(mptmp, "%s:%d", msr->remote_addr, msr->remote_port);;
    rvar->value_len = strlen(rvar->value);

    /* Add variable to the collection. */
    apr_table_addn(vartab, rvar->name, (void *)rvar);

    return 1;
}
```

The following parameters are provided:

1. modsec_rec *msr: the structure where all transaction data is stored

2. msre_var *var: variable template

3. apr_table_t *vartab: the collection used to store the variables being prepared for inspection

4. apr_pool_t *mptmp: the memory pool from which you can allocate memory

Creating new variables is a four-step process:

1. Create the variable data. How you do that depends on the nature of the data, but it can be as easy as using a single apr_sprintf() call (as in the example).

2. Create a new msre_var structure, duplicating from the one already provided in var, and populate the value and value_len fields.

3. Using apr_table_addn(), add the newly created msre_var structure to the vartab collection.

4. Return 1 to indicate that you've added one variable to the collection. If you create more than one variable (by just repeating steps 1 through 3, keep track of how many new variables there are and return the correct value at the end of the function).

Variable registration is slightly more involved, but only because you need to help ModSecurity do most of the runtime work for you.

```
static int hook_pre_config(apr_pool_t *mp, apr_pool_t *mp_log, ↩
apr_pool_t *mp_temp) {
    void (*register_fn)(const char *name, unsigned int type,
                        unsigned int argc_min, unsigned int argc_max,
                        void *fn_validate, void *fn_generate,
                        unsigned int is_cacheable, unsigned int availability);

    /* Look for the registration function
     * exported by ModSecurity.
     */
    register_fn = APR_RETRIEVE_OPTIONAL_FN(modsec_register_variable);
    if (register_fn) {
        /* Use it to register our new
         * variable under the
         * name "REMOTE_ADDR_PORT".
         */
        register_fn(
            "REMOTE_ADDR_PORT",
            VAR_SIMPLE,
            0, 0,
            NULL,
            var_remote_addr_port_generate,
            VAR_DONT_CACHE,
            PHASE_REQUEST_HEADERS
        );
    } else {
        ap_log_error(APLOG_MARK, APLOG_ERR | APLOG_NOERRNO, 0, NULL,
            "mod_var_remote_addr_port: Unable to find modsec_register_variable.");
    }

    return OK;
}
```

To register a variable you need to use 8 parameters, but apart from that, the registration process does not hold any surprises:

1. `const char *name`: variable name.

2. `unsigned int type`: variable type; use `VAR_SIMPLE` to indicate that you will return only one value, or `VAR_LIST` to indicate the possibly of returning multiple values.

3. `unsigned int argc_min`: variable parameter definition; use 0 if you don't need to use a parameter, or 1 if you do.

4. `unsigned int argc_max`: variable parameter definition; use 0 if you do not allow a parameter, or 1 if you do.

5. `void *fn_validate`: optional pointer to the parameter validation function.

6. `void *fn_generate`: pointer to the generation function.

7. `unsigned int is_cacheable`: is the variable cacheable? If generating the variable is expensive and the value is not likely to change during the duration of a transaction, use `VAR_CACHE`. Otherwise, use `VAR_DONT_CACHE`.

8. `unsigned int availability`: the phase in which the variable becomes available: `PHASE_REQUEST_HEADERS`, `PHASE_REQUEST_BODY`, `PHASE_RESPONSE_HEADERS`, `PHASE_RESPONSE_BODY` or `PHASE_LOGGING`. ModSecurity should use this value to ensure that the variable isn't referenced in the rules before it is available. (I say "should" because ModSecurity does not do that at the moment.)

As you know, in ModSecurity variables can have parameters. For example, you use `ARGS:p` to request the parameter named p, and `ARGS:/^p/` to request all the parameters that start with p. If you allow parameters for your variables, the single parameter will be placed in `var->param`. How you interpret the parameter depends on the nature of the variable. For inspiration, you can look up the `var_args_generate()` function in `re_variables.c`, which implements the `ARGS` collection.

Finally, if you think you can speed up variable retrieval by using configure-time initialization, supply a separate validation function when you register your variable. For example:

```
static char *var_generic_list_validate(msre_ruleset *ruleset, msre_var *var) {
    /* Is it OK if there's no parameter provided? Return NULL if
     * it is. If you require a parameter and you correctly registered
     * the variable, your validation function will never be invoked.
     */
    if (var->param == NULL) return NULL;

    /* Validate the value in var->param. */
    // ...

    /* Perform your initialization work. */
    // ...

    /* Store initialization data for subsequent retrieval. */
    var->param_data = my_opaque_pointer;

    /* No error. */
    return NULL;
}
```

If you need more examples, all the ModSecurity variables are implemented in the file `re_variables.c`.

Summary

In this final chapter of the book (not counting the reference manual that follows in the second part), I led you through the process of adding new elements to the ModSecurity rule language. The extension mechanism of ModSecurity really is a case of standing on the shoulders of giants: you get to use a polished and well-documented extension mechanism implemented for Apache, while the developers (of ModSecurity) get to support extensions with only a dozen lines of code.

With this chapter, you've reached the end of the book, and you now know pretty much everything you need to about ModSecurity. This may be where your real work begins, because although you now know the tool, keeping up with web application security—which you need to understand in order to use ModSecurity in the right way—is often a full-time job.

But it's a fun one!

‖ Reference Manual

This part of the book contains the original ModSecurity Reference Manual, reprinted with the permission of Breach Security, Inc. The version included here is the most complete version as of February 2010, when this book is about to go to print. It contains the information on the most recent version of ModSecurity, 2.5.12, as well as the improvements currently available only in the development trunk.

15 Directives

This section documents the configuration directives currently available in ModSecurity.

SecAction

Description: Unconditionally processes the action list it receives as the first and only parameter. The syntax of the parameter is identical to that of the third parameter of SecRule.

Syntax: SecAction "action1,action2,action3,..."

Scope: Any

Version: 2.0.0

This directive is commonly used to set variables and initialize persistent collections using the initcol action. For example:

```
SecAction nolog,phase:1,initcol:RESOURCE=%{REQUEST_FILENAME}
```

SecArgumentSeparator

Description: Specifies which character to use as the separator for application/x-www-form-urlencoded content.

Syntax: SecArgumentSeparator character

Default: &

Scope: Main

Version: 2.0.0

This directive is needed if a backend web application is using a nonstandard argument separator. Applications are sometimes (very rarely) written to use a semicolon separator. You should not change the default setting unless you establish that the application you are working with requires a different separator. If this directive is not set properly for each web application, then

ModSecurity will not be able to parse the arguments appropriately and the effectiveness of the rule matching will be significantly decreased.

SecAuditEngine

Description: Configures the audit logging engine.

Syntax: SecAuditEngine On|Off|RelevantOnly

Default: Off

Scope: Any

Version: 2.0.0

The SecAuditEngine directive is used to configure the audit engine, which logs complete transactions. ModSecurity is currently able to log most, but not all transactions. Transactions involving errors (e.g., 400 and 404 transactions) use a different execution path, which ModSecurity does not support.

> **Note**
>
> If you need to change the audit log engine configuration on a per-transaction basis (e.g., in response to some transaction data), use the ctl action.

The following example demonstrates how SecAuditEngine is used:

```
SecAuditEngine RelevantOnly
SecAuditLog logs/audit/audit.log
SecAuditLogParts ABCFHZ
SecAuditLogType concurrent
SecAuditLogStorageDir logs/audit
SecAuditLogRelevantStatus ^(?:5|4\d[^4])
```

The possible values for the audit log engine are as follows:

- On: log all transactions
- Off: do not log any transactions
- RelevantOnly: only the log transactions that have triggered a warning or an error, or have a status code that is considered to be relevant (as determined by the SecAuditLogRelevantStatus directive)

SecAuditLog

Description: Defines the path to the main audit log file (serial logging format) or the concurrent logging index file (concurrent logging format). When used in combination with mlogc (only possible with concurrent logging), this directive defines the mlogc location and command line.

Syntax: `SecAuditLog /path/to/audit.log`

Scope: Any

Version: 2.0.0

This file will be used to store the audit log entries if serial audit logging format is used. If concurrent audit logging format is used this file will be used as an index, and contain a record of all audit log files created. If you are planning to use concurrent audit logging to send your audit log data off to a remote server you will need to deploy the ModSecurity Log Collector (`mlogc`), like this:

```
SecAuditLog "|/path/to/mlogc /path/to/mlogc.conf"
```

> **Note**
>
> This audit log file is opened on startup when the server typically still runs as `root`. You should not allow non-root users to have write privileges for this file or for the directory it is stored in.

SecAuditLog2

Description: Defines the path to the secondary audit log index file when concurrent logging is enabled. See `SecAuditLog` for more details.

Syntax: `SecAuditLog2 /path/to/audit.log`

Scope: Any

Version: 2.1.2

The purpose of `SecAuditLog2` is to make logging to two remote servers possible, which is typically achieved by running two instances of the `mlogc` tool, each with a different configuration (in addition, one of the instances will need to be instructed not to delete the files it submits). This directive can be used only if `SecAuditLog` was previously configured and only if concurrent logging format is used.

SecAuditLogDirMode

Description: Configures the mode (permissions) of any directories created for the concurrent audit logs, using an octal mode value as parameter (as used in `chmod`).

Syntax: `SecAuditLogDirMode octal_mode|"default"`

Default: 0600

Scope: Any

Version: 2.5.10

The default mode for new audit log directories (0600) only grants read/write access to the owner (typically the account under which Apache is running, for example apache). If access from other accounts is needed (e.g., for use with mpm-itk), then you may use this directive to grant additional read and/or write privileges. You should use this directive with caution to avoid exposing potentially sensitive data to unauthorized users. Using the value default as parameter reverts the configuration back to the default setting. This feature is not available on operating systems not supporting octal file modes.

Example:

```
SecAuditLogDirMode 02750
```

> **Note**
>
> The process umask may still limit the mode if it is being more restrictive than the mode set using this directive.

SecAuditLogFileMode

Description: Configures the mode (permissions) of any files created for concurrent audit logs using an octal mode (as used in chmod). See SecAuditLogDirMode for controlling the mode of created audit log directories.

Syntax: SecAuditLogFileMode octal_mode|"default"

Example Usage: SecAuditLogFileMode 00640

Scope: Any

Version: 2.5.10

This feature is not available on operating systems not supporting octal file modes. The default mode (0600) only grants read/write access to the account writing the file. If access from another account is needed (using mpm-itk is a good example), then this directive may be required. However, use this directive with caution to avoid exposing potentially sensitive data to unauthorized users. Using the value "default" will revert back to the default setting.

> **Note**
>
> The process umask may still limit the mode if it is being more restrictive than the mode set using this directive.

SecAuditLogParts

Description: Defines which parts of each transaction are going to be recorded in the audit log. Each part is assigned a single letter; when a letter appears in the list then the equivalent part will be recorded. See below for the list of all parts.

Syntax: `SecAuditLogParts PARTLETTERS`

Example Usage: `SecAuditLogParts ABCFHZ`

Scope: Any

Version: 2.0.0

Default: `ABCFHZ`.

> **Note**
>
> The format of the audit log format is documented in detail in the section called "Audit Log" in Chapter 20.

Available audit log parts:

- `A`: Audit log header (mandatory).

- `B`: Request headers.

- `C`: Request body (present only if the request body exists and ModSecurity is configured to intercept it).

- `D`: Reserved for intermediary response headers; not implemented yet.

- `E`: Intermediary response body (present only if ModSecurity is configured to intercept response bodies, and if the audit log engine is configured to record it). Intermediary response body is the same as the actual response body unless ModSecurity intercepts the intermediary response body, in which case the actual response body will contain the error message (either the Apache default error message, or the `ErrorDocument` page).

- `F`: Final response headers (excluding the `Date` and `Server` headers, which are always added by Apache in the late stage of content delivery).

- `G`: Reserved for the actual response body; not implemented yet.

- `H`: Audit log trailer.

- `I`: This part is a replacement for part `C`. It will log the same data as `C` in all cases except when `multipart/form-data` encoding in used. In this case, it will log a fake `application/x-www-form-urlencoded` body that contains the information about parameters but not about the files. This is handy if you don't want to have (often large) files stored in your audit logs.

- `J`: Reserved. This part, when implemented, will contain information about the files uploaded using `multipart/form-data` encoding.

- `K`: This part contains a full list of every rule that matched (one per line) in the order they were matched. The rules are fully qualified and will thus show inherited actions and default operators. Supported as of v2.5.0.

- Z: Final boundary, signifies the end of the entry (mandatory).

SecAuditLogRelevantStatus

Description: Configures which response status code is to be considered relevant for the purpose of audit logging.

Syntax: SecAuditLogRelevantStatus REGEX

Example Usage: SecAuditLogRelevantStatus ^(?:5|4\d[^4])

Scope: Any

Version: 2.0.0

The main purpose of this directive is to allow you to configure audit logging for only the transactions that have the status code that matches the supplied regular expression. For example, you might want to log all application errors (status code 500). Although you could achieve the same effect with a rule in phase 5, SecAuditLogRelevantStatus is sometimes better, because it continues to work even when SecRuleEngine is disabled.

SecAuditLogStorageDir

Description: Configures the directory where concurrent audit log entries are to be stored.

Syntax: SecAuditLogStorageDir /path/to/storage/dir

Example Usage: SecAuditLogStorageDir /usr/local/apache/logs/audit

Scope: Any

Version: 2.0.0

This directive is only needed when concurrent audit logging is used. The directory must already exist and must be writable by the web server user. Audit log entries are created at runtime, after Apache switches to a non-root account.

As with all logging mechanisms, ensure that you specify a file system location that has adequate disk space and is not on the main system partition.

SecAuditLogType

Description: Configures the type of audit logging mechanism to be used.

Syntax: SecAuditLogType Serial|Concurrent

Example Usage: SecAuditLogType Serial

Scope: Any

Version: 2.0.0

The possible values are:

Serial
> Audit log entries will be stored in a single file, specified by `SecAuditLog`. This is convenient for casual use, but it can slow down the server, because only one audit log entry can be written to the file at any one time.

Concurrent
> One file per transaction is used for audit logging. This approach is more scalable when heavy logging is required (multiple transactions can be recorded in parallel). It is also the only choice if you need to use remote logging.

SecCacheTransformations

Description: Controls the caching of transformations, which may speed up the processing of complex rule sets. Caching is off by default starting with 2.5.6, when it was deprecated and downgraded back to experimental.

Syntax: `SecCacheTransformations On|Off [options]`

Example Usage: `SecCacheTransformations On "minlen:64,maxlen:0"`

Scope: Any

Version: 2.5.0; deprecated in 2.5.6.

The first directive parameter can be one of the following:

- `On`: Cache transformations (per transaction, per phase) allowing identical transformations to be performed only once.
- `Off`: Do not cache any transformations, leaving all transformations to be performed every time they are needed.

The following options are allowed (multiple options must be comma-separated):

- `incremental:on|off`: Enabling this option will cache every transformation instead of just the final transformation. The default is `off`.
- `maxitems:N`: Do not allow more than N transformations to be cached. Cache will be disabled once this number is reached. A zero value is interpreted as unlimited. This option may be useful to limit caching for a form with a large number of variables. The default value is 512.
- `minlen:N`: Do not cache the transformation if the variable's length is less than N bytes. The default setting is 32.
- `maxlen:N`: Do not cache the transformation if the variable's length is more than N bytes. A zero value is interpreted as unlimited. The default setting is 1024.

SecChrootDir

Description: Configures the directory path that will be used to jail the web server process.

Syntax: SecChrootDir /path/to/chroot/dir

Example Usage: SecChrootDir /chroot

Scope: Main

Version: 2.0.0

This feature is not available on Windows builds. The internal chroot functionality provided by ModSecurity works great for simple setups. One example of a simple setup is Apache serving only static files, or running applications using built-in modules. Some problems you might encounter with more complex setups:

1. DNS lookups do not work (this is because this feature requires a shared library that is loaded on demand, after chroot takes place).

2. You cannot send email from PHP, because it wants to use sendmail and sendmail resides outside the jail.

3. In some cases, when you separate Apache from its configuration, restarts and graceful reloads no longer work.

The best way to use SecChrootDir is the following:

1. Create /chroot to be your main jail directory.

2. Create /chroot/opt/apache inside jail.

3. Create a symlink from /opt/apache to /chroot/opt/apache.

4. Now install Apache into /chroot/opt/apache.

You should be aware that the internal chroot feature might not be 100% reliable. Due to the large number of default and third-party modules available for the Apache web server, it is not possible to verify the internal chroot works reliably with all of them. A module, working from within Apache, can do things that make it easy to break out of the jail. In particular, if you are using any of the modules that fork in the module initialisation phase (e.g., mod_fastcgi, mod_fcgid, mod_cgid), you are advised to examine each Apache process and observe its current working directory, process root, and the list of open files. Consider what your options are and make your own decision.

SecComponentSignature

Description: Appends component signature to the ModSecurity signature.

Syntax: SecComponentSignature "COMPONENT_NAME/X.Y.Z (COMMENT)"

Example usage: SecComponentSignature "Core Rules/1.2.3"

Scope: Main

Version: 2.5.0

This directive should be used to make the presence of significant rule sets known. The entire signature will be recorded in the transaction audit log.

SecContentInjection

Description: Enables content injection using actions `append` and `prepend`.

Syntax: `SecContentInjection On|Off`

Example Usage: `SecContentInjection On`

Scope: Any

Version: 2.5.0

This directive provides an easy way to control content injection, no matter what the rules want to do. It is not necessary to have response body buffering enabled in order to use content injection.

SecCookieFormat

Description: Selects the cookie format that will be used in the current configuration context.

Syntax: `SecCookieFormat 0|1`

Example Usage: `SecCookieFormat 0`

Scope: Any

Version: 2.0.0

The possible values are:

- 0: Use version 0 (Netscape) cookies. This is what most applications use. It is the default value.
- 1: Use version 1 cookies.

SecDataDir

Description: Path where persistent data (e.g., IP address data, session data, and so on) is to be stored.

Syntax: `SecDataDir /path/to/dir`

Example Usage: `SecDataDir /usr/local/apache/logs/data`

Scope: Main

This directive must be provided before `initcol`, `setsid`, and `setuid` can be used. The directory to which the directive points must be writable by the web server user.

SecDebugLog

Description: Path to the ModSecurity debug log file.

Syntax: `SecDebugLog /path/to/modsec-debug.log`

Example Usage: `SecDebugLog /usr/local/apache/logs/modsec-debug.log`

Scope: Any

Version: 2.0.0

SecDebugLogLevel

Description: Configures the verboseness of the debug log data.

Syntax: `SecDebugLogLevel 0|1|2|3|4|5|6|7|8|9`

Example Usage: `SecDebugLogLevel 4`

Scope: Any

Version: 2.0.0

Messages at levels 1–3 are always copied to the Apache error log. Therefore you can always use level 0 as the default logging level in production if you are very concerned with performance. Having said that, the best value to use is 3. Higher logging levels are not recommended in production, because the heavy logging affects performance adversely.

The possible values for the debug log level are:

- 0: no logging
- 1: errors (intercepted requests) only
- 2: warnings
- 3: notices
- 4: details of how transactions are handled
- 5: as above, but including information about each piece of information handled
- 9: log everything, including very detailed debugging information

SecDefaultAction

Description: Defines the default list of actions, which will be inherited by the rules in the same configuration context.

Syntax: SecDefaultAction "action1,action2,action3"

Example Usage: SecDefaultAction "phase:2,log,auditlog,deny,status:403"

Scope: Any

Version: 2.0.0

Default: phase:2,log,auditlog,pass

Every rule following a previous SecDefaultAction directive in the same configuration context will inherit its settings unless more specific actions are used. Every SecDefaultAction directive must specify a disruptive action and a processing phase and cannot contain metadata actions.

> **Warning**
>
> SecDefaultAction is **not** inherited across configuration contexts. (For an example of why this may be a problem, read the following ModSecurity Blog entry http://blog.modsecurity.org/2008/07/modsecurity-tri.html.)

SecGeoLookupDb

Description: Defines the path to the database that will be used for geolocation lookups.

Syntax: SecGeoLookupDb /path/to/db

Example Usage: SecGeoLookupDb /path/to/GeoLiteCity.dat

Scope: Any

Version: 2.5.0

ModSecurity relies on the free geolocation databases (GeoLite City and GeoLite Country) that can be obtained from MaxMind [http://www.maxmind.com].

SecGuardianLog

Description: Configures an external program that will receive the information about every transaction via piped logging.

Syntax: SecGuardianLog |/path/to/httpd-guardian

Example Usage: SecGuardianLog |/usr/local/apache/bin/httpd-guardian

Scope: Main

Version: 2.0.0

Guardian logging is designed to send the information about every request to an external program. Because Apache is typically deployed in a multiprocess fashion, which makes information sharing between processes difficult, the idea is to deploy a single external process to observe all requests in a stateful manner, providing additional protection.

Currently the only tool known to work with guardian logging is `httpd-guardian`, which is part of the Apache httpd tools project [http://www.apachesecurity.net/tools/]. The `httpd-guardian` tool is designed to defend against denial of service attacks. It uses the `blacklist` tool (from the same project) to interact with an iptables-based (on a Linux system) or pf-based (on a BSD system) firewall, dynamically blacklisting the offending IP addresses. It can also interact with SnortSam [http://www.snortsam.net]. Assuming `httpd-guardian` is already configured (look into the source code for the detailed instructions), you only need to add one line to your Apache configuration to deploy it:

```
SecGuardianLog |/path/to/httpd-guardian
```

SecMarker

Description: Adds a fixed rule marker that can be used as a target in a `skipAfter` action. A SecMarker directive essentially creates a rule that does nothing and whose only purpose is to carry the given ID.

Syntax: `SecMarker ID`

Example Usage: `SecMarker 9999`

Scope: Any

Version: 2.5.0

The SecMarker directive is available to allow you to choose the best way to implement a skip-over. In many cases, however, there will be a rule nearby that you can use. In the following example, which does use `SecMarker`, the `skipAfter` could have just as well used rule 15.

```
SecRule REQUEST_URI "^/$" \
    "chain,t:none,t:urlDecode,t:lowercase,t:normalizePath,skipAfter:99"
SecRule REMOTE_ADDR "^127\.0\.0\.1$" "chain"
SecRule REQUEST_HEADERS:User-Agent \
    "^Apache \(internal dummy connection\)$" "t:none"
SecRule &REQUEST_HEADERS:Host "@eq 0" \
    "deny,log,status:400,id:08,severity:4,msg:'Missing a Host Header'"
SecRule &REQUEST_HEADERS:Accept "@eq 0" \
    "log,deny,log,status:400,id:15,msg:'Request Missing an Accept Header'"

SecMarker 99
```

SecPcreMatchLimit

Description: Sets the match limit in the PCRE library.

Syntax: `SecPcreMatchLimit value`

Example Usage: `SecPcreMatchLimit 1500`

Scope: Main

Version: 2.5.12

Default: 1500

The default can be changed when ModSecurity is prepared for compilation: the `--enable-pcre-match-limit=val` configure option will set a custom default and the `--disable-pcre-match-limit` option will revert back to the default of the PCRE library.

For more information, refer to the `pcre_extra` field in the `pcreapi` man page.

SecPcreMatchLimitRecursion

Description: Sets the match limit recursion in the PCRE library.

Syntax: `SecPcreMatchLimitRecursion value`

Example Usage: `SecPcreMatchLimitRecursion 1500`

Scope: Main

Version: 2.5.12

Default: 1500

The default can be changed when ModSecurity is prepared for compilation: the `--enable-pcre-match-limit-recursion=val` configure option will set a custom default and the `--disable-pcre-match-limit-recursion` option will revert back to the default of the PCRE library.

For more information, refer to the `pcre_extra` field in the `pcreapi` man page.

SecPdfProtect

Description: Enables the PDF XSS protection functionality. Once enabled access to PDF files is tracked. Direct access attempts are redirected to links that contain one-time tokens. Requests with valid tokens are allowed through, unmodified. Requests with invalid tokens are also allowed through, but with forced download of the PDF files. This implementation uses response headers to detect PDF files and thus can be used with dynamically generated PDF files that do not have the `.pdf` extension in the request URI.

Syntax: `SecPdfProtect On|Off`

Example Usage: `SecPdfProtect On`

Scope: Any

Version: 2.5.0; removed from trunk

SecPdfProtectMethod

Description: Configure desired protection method to be used when requests for PDF files are detected. Possible values are `TokenRedirection` and `ForcedDownload`. The token redirection approach will attempt to redirect with tokens where possible. This allows PDF files to continue to be opened inline but works only for GET requests. Forced download always causes PDF files to be delivered as opaque binaries and attachments. The latter will always be used for non-GET requests. Forced download is considered to be more secure but may cause usability problems for users ("This PDF won't open anymore!").

Syntax: `SecPdfProtectMethod method`

Example Usage: `SecPdfProtectMethod TokenRedirection`

Scope: Any

Version: 2.5.0; removed from trunk

Default: `TokenRedirection`

SecPdfProtectSecret

Description: Defines the secret that will be used to construct one-time tokens. You should use a reasonably long value for the secret (e.g., 16 characters is good). Once selected, the secret should not be changed, as it will break the tokens that were sent prior to change. But it's not a big deal even if you change it. It will just force download of PDF files with tokens that were issued in the last few seconds.

Syntax: `SecPdfProtectSecret secret`

Example Usage: `SecPdfProtectSecret MyRandomSecretString`

Scope: Any

Version: 2.5.0; removed from trunk

SecPdfProtectTimeout

Description: Defines the token timeout. After token expires, it can no longer be used to allow access to a PDF file. Request will be allowed through but the PDF will be delivered as an attachment.

Syntax: `SecPdfProtectTimeout timeout`

Example Usage: `SecPdfProtectTimeout 10`

Scope: Any

Version: 2.5.0; removed from trunk

Default: 10

SecPdfProtectTokenName

Description: Defines the name of the token. The only reason you would want to change the name of the token is if you wanted to hide the fact that you are running ModSecurity. It's a good reason, but it won't really help, as the adversary can look into the algorithm used for PDF protection and figure it out anyway. It does raise the bar slightly, so go ahead if you want to.

Syntax: SecPdfProtectTokenName name

Example Usage: SecPdfProtectTokenName PDFTOKEN

Scope: Any

Version: 2.5.0; removed from trunk

Default: PDFTOKEN

SecRequestBodyAccess

Description: Configures whether request bodies will be buffered and processed by ModSecurity.

Syntax: SecRequestBodyAccess On|Off

Example Usage: SecRequestBodyAccess On

Scope: Any

Version: 2.0.0

This directive is required if you want to inspect the data transported request bodies (e.g., POST parameters). Request buffering is also required in order to make reliable blocking possible.

The possible values are:

- On: buffer request bodies
- Off: do not buffer request bodies

SecRequestBodyLimit

Description: Configures the maximum request body size ModSecurity will accept for buffering.

Syntax: SecRequestBodyLimit LIMIT_IN_BYTES

Example Usage: SecRequestBodyLimit 134217728

Scope: Any

Version: 2.0.0

Default: 134217728 (131072 KB)

Anything over the limit will be rejected with status code 413 (Request Entity Too Large). There is a hard limit of 1 GB.

SecRequestBodyNoFilesLimit

Description: Configures the maximum request body size ModSecurity will accept for buffering, excluding the size of any files being transported in the request. This directive is useful to reduce susceptibility to DoS attacks when someone is sending request bodies of very large sizes. Web applications that require file uploads must configure `SecRequestBodyLimit` to a high value, but because large files are streamed to disk, file uploads will not increase memory consumption. However, it's still possible for someone to take advantage of a large request body limit and send non-upload requests with large body sizes. This directive eliminates that loophole.

Syntax: `SecRequestBodyNoFilesLimit NUMBER_IN_BYTES`

Example Usage: `SecRequestBodyLimit 131072`

Scope: Any

Version: 2.5.0

Default: 1048576 (1 MB)

Generally speaking, the default value is not small enough. For most applications, you should be able to reduce it down to 128 KB or lower. Anything over the limit will be rejected with status code 413 (Request Entity Too Large). There is a hard limit of 1 GB.

SecRequestBodyInMemoryLimit

Description: Configures the maximum request body size that ModSecurity will store in memory.

Syntax: `SecRequestBodyInMemoryLimit LIMIT_IN_BYTES`

Example Usage: `SecRequestBodyInMemoryLimit 131072`

Scope: Any

Version: 2.0.0

Default: 131072 (128 KB)

When a `multipart/form-data` request is being processed, once the in-memory limit is reached, the request body will start to be streamed into a temporary file on disk.

SecResponseBodyLimit

Description: Configures the maximum response body size that will be accepted for buffering.

Syntax: SecResponseBodyLimit LIMIT_IN_BYTES

Example Usage: SecResponseBodyLimit 524228

Scope: Any

Version: 2.0.0

Default: 524288 (512 KB)

Anything over this limit will be rejected with status code 500 (Internal Server Error). This setting will not affect the responses with MIME types that are not selected for buffering. There is a hard limit of 1 GB.

SecResponseBodyLimitAction

Description: Controls what happens once a response body limit, configured with SecResponseBodyLimit, is encountered. By default, ModSecurity will reject a response body that is longer than specified. Some web sites, however, will produce very long responses, making it difficult to come up with a reasonable limit. Such sites would have to raise the limit significantly to function properly, defying the purpose of having the limit in the first place (to control memory consumption). With the ability to choose what happens once a limit is reached, site administrators can choose to inspect only the first part of the response, the part that can fit into the desired limit, and let the rest through. Some could argue that allowing parts of responses to go uninspected is a weakness. This is true in theory, but applies only to cases in which the attacker controls the output (e.g., can make it arbitrary long). In such cases, however, it is not possible to prevent leakage anyway. The attacker could compress, obfuscate, or even encrypt data before it is sent back, and therefore bypass any monitoring device.

Syntax: SecResponseBodyLimitAction Reject|ProcessPartial

Example Usage: SecResponseBodyLimitAction ProcessPartial

Scope: Any

Version: 2.5.0

SecResponseBodyMimeType

Description: Configures which MIME types are to be considered for response body buffering.

Syntax: SecResponseBodyMimeType MIMETYPE MIMETYPE ...

Example Usage: SecResponseBodyMimeType text/plain text/html

Scope: Any

Version: 2.0.0

Default: text/plain text/html

Multiple SecResponseBodyMimeType directives can be used to add MIME types. Use SecResponseBodyMimeTypesClear to clear previously configured MIME types and start over.

SecResponseBodyMimeTypesClear

Description: Clears the list of MIME types considered for response body buffering, allowing you to start populating the list from scratch.

Syntax: SecResponseBodyMimeTypesClear

Example Usage: SecResponseBodyMimeTypesClear

Scope: Any

Version: 2.0.0

SecResponseBodyAccess

Description: Configures whether response bodies are to be buffered.

Syntax: SecResponseBodyAccess On|Off

Example Usage: SecResponseBodyAccess On

Scope: Any

Version: 2.0.0

Default: Off

This directive is required if you plan to inspect HTML responses and implement response blocking.

Possible values are:

- On: buffer response bodies (but only if the response MIME type matches the list configured with SecResponseBodyMimeType).
- Off: do not buffer response bodies.

SecRule

Description: Creates a rule that will analyze the selected variables using the selected operator.

Syntax: SecRule VARIABLES OPERATOR [ACTIONS]

Example Usage: SecRule ARGS "@rx attack" "phase:1,log,deny"

Scope: Any

Version: 2.0.0

Every rule must provide one or more variables along with the operator that should be used to inspect them. If no actions are provided, the default list will be used. (There is always a default list, even if one was not explicitly set with SecDefaultAction.) If there are actions specified in a rule, they will be merged with the default list to form the final actions that will be used. (The actions in the rule will overwrite those in the default list.) Refer to SecDefaultAction for more information.

SecRuleInheritance

Description: Configures whether the current context will inherit the rules from the parent context.

Syntax: SecRuleInheritance On|Off

Example Usage: SecRuleInheritance Off

Scope: Any

Version: 2.0.0

Default: On

Sometimes when you create a more specific configuration context (for example using the <Location> container), you may wish to use a different set of rules than those used in the parent context. By setting SecRuleInheritance to Off, you prevent the parent rules to be inherited, which allows you to start from scratch. In ModSecurity 2.5.x it is not possible to override phase 1 rules from a <Location> configuration context. There are no limitations in that respect in the current development version (and there won't be in the next major version).

The possible values are:

- On: inherit rules from the parent context
- Off: do not inherit rules from the parent context

> **Note**
>
> Configuration contexts are an Apache concept. Directives <Directory>, <Files>, <Location>, and <VirtualHost> are all used to create configuration contexts. For more information, please go to the Apache documentation, under Configuration Sections [http://httpd.apache.org/docs/2.0/sections.html].

This directive does not affect how configuration options are inherited.

SecRuleEngine

Description: Configures the rules engine.

Syntax: SecRuleEngine On|Off|DetectionOnly

Example Usage: SecRuleEngine On

Scope: Any

Version: 2.0.0

Default: Off

The possible values are:

- On: process rules
- Off: do not process rules
- DetectionOnly: process rules but never intercept transactions, even when rules are configured to block

SecRuleRemoveById

Description: Removes the matching rules from the current configuration context.

Syntax: SecRuleRemoveById ID ID RANGE ...

Example Usage: SecRuleRemoveByID 1 2 "9000-9010"

Scope: Any

Version: 2.0.0

This directive supports multiple parameters, each of which can be a rule ID or a range. Parameters that contain spaces must be delimited using double quotes.

SecRuleRemoveByMsg

Description: Removes the matching rules from the current configuration context.

Syntax: SecRuleRemoveByMsg REGEX

Example Usage: SecRuleRemoveByMsg "FAIL"

Scope: Any

Version: 2.0.0

Normally, you would use SecRuleRemoveById to remove rules, but that requires the rules to have IDs defined. If they don't, then you can remove them with SecRuleRemoveByMsg, which matches a regular expression against rule messages.

SecRuleScript

Description: This directive creates a special rule that executes a Lua script to decide whether to match. The main difference from SecRule is that there are no targets or operators. The script can fetch any variable from the ModSecurity context and use any Lua code to test them. The second optional parameter is the list of actions, whose meaning is identical to that of SecRule.

Syntax: SecRuleScript /path/to/script.lua [ACTIONS]

Example Usage: SecRuleScript "/path/to/file.lua" "block"

Scope: Any

Version: 2.5.0

All Lua scripts are compiled at configuration time and cached in memory. To reload scripts, you must reload the entire ModSecurity configuration by restarting Apache. You can find out more about Lua by visiting its web site [http://www.lua.org].

Example Lua script:

```lua
-- Your script must define the main entry
-- point, as below.
function main()
    -- Log something at level 1. Normally you shouldn't be
    -- logging anything, especially not at level 1, but this is
    -- just to show you can. Useful for debugging.
    m.log(1, "Hello world!");

    -- Retrieve one variable.
    local var1 = m.getvar("REMOTE_ADDR");

    -- Retrieve one variable, applying one transformation function.
    -- The second parameter is a string.
    local var2 = m.getvar("ARGS", "lowercase");

    -- Retrieve one variable, applying several transformation functions.
    -- The second parameter is now a list. You should note that m.getvar()
    -- requires the use of comma to separate collection names from
    -- variable names. This is because only one variable is returned.
    local var3 = m.getvar("ARGS.p", { "lowercase", "compressWhitespace" } );

    -- If you want this rule to match return a string
    -- containing the error message. The message must contain the name
    -- of the variable where the problem is located.
    -- return "Variable ARGS:p looks suspicious!"

    -- Otherwise, simply return nil.
    return nil;
end
```

In this first example, we were only retrieving one variable at the time. In this case, the name of the variable is known to you. In many cases, however, you will want to examine variables whose names you won't know in advance, such as script parameters.

Example showing use of m.getvars() to retrieve many variables at once:

```
function main()
    -- Retrieve script parameters.
    local d = m.getvars("ARGS", { "lowercase", "htmlEntityDecode" } );

    -- Loop through the parameters.
    for i = 1, #d do
        -- Examine parameter value.
        if (string.find(d[i].value, "<script")) then
            -- Always specify the name of the variable where the
            -- problem is located in the error message.
            return ("Suspected XSS in variable " .. d[i].name .. ".");
        end
    end

    -- Nothing wrong found.
    return nil;
end
```

> **Note**
>
> Although the current implementation of the Lua rules is solid (and production ready), Lua support is marked as *experimental*, because the programming interface may change in a future version of ModSecurity.

SecRuleUpdateActionById

Description: Updates the action list of the specified rule.

Syntax: SecRuleRemoveById RULEID ACTIONLIST

Example Usage: SecRuleUpdateActionById 12345 "deny,status:403"

Scope: Any

Version: 2.5.0

This directive will overwrite the action list of the specified rule with the actions provided in the second parameter. It has two limitations: it cannot be used to change the ID or phase of a rule. Only the actions that can appear only once are overwritten. The actions that are allowed to appear multiple times in a list, will be appended to the end of the list.

```
SecRule ARGS attack \
    "phase:2,id:12345,t:lowercase,log,pass,msg:'Message text'"

SecRuleUpdateActionById 12345 \
    "t:none,t:compressWhitespace,deny,status:403,msg:'New message text'"
```

The effective resulting rule in the previous example will be as follows:

```
SecRule ARGS attack \
    "phase:2,id:12345,t:lowercase,t:none,t:compressWhitespace,\
    deny,status:403,msg:'New Message text'"
```

The addition of t:none will neutralize any previous transformation functions specified (t:lowercase, in the example).

SecServerSignature

Description: Instructs ModSecurity to change the data Apache sends out in the Server response header.

Syntax: SecServerSignature "NEW_SERVER_SIGNATURE"

Example Usage: SecServerSignature "Acme Web Server 19.99"

Scope: Main

Version: 2.0.0

In order for this directive to work, you must set the Apache ServerTokens directive to Full. ModSecurity will overwrite the server signature data held in this memory space with the data set in this directive. If ServerTokens is not set to Full, then the memory space is most likely not large enough to hold the new data we are looking to insert.

SecTmpDir

Description: Configures the directory where temporary files will be created.

Syntax: SecTmpDir /path/to/dir

Example Usage: SecTmpDir /tmp

Scope: Any

Version: 2.0.0

The location specified needs to be writable by the Apache user process. This is the directory location where ModSecurity will swap data to disk if it runs out of memory (more data than what was specified in the SecRequestBodyInMemoryLimit directive) during inspection.

SecUploadDir

Description: Configures the directory where intercepted files will be stored.

Syntax: SecUploadDir /path/to/dir

Example Usage: SecUploadDir /tmp

Scope: Any

Version: 2.0.0

This directory must be on the same filesystem as the temporary directory defined with SecTmpDir. This directive is used with SecUploadKeepFiles.

SecUploadFileLimit

Description: Configures the maximum number of file uploads processed in a multipart POST.

Syntax: SecUploadFileLimit LIMIT

Example Usage: SecUploadFileLimit 10

Scope: Any

Version: 2.5.12

Default: 100

The default limit is set to 100 files, but you are encouraged to reduce this value. Any file over the limit will not be extracted and the MULTIPART_FILE_LIMIT_EXCEEDED and MULTIPART_STRICT_ERROR flags will be set. To prevent bypassing any file checks, you must check for one of these flags.

> **Note**
>
> If the limit is exceeded, the part name and file name will still be recorded in FILES_NAME and FILES, the file size will be recorded in FILES_SIZES, but there will be no record in FILES_TMPNAMES, as a temporary file was not created.

SecUploadFileMode

Description: Configures the mode (permissions) of any uploaded files using an octal mode (as used in chmod).

Syntax: SecUploadFileMode octal_mode|"default"

Example Usage: SecUploadFileMode 0640

Scope: Any

Version: 2.1.6

This feature is not available on operating systems not supporting octal file modes. The default mode (0600) grants read/write access to the account writing the file only. If access from another account is needed (using clamd is a good example), then this directive may be required. However, use this directive with caution to avoid exposing potentially sensitive data to unauthorized users. Using the value "default" will revert back to the default setting.

SecUploadKeepFiles

Description: Configures whether the intercepted files will be kept after transaction is processed.

Syntax: SecUploadKeepFiles On|Off|RelevantOnly

Example Usage: SecUploadKeepFiles On

Scope: Any

Version: 2.0.0

This directive requires the storage directory to be defined (using SecUploadDir).

Possible values are:

- On: keep uploaded files
- Off: do not keep uploaded files
- RelevantOnly: keep only those files that belong to requests that are deemed relevant

SecWebAppId

Description: Creates an application namespace, allowing for separate persistent session and user storage.

Syntax: SecWebAppId "NAME"

Example Usage: SecWebAppId "WebApp1"

Scope: Any

Version: 2.0.0

Default: default

Application namespaces are used to avoid collisions between session IDs and user IDs when multiple applications are deployed on the same server. If it isn't used, a collision between session IDs might occur.

```
<VirtualHost *:80>
    ServerName app1.example.com
    SecWebAppId "App1"
    ...
</VirtualHost>
```

```
<VirtualHost *:80>
    ServerName app2.example.com
    SecWebAppId "App2"
    ...
</VirtualHost>
```

In the two examples configurations shown, SecWebAppId is being used in conjunction with the Apache VirtualHost directives. Applications namespace information is also recorded in the audit logs (using the WebApp-Info header of the H part).

16 Variables

This section documents the variables currently available in ModSecurity.

ARGS

ARGS is a collection that contains all request parameters, regardless of where they appear in request (e.g., in the query string or in the request body).

```
SecRule ARGS attack
```

ARGS_COMBINED_SIZE

Contains the combined size of all request parameters. Files are excluded from the calculation. This variable can be useful, for example, to create a rule to ensure that the total size of the argument data is below a certain threshold. The following rule detects a request whose parameters are more than 2500 bytes long:

```
SecRule ARGS_COMBINED_SIZE "@gt 2500"
```

ARGS_NAMES

Contains all request parameter names. You can search for specific parameter names that you want to inspect. In a positive policy scenario, you can also whitelist (using an inverted rule with the exclamation mark) only the authorized argument names.

This example rule allows only two argument names: p and a:

```
SecRule ARGS_NAMES "!^(p|a)$"
```

ARGS_GET

ARGS_GET is similar to ARGS, but contains only query string parameters.

ARGS_GET_NAMES

ARGS_GET_NAMES is similar to ARGS_NAMES, but contains only the names of query string parameters.

ARGS_POST

ARGS_POST is similar to ARGS, but contains only request body parameters.

ARGS_POST_NAMES

ARGS_POST_NAMES is similar to ARGS_NAMES, but contains only the names of request body parameters.

AUTH_TYPE

This variable holds the authentication method used to validate a user, if any of the methods built into HTTP are used. In a reverse-proxy deployment, this information will not be available if the authentication is handled in the backend web server.

```
SecRule AUTH_TYPE "Basic"
```

DURATION

Contains the number of milliseconds elapsed since the beginning of the current transaction. Available starting with 2.6.0.

ENV

Collection that provides access to environment variables. Requires a single parameter to specify the name of the desired variable.

```
# Set environment variable
SecRule REQUEST_FILENAME "printenv" \
    "phase:2,pass,setenv:tag=suspicious"

# Inspect environment variable
SecRule ENV:tag "suspicious"
```

Use setenv to set environment variables.

FILES

Contains a collection of original file names (as they were called on the remote user's filesystem). Available only on inspected multipart/form-data requests.

```
SecRule FILES "@rx \.conf$"
```

FILES_COMBINED_SIZE

Contains the total size of the files transported in request body. Available only on inspected multipart/form-data requests.

```
SecRule FILES_COMBINED_SIZE "@gt 100000"
```

FILES_NAMES

Contains a list of form fields that were used for file upload. Available only on inspected multipart/form-data requests.

```
SecRule FILES_NAMES "^upfile$"
```

FILES_SIZES

Contains a list of individual file sizes. Useful for implementing a size limitation on individual uploaded files. Available only on inspected multipart/form-data requests.

```
SecRule FILES_SIZES "@gt 100"
```

FILES_TMPNAMES

Contains a list of temporary files' names on the disk. Useful when used together with @inspectFile. Available only on inspected multipart/form-data requests.

```
SecRule FILES_TMPNAMES "@inspectFile /path/to/inspect_script.pl"
```

GEO

GEO is a collection that contains the data obtained by the most recent execution of the @geoLookup operator.

Available since ModSecurity 2.5.0.

Fields:

- COUNTRY_CODE: Two-character country code. For example, US, GB, and so on.
- COUNTRY_CODE3: Up to three-character country code. For example, GBR.
- COUNTRY_NAME: The full country name.
- COUNTRY_CONTINENT: The two-character continent on which the country is located.
- REGION: The two-character region. For the U.S., this is the state; for Canada, it is the province; and so on.
- CITY: The city name if supported by the database.
- POSTAL_CODE: The postal code if supported by the database.
- LATITUDE: The latitude if supported by the database.
- LONGITUDE: The longitude if supported by the database.
- DMA_CODE: The metropolitan area code if supported by the database (U.S. only).
- AREA_CODE: The phone system area code (U.S. only).

Example:

```
SecGeoLookupDb /path/to/GeoLiteCity.dat
...
SecRule REMOTE_ADDR "@geoLookup" "chain,drop,msg:'Non-GB IP address'"
SecRule GEO:COUNTRY_CODE "!@streq GB"
```

HIGHEST_SEVERITY

This variable holds the highest severity of any rules that have matched so far. Severities are numeric values and thus can be used with comparison operators such as @lt, and so on. A value of 255 indicates that no severity has been set.

```
SecRule HIGHEST_SEVERITY "@le 2" \
    "phase:2,deny,status:500,msg:'severity %{HIGHEST_SEVERITY}'"
```

> **Note**
> Higher severities have a lower numeric value.

MATCHED_VAR

This variable holds the value of the most-recently matched variable. It is similar to the TX:0, but it is automatically supported by all operators and there is no need to specify the capture action.

```
SecRule ARGS pattern chain,deny
...
SecRule MATCHED_VAR "further scrutiny"
```

MATCHED_VAR_NAME

This variable holds the full name of the most-recently matched variable.

```
SecRule ARGS pattern \
    "setvar:tx.mymatch=%{MATCHED_VAR_NAME}"
...
SecRule TX:MYMATCH "@eq ARGS:param" deny
```

MODSEC_BUILD

This variable holds the ModSecurity build number. This variable is intended to be used to check the build number prior to using a feature that is available only in a certain build. Example:

```
SecRule MODSEC_BUILD "!@ge 02050102" \
    "skipAfter:12345"
SecRule ARGS "@pm some key words" \
    "id:12345,deny,status:500"
```

MULTIPART_CRLF_LF_LINES

This flag variable will be set to 1 whenever a multipart request uses mixed line terminators. The multipart/form-data RFC requires that the CRLF sequence be used to terminate lines. Because some client implementations use only LF to terminate lines, you might want to allow them to proceed under certain circumstances (if you want to do this, you will need to stop using MULTIPART_STRICT_ERROR and check each multipart flag variable individually, avoiding MULTIPART_LF_LINE). However, mixing CRLF and LF line terminators is dangerous, as it can allow for evasion. Therefore, in such cases, you will have to add a check for MULTIPART_CRLF_LF_LINES.

MULTIPART_STRICT_ERROR

MULTIPART_STRICT_ERROR will be set to 1 when any of the following variables is also set to 1: REQBODY_PROCESSOR_ERROR, MULTIPART_BOUNDARY_QUOTED, MULTIPART_BOUNDARY_WHITESPACE, MULTIPART_DATA_BEFORE, MULTIPART_DATA_AFTER, MULTIPART_HEADER_FOLDING, MULTIPART_LF_LINE, MULTIPART_SEMICOLON_MISSING MULTIPART_INVALID_QUOTING, MULTIPART_INVALID_HEADER_FOLDING, and MULTIPART_FILE_LIMIT_EXCEEDED. Each of these variables covers one unusual (although sometimes legal) aspect of the request body in multipart/form-data format. Your policies should *always* contain a rule to check either this variable (easier) or one or more individual variables (if you know exactly what you want to accomplish). Depending on the rate of false positives

---

and your default policy, you should decide whether to block or just warn when the rule is triggered.

The best way to use this variable is as in the following example:

```
SecRule MULTIPART_STRICT_ERROR "!@eq 0" \
"phase:2,t:none,log,deny,msg:'Multipart request body \
failed strict validation: \
PE %{REQBODY_PROCESSOR_ERROR}, \
BQ %{MULTIPART_BOUNDARY_QUOTED}, \
BW %{MULTIPART_BOUNDARY_WHITESPACE}, \
DB %{MULTIPART_DATA_BEFORE}, \
DA %{MULTIPART_DATA_AFTER}, \
HF %{MULTIPART_HEADER_FOLDING}, \
LF %{MULTIPART_LF_LINE}, \
SM %{MULTIPART_SEMICOLON_MISSING}, \
IQ %{MULTIPART_INVALID_QUOTING}, \
IF %{MULTIPART_INVALID_HEADER_FOLDING}, \
FE %{MULTIPART_FILE_LIMIT_EXCEEDED}'"
```

The multipart/form-data parser was upgraded in ModSecurity v2.1.3 to actively look for signs of evasion. Many variables (as listed earlier) were added to expose various facts discovered during the parsing process. The MULTIPART_STRICT_ERROR variable is handy to check on all abnormalities at once. The individual variables allow detection to be fine-tuned according to your circumstances in order to reduce the number of false positives.

MULTIPART_UNMATCHED_BOUNDARY

Set to 1 when, during the parsing phase of a multipart/request-body, ModSecurity encounters what seems like a boundary but is not. Such an event may occur when evasion of ModSecurity is attempted.

The best way to use this variable is as in the following:

```
SecRule MULTIPART_UNMATCHED_BOUNDARY "!@eq 0" \
    "phase:2,t:none,log,deny,\
    msg:'Multipart parser detected a possible unmatched boundary.'"
```

Change the rule from blocking to logging-only if many false positives are encountered.

PATH_INFO

Contains the extra request URI information, also known as path info. (For example, in the URI /index.php/123, /123 is the path info.) Available only in embedded deployments.

```
SecRule PATH_INFO "^/(bin|etc|sbin|opt|usr)"
```

PERF_COMBINED

Contains the time, in microseconds, spent in ModSecurity during the current transaction. The value in this variable is arrived to by adding all the performance variables except PERF_SREAD (the time spent reading from persistent storage is already included in the phase measurements). Available starting with 2.6.

PERF_GC

Contains the time, in microseconds, spent performing garbage collection. Available starting with 2.6.

PERF_LOGGING

Contains the time, in microseconds, spent in audit logging. This value is known only after the handling of a transaction is finalized, which means that it can only be logged using mod_log_config and the %{VARNAME}M syntax. Available starting with 2.6.

PERF_PHASE1

Contains the time, in microseconds, spent processing phase 1. Available starting with 2.6.

PERF_PHASE2

Contains the time, in microseconds, spent processing phase 2. Available starting with 2.6.

PERF_PHASE3

Contains the time, in microseconds, spent processing phase 3. Available starting with 2.6.

PERF_PHASE4

Contains the time, in microseconds, spent processing phase 4. Available starting with 2.6.

PERF_PHASE5

Contains the time, in microseconds, spent processing phase 5. Available starting with 2.6.

PERF_SREAD

Contains the time, in microseconds, spent reading from persistent storage. Available starting with 2.6.

PERF_SWRITE

Contains the time, in microseconds, spent writing to persistent storage. Available starting with 2.6.

QUERY_STRING

Contains the query string part of a request URI. The value in QUERY_STRING is always provided raw, without URL decoding taking place.

```
SecRule QUERY_STRING "attack"
```

REMOTE_ADDR

This variable holds the IP address of the remote client.

```
SecRule REMOTE_ADDR "^192\.168\.1\.101$"
```

REMOTE_HOST

If the Apache directive HostnameLookups is set to On, then this variable will hold the remote hostname resolved through DNS. If the directive is set to Off, this variable it will hold the remote IP address (same as REMOTE_ADDR). Possible uses for this variable would be to deny known bad client hosts or network blocks, or conversely, to allow in authorized hosts.

```
SecRule REMOTE_HOST "\.evil\.network\org$"
```

REMOTE_PORT

This variable holds information on the source port that the client used when initiating the connection to our web server.

In the following example, we are evaluating to see whether the REMOTE_PORT is less than 1024, which would indicate that the user is a privileged user:

```
SecRule REMOTE_PORT "@lt 1024"
```

REMOTE_USER

This variable holds the username of the authenticated user. If there are no password access controls in place (Basic or Digest authentication), then this variable will be empty.

```
SecRule REMOTE_USER "^admin$"
```

In a reverse-proxy deployment, this information will not be available if the authentication is handled in the backend web server.

REQBODY_PROCESSOR

Contains the name of the currently used request body processor. The possible values are UR-LENCODED, MULTIPART, and XML.

```
SecRule REQBODY_PROCESSOR "^XML$ chain
SecRule XML "@validateDTD /opt/apache-frontend/conf/xml.dtd"
```

REQBODY_PROCESSOR_ERROR

Contains the status of the request body processor used for request body parsing. The values can be 0 (no error) or 1 (error). This variable will be set by request body processors (typically the multipart/request-data parser or the XML parser) when they fail to do their work.

```
SecRule REQBODY_PROCESSOR_ERROR "@eq 1" deny,phase:2
```

> **Note**
>
> Your policies *must* have a rule to check for request body processor errors at the very beginning of phase 2. Failure to do so will leave the door open for impedance mismatch attacks. It is possible, for example, that a payload that cannot be parsed by ModSecurity can be successfully parsed by more tolerant parser operating in the application. If your policy dictates blocking, then you should reject the request if error is detected. When operating in detection-only mode, your rule should alert with high severity when request body processing fails.

REQBODY_PROCESSOR_ERROR_MSG

If there's been an error during request body parsing, the variable will contain the following error message:

```
SecRule REQBODY_PROCESSOR_ERROR_MSG "failed to parse"
```

REQUEST_BASENAME

This variable holds just the filename part of REQUEST_FILENAME (e.g., index.php).

```
SecRule REQUEST_BASENAME "^login\.php$" phase:2,t:none,t:lowercase
```

> **Note**
>
> Please note that anti-evasion transformations are not applied to this variable by default. REQUEST_BASENAME will recognise both / and \ as path separators. You should understand that the value of this variable depends on what was provided in request, and that it does not have to correspond to the resource (on disk) that will be used by the web server.

REQUEST_BODY

Holds the raw request body. This variable is available only if the URLENCODED request body processor was used, which will occur by default when the application/x-www-form-urlencoded content type is detected, or if the use of the URLENCODED request body parser was forced. As of 2.5.7, it is possible to force the presence of the REQUEST_BODY variable, but only when there is no request body processor defined using the ctl:forceRequestBodyVariable option in the REQUEST_HEADERS phase.

REQUEST_BODY_LENGTH

Contains the number of bytes read from a request body. Available starting with v2.6.

REQUEST_COOKIES

This variable is a collection of all of request cookies (values only).

```
SecRule &REQUEST_COOKIES "@eq 0"
```

REQUEST_COOKIES_NAMES

This variable is a collection of the names of all request cookies. For example, the following rule will trigger if the JSESSIONID cookie is not present:

```
SecRule &REQUEST_COOKIES_NAMES:JSESSIONID "@eq 0"
```

REQUEST_FILENAME

This variable holds the relative request URL without the query string part (e.g., /index.php).

```
SecRule REQUEST_FILENAME "^/cgi-bin/login\.php$" phase:2,t:none,t:normalizePath
```

> **Note**
>
> Please note that anti-evasion transformations are not used on REQUEST_FILENAME, which means that you will have to specify them in the rules that use this variable.

REQUEST_HEADERS

This variable can be used as either a collection of all of the request headers or can be used to inspect selected headers (by using the REQUEST_HEADERS:Header-Name syntax).

```
SecRule REQUEST_HEADERS:Host "^[\d\.]+$" \
    "deny,log,status:400,msg:'Host header is a numeric IP address'"
```

REQUEST_HEADERS_NAMES

This variable is a collection of the names of all of the request headers.

```
SecRule REQUEST_HEADERS_NAMES "^x-forwarded-for" \
    "log,deny,status:403,t:lowercase,msg:'Proxy Server Used'"
```

REQUEST_LINE

This variable holds the complete request line sent to the server (including the request method and HTTP version information).

```
# Allow only POST, GET and HEAD request methods, as well as only
# the valid protocol versions
SecRule REQUEST_LINE "!(^((?:(?:POS|GE)T|HEAD))|HTTP/(0\.9|1\.0|1\.1)$)" \
    "phase:1,log,block,t:none"
```

REQUEST_METHOD

This variable holds the request method used in the transaction.

```
SecRule REQUEST_METHOD "^(?:CONNECT|TRACE)$"
```

REQUEST_PROTOCOL

This variable holds the request protocol version information.

```
SecRule REQUEST_PROTOCOL "!^HTTP/(0\.9|1\.0|1\.1)$"
```

REQUEST_URI

This variable holds the full request URL including the query string data (e.g., /index.php?p=X). However, it will never contain a domain name, even if it was provided on the request line.

```
SecRule REQUEST_URI "attack" \
```

```
"phase:1,t:none,t:urlDecode,t:lowercase,t:normalizePath"
```

> **Note**
>
> Please note that anti-evasion transformations are not used on REQUEST_URI, which means that you will have to specify them in the rules that use this variable.

REQUEST_URI_RAW

Same as REQUEST_URI but will contain the domain name if it was provided on the request line (e.g., http://www.example.com/index.php?p=X).

```
SecRule REQUEST_URI_RAW "http:/" \
    "phase:1,t:none,t:urlDecode,t:lowercase,t:normalizePath"
```

> **Note**
>
> Please note that anti-evasion transformations are not used on REQUEST_URI_RAW, which means that you will have to specify them in the rules that use this variable.

RESPONSE_BODY

This variable holds the data for the response body, but only when response body buffering is enabled.

```
SecRule RESPONSE_BODY "ODBC Error Code"
```

RESPONSE_CONTENT_LENGTH

Response body length in bytes. Can be available starting with phase 3, but it does not have to be (as the length of response body is not always known in advance). If the size is not known, this variable will contain a zero. If RESPONSE_CONTENT_LENGTH contains a zero in phase 5 that means the actual size of the response body was 0. The value of this variable can change between phases if the body is modified. For example, in embedded mode, mod_deflate can compress the response body between phases 4 and 5.

RESPONSE_CONTENT_TYPE

Response content type. Available only starting with phase 3. The value available in this variable is taken directly from the internal structures of Apache, which means that it may contain the information that is not yet available in response headers. In embedded deployments, you should always refer to this variable, rather than to RESPONSE_HEADERS:Content-Type.

RESPONSE_HEADERS

This variable refers to response headers, in the same way as REQUEST_HEADERS does to request headers.

```
SecRule RESPONSE_HEADERS:X-Cache "MISS"
```

This variable may not have access to some headers when running in embedded mode. Headers such as Server, Date, Connection, and Content-Type could be added just prior to sending the data to the client. This data should be available in phase 5 or when deployed in proxy mode.

RESPONSE_HEADERS_NAMES

This variable is a collection of the response header names.

```
SecRule RESPONSE_HEADERS_NAMES "Set-Cookie"
```

The same limitations apply as the ones discussed in RESPONSE_HEADERS.

RESPONSE_PROTOCOL

This variable holds the HTTP response protocol information.

```
SecRule RESPONSE_PROTOCOL "^HTTP\/0\.9"
```

RESPONSE_STATUS

This variable holds the HTTP response status code:

```
SecRule RESPONSE_STATUS "^[45]"
```

This variable may not work as expected in embedded mode, as Apache sometimes handles certain requests differently, and without invoking ModSecurity (all other modules).

RULE

This is a special collection that provides access to the id, rev, severity, logdata, and msg fields of the rule that triggered the action. It can be used to refer to only the same rule in which it resides.

```
SecRule &REQUEST_HEADERS:Host "@eq 0" \
    "log,deny,setvar:tx.varname=%{RULE.id}"
```

SCRIPT_BASENAME

This variable holds just the local filename part of SCRIPT_FILENAME. Not available in proxy mode.

```
SecRule SCRIPT_BASENAME "^login\.php$"
```

SCRIPT_FILENAME

This variable holds the full internal path to the script that will be used to serve the request. Not available in proxy mode.

```
SecRule SCRIPT_FILENAME "^/usr/local/apache/cgi-bin/login\.php$"
```

SCRIPT_GID

This variable holds the numerical identifier of the group owner of the script. Not available in proxy mode.

```
SecRule SCRIPT_GID "!^46$"
```

SCRIPT_GROUPNAME

This variable holds the name of the group owner of the script. Not available in proxy mode.

```
SecRule SCRIPT_GROUPNAME "!^apache$"
```

SCRIPT_MODE

This variable holds the script's permissions mode data (e.g., 644). Not available in proxy mode.

```
# Do not allow scripts that can be written to
SecRule SCRIPT_MODE "^(2|3|6|7)$"
```

SCRIPT_UID

This variable holds the numerical identifier of the owner of the script. Not available in proxy mode.

```
# Do not run any scripts that are owned
# by Apache (Apache's user id is 46)
SecRule SCRIPT_UID "!^46$"
```

SCRIPT_USERNAME

This variable holds the username of the owner of the script. Not available in proxy mode.

```
# Do not run any scripts owned by Apache
SecRule SCRIPT_USERNAME "^apache$"
```

SERVER_ADDR

This variable contains the IP address of the server.

```
SecRule SERVER_ADDR "^192\.168\.1\.100$"
```

SERVER_NAME

This variable contains the transaction's hostname or IP address, taken from the request itself (which means that, in principle, it should not be trusted).

```
SecRule SERVER_NAME "hostname\.com$"
```

SERVER_PORT

This variable contains the local port that the web server (or reverse proxy) is listening on.

```
SecRule SERVER_PORT "^80$"
```

SESSION

This variable is a collection that contains session information. It becomes available only after setsid is executed.

The following example shows how to initialize SESSION using setsid, how to use setvar to increase the SESSION.score values, how to set the SESSION.blocked variable, and finally, how to deny the connection based on the SESSION:blocked value:

```
# Initialize session storage
SecRule REQUEST_COOKIES:PHPSESSID !^$ \
    "phase:2,nolog,pass,setsid:%{REQUEST_COOKIES.PHPSESSID}"

# Increment session score on attack
SecRule REQUEST_URI "^/cgi-bin/finger$" \
    "phase:2,t:none,t:lowercase,t:normalizePath,pass,setvar:SESSION.score=+10"

# Detect too many attacks in a session
```

```
SecRule SESSION:score "@gt 50" \
    "phase:2,pass,setvar:SESSION.blocked=1"

# Enforce session block
SecRule SESSION:blocked "@eq 1" \
    "phase:2,deny,status:403"
```

SESSIONID

This variable contains the value set with setsid. See SESSION (above) for a complete example.

TIME

This variable holds a formatted string representing the time (hour:minute:second).

```
SecRule TIME "^(([1](8|9))|([2](0|1|2|3))):\d{2}:\d{2}$"
```

TIME_DAY

This variable holds the current date (1–31). The following rule triggers on a transaction that's happening anytime between the 10th and 20th in a month:

```
SecRule TIME_DAY "^(([1](0|1|2|3|4|5|6|7|8|9))|20)$"
```

TIME_EPOCH

This variable holds the time in seconds since 1970.

TIME_HOUR

This variable holds the current hour value (0–23). The following rule triggers when a request is made "off hours":

```
SecRule TIME_HOUR "^(0|1|2|3|4|5|6|[1](8|9)|[2](0|1|2|3))$"
```

TIME_MIN

This variable holds the current minute value (0–59). The following rule triggers during the last half hour of every hour:

```
SecRule TIME_MIN "^(3|4|5)"
```

TIME_MON

This variable holds the current month value (0–11). The following rule matches if the month is either November (value 10) or December (value 11):

```
SecRule TIME_MON "^1"
```

TIME_SEC

This variable holds the current second value (0–59).

```
SecRule TIME_SEC "@gt 30"
```

TIME_WDAY

This variable holds the current weekday value (0–6). The following rule triggers only on Saturday and Sunday:

```
SecRule TIME_WDAY "^(0|6)$"
```

TIME_YEAR

This variable holds the current four-digit year value.

```
SecRule TIME_YEAR "^2006$"
```

TX

This is the transient transaction collection, which is used to store pieces of data, create a transaction anomaly score, and so on. The variables placed into this collection are available only until the transaction is complete.

```
# Increment transaction attack score on attack
SecRule ARGS attack \
    "phase:2,nolog,pass,setvar:TX.score=+5"
```

```
# Block the transactions whose scores are too high
SecRule TX:SCORE "@gt 20" \
    "phase:2,log,deny"
```

Some variable names in the TX collection are reserved and cannot be used:

- TX:0: the matching value when using the @rx or @pm operator with the capture action

---

- `TX:1-TX:9`: the captured subexpression value when using the `@rx` operator with capturing parens and the capture action
- `TX:MSC_.*`: ModSecurity processing flags
  - `MSC_PCRE_LIMITS_EXCEEDED`: Set to nonzero if PCRE match limits are exceeded. See `SecPcreMatchLimit` and `SecPcreMatchLimitRecursion` for more information.

URLENCODED_ERROR

This flag is raised when an invalid URL encoding is encountered during the parsing of a query string (on every request) or during the parsing of an `application/x-www-form-urlencoded` request body (only on the requests that use the `URLENCODED` request body processor).

USERID

This variable contains the value set with `setuid`.

```
# Initialize user tracking
SecAction "nolog,pass,setuid:%{REMOTE_USER}"

# Is the current user the administrator?
SecRule USERID "admin"
```

WEBAPPID

This variable contains the current application name, which is set in configuration using SecWebAppId.

WEBSERVER_ERROR_LOG

Contains zero or more error messages produced by the web server. This variable is best accessed from phase 5 (logging).

```
SecRule WEBSERVER_ERROR_LOG "File does not exist" \
    "phase:5,nolog,pass,setvar:TX.score=+5"
```

XML

Special collection used to interact with the XML parser. It can be used standalone as a target for the `validateDTD` and `validateSchema` operator. Otherwise, it must contain a valid XPath expression, which will then be evaluated against a previously parsed XML DOM tree.

```
# Parse request body as XML
SecRule REQUEST_HEADERS:Content-Type ^text/xml$ \
    "phase:1,t:lowercase,nolog,pass,ctl:requestBodyProcessor=XML"

# Skip over the XML processing rules when not processing XML
SecRule REQBODY_PROCESSOR "!^XML$" \
    "phase:2,nolog,pass,skipAfter:12345"

# Run XPath expression
SecRule XML:/employees/employee/name/text() Fred \
    "phase:2,block"

# Run XPath expression, with namespace
SecRule XML:/xq:employees/employee/name/text() Fred \
    "phase:2,block,id:12345,xmlns:xq=http://www.example.com/employees"
```

17 Transformation Functions

Transformation functions are used to alter input data before it is used in matching (i.e., operator execution). The input data is never modified, actually—whenever you request a transformation function to be used, ModSecurity will create a copy of the data, transform it, and then run the operator against the result.

> **Note**
>
> There are no default transformation functions, as there were in the first generation of ModSecurity (1.x).

In the following example, the request parameter values are converted to lowercase before matching:

```
SecRule ARGS "xp_cmdshell" "t:lowercase"
```

Multiple transformation actions can be used in the same rule, forming a *transformation pipeline*. The transformations will be performed in the order in which they appear in the rule.

In most cases, the order in which transformations are performed is very important. In the following example, a series of transformation functions is performed to counter evasion. Performing the transformations in any other order would allow a skillful attacker to evade detection:

```
SecRule ARGS "(asfunction|javascript|vbscript|data|mocha|livescript):" \
    "t:none,t:htmlEntityDecode,t:lowercase,t:removeNulls,t:removeWhitespace"
```

> **Warning**
>
> It is currently possible to use SecDefaultAction to specify a default list of transformation functions, which will be applied to all rules that follow the SecDefaultAction directive. However, this practice is not recommended, because it means that mistakes are very easy to make. It is recommended that you always specify the transformation functions that are needed by a particular rule, starting the list with t:none (which clears the possibly inherited transformation functions).

The remainder of this section documents the transformation functions currently available in ModSecurity.

base64Decode

Decodes a Base64-encoded string.

base64Encode

Encodes input string using Base64 encoding.

compressWhitespace

Converts any of the whitespace characters (0x20, \f, \t, \n, \r, \v, 0xa0) to spaces (ASCII 0x20), compressing multiple consecutive space characters into one.

cssDecode

Decodes characters encoded using the CSS 2.x escape rules [http://www.w3.org/TR/CSS2/ syndata.html#characters]. This function uses only up to two bytes in the decoding process, meaning that it is useful to uncover ASCII characters encoded using CSS encoding (that wouldn't normally be encoded), or to counter evasion, which is a combination of a backslash and non-hexadecimal characters (e.g., ja\vascript is equivalent to javascript).

escapeSeqDecode

Decodes ANSI C escape sequences: \a, \b, \f, \n, \r, \t, \v, \\, \?, \', \", \xHH (hexadecimal), \0000 (octal). Invalid encodings are left in the output.

hexDecode

Decodes a string that has been encoded using the same algorithm as the one used in hexEncode (see following entry).

hexEncode

Encodes string (possibly containing binary characters) by replacing each input byte with two hexadecimal characters. For example, xyz is encoded as 78797a.

htmlEntityDecode

Decodes the characters encoded as HTML entities. The following variants are supported:

- &#xHH and &#xHH; (where H is any hexadecimal number)
- &#DDD and &#DDD; (where D is any decimal number)
- &quot and "
-   and
- &lt and <
- &gt and >

This function always converts one HTML entity into one byte, possibly resulting in a loss of information (if the entity refers to a character that cannot be represented with the single byte). It is thus useful to uncover bytes that would otherwise not need to be encoded, but it cannot do anything meaningful with the characters from the range above 0xff.

jsDecode

Decodes JavaScript escape sequences. If a \uHHHH code is in the range of FF01-FF5E (the full width ASCII codes), then the higher byte is used to detect and adjust the lower byte. Otherwise, only the lower byte will be used and the higher byte zeroed (leading to possible loss of information).

length

Looks up the length of the input string in bytes, placing it (as string) in output. For example, if it gets ABCDE on input, this transformation function will return 5 on output.

lowercase

Converts all characters to lowercase using the current C locale.

md5

Calculates an MD5 hash from the data in input. The computed hash is in a raw binary form and may need encoded into text to be printed (or logged). Hash functions are commonly used in combination with hexEncode (for example: t:md5,t:hexEncode).

none

Not an actual transformation function, but an instruction to ModSecurity to remove all transformation functions associated with the current rule.

---

normalisePath

Removes multiple slashes, directory self-references, and directory back-references (except when at the beginning of the input) from input string.

normalisePathWin

Same as normalisePath, but first converts backslash characters to forward slashes.

parityEven7bit

Calculates even parity of 7-bit data replacing the 8th bit of each target byte with the calculated parity bit.

parityOdd7bit

Calculates odd parity of 7-bit data replacing the 8th bit of each target byte with the calculated parity bit.

parityZero7bit

Calculates zero parity of 7-bit data replacing the 8th bit of each target byte with a zero-parity bit, which allows inspection of even/odd parity 7-bit data as ASCII7 data.

removeNulls

Removes all NUL bytes from input.

removeWhitespace

Removes all whitespace characters from input.

replaceComments

Replaces each occurrence of a C-style comment (/* ... */) with a single space (multiple consecutive occurrences of which will not be compressed). Unterminated comments will also be replaced with a space (ASCII 0x20). However, a standalone termination of a comment (*/) will not be acted upon.

replaceNulls

Replaces NUL bytes in input with space characters (ASCII 0x20).

urlDecode

Decodes a URL-encoded input string. Invalid encodings (i.e., the ones that use non-hexadecimal characters, or the ones that are at the end of string and have one or two bytes missing) are not converted, but no error is raised. To detect invalid encodings, use the @validateUrlEncoding operator on the input data first. The transformation function should not be used against variables that have already been URL-decoded (such as request parameters) unless it is your intention to perform URL decoding twice!

urlDecodeUni

Like urlDecode, but with support for the Microsoft-specific %u encoding. If the code is in the range of FF01-FF5E (the full-width ASCII codes), then the higher byte is used to detect and adjust the lower byte. Otherwise, only the lower byte will be used and the higher byte zeroed.

urlEncode

Encodes input string using URL encoding.

sha1

Calculates a SHA1 hash from the input string. The computed hash is in a raw binary form and may need encoded into text to be printed (or logged). Hash functions are commonly used in combination with hexEncode (for example, t:sha1,t:hexEncode).

trimLeft

Removes whitespace from the left side of the input string.

trimRight

Removes whitespace from the right side of the input string.

trim

Removes whitespace from both the left and right sides of the input string.

18 Actions

This section documents the actions currently available in ModSecurity.

allow

Stops rule processing.

```
# Allow unrestricted access from 192.168.1.100
SecRule REMOTE_ADDR "^192\.168\.1\.100$" phase:1,nolog,allow
```

Prior to ModSecurity 2.5, the `allow` action would affect only the processing of the phase in which it is executed. An `allow` in phase 1 would skip the processing of the remaining rules in phase 1, but the rules from phase 2 would execute as normal. Starting with version 2.5.0, `allow` was enhanced to enable fine-grained control of what is done. The following rules now apply:

1. If used on its own, like in the previous example, `allow` will affect the entire transaction, stopping processing of the current phase but also skipping over all other phases apart from the logging phase. (The logging phase is special; it is designed to always execute.)

2. If used with parameter "phase," `allow` will cause the engine to stop processing the current phase. Other phases will continue as normal.

3. If used with parameter "request," `allow` will cause the engine to stop processing the current phase. The next phase to be processed will be the phase RESPONSE_HEADERS.

Examples:

```
# Do not process request but process response
SecAction phase:1,nolog,allow:request

# Do not process transaction (request and response)
SecAction phase:1,nolog,allow
```

If you want to allow a response through, put a rule into the RESPONSE_HEADERS phase and simply use `allow` on its own:

```
# Allow response through.
SecAction phase:3,nolog,allow
```

append

Appends text given as parameter to the end of response body. Content injection must be enabled (using the SecContentInjection directive). No content type checks are made, which means that before using any of the content injection actions, you must check whether the content type of the response is adequate for injection.

The following rule injects content into the response body after checking its content type:

```
SecRule RESPONSE_CONTENT_TYPE "^text/html" "nolog,pass,append:'<hr>Footer'"
```

> **Warning**
>
> Although macro expansion is allowed in the additional content, you are strongly cautioned against inserting user-defined data fields into output. Doing so would create a cross-site scripting vulnerability.

auditlog

Marks the current transaction to be logged in the audit log.

```
# Always log transactions from 192.168.1.100
SecRule REMOTE_ADDR "^192\.168\.1\.100$" phase:1,nolog,auditlog
```

block

Performs the default disruptive action.

This action is essentially a placeholder that is intended to be used by rule writers to request a blocking action, but without specifying how the blocking is to be done. The idea is that such decisions are best left to rule users, as well as to allow users, to override blocking if they so desire.

```
# Specify how blocking is to be done
SecDefaultAction phase:2,deny,status:403,log,auditlog

# Detect attacks where we want to block
SecRule ARGS attack1 phase:2,block

# Detect attacks where we want only to warn
SecRule ARGS attack2 phase:2,pass
```

It is possible to use the SecRuleUpdateActionById directive to override how a rule handles blocking. This is useful in three cases:

- If a rule has blocking hard-coded, and you want it to use the policy you determine
- If a rule was written to block, but you want it to only warn
- If a rule was written to only warn, but you want it to block

The following example demonstrates the first case, in which the hard-coded block is removed in favor of the user-controllable `block`:

```
# Specify how blocking is to be done
SecDefaultAction phase:2,deny,status:403,log,auditlog

# Detect attacks and block
SecRule ARGS attack1 phase:2,id:1,deny

# Change how rule ID 1 blocks
SecRuleUpdateActionById 1 block
```

capture

When used together with the regular expression operator (@rx), the capture action will create copies of the regular expression captures and place them into the transaction variable collection.

```
SecRule REQUEST_BODY "^username=(\w{25,})" \
    phase:2,capture,t:none,chain
SecRule TX:1 "(?:(?:a(dmin|nonymous)))"
```

Up to 10 captures will be copied on a successful pattern match, each with a name consisting of a digit from 0 to 9. The TX.0 variable always contains the entire area that the regular expression matched. All the other variables contain the captured values, in the order in which the capturing parentheses appear in the regular expression.

chain

Chains the current rule with the rule that immediately follows it, creating a *rule chain*. Chained rules allow for more complex processing logic.

```
# Refuse to accept POST requests that do not contain Content-Length header.
# (Do note that this rule should be preceded by a rule
# that verifies only valid request methods are used.)
SecRule REQUEST_METHOD "^POST$" phase:1,chain,t:none
SecRule &REQUEST_HEADERS:Content-Length "@eq 0" t:none
```

> **Note**
>
> Rule chains allow you to simulate logical AND. The disruptive actions specified in the first portion of the chained rule will be triggered only if all of the variable checks

> return positive hits. If any one aspect of a chained rule comes back negative, then the entire rule chain will fail to match. Also note that disruptive actions, execution phases, metadata actions (id, rev, msg), skip, and skipAfter actions can be specified only by the chain starter rule.

The following directives can be used in rule chains:

- SecAction
- SecRule
- SecRuleScript

Special rules control the usage of actions in chained rules:

- Any actions that affect the rule flow (i.e., the disruptive actions, skip and skipAfter) can be used only in the chain starter. They will be executed only if the entire chain matches.
- Non-disruptive rules can be used in any rule; they will be executed if the rule that contains them matches and not only when the entire chain matches.
- The metadata actions (e.g., id, rev, msg) can be used only in the chain starter.

ctl

Changes ModSecurity configuration on transient, per-transaction basis. Any changes made using this action will affect only the transaction in which the action is executed. The default configuration, as well as the other transactions running in parallel, will be unaffected.

```
# Parse requests with Content-Type "text/xml" as XML
SecRule REQUEST_CONTENT_TYPE ^text/xml \
    "nolog,pass,ctl:requestBodyProcessor=XML"
```

The following configuration options are supported:

1. auditEngine
2. auditLogParts
3. debugLogLevel
4. ruleRemoveById
5. requestBodyAccess
6. forceRequestBodyVariable
7. requestBodyLimit
8. requestBodyProcessor
9. responseBodyAccess
10. responseBodyLimit

11. ruleEngine

With the exception of the `requestBodyProcessor` and `forceRequestBodyVariable` settings, each configuration option corresponds to one configuration directive and the usage is identical.

The `requestBodyProcessor` option allows you to configure the request body processor. By default, ModSecurity will use the `URLENCODED` and `MULTIPART` processors to process an `application/x-www-form-urlencoded` and a `multipart/form-data` body, respectively. A third processor, `XML`, is also supported, but it is never used implicitly. Instead, you must tell ModSecurity to use it by placing a few rules in the `REQUEST_HEADERS` processing phase. After the request body is processed as XML, you will be able to use the XML-related features to inspect it.

Request body processors will not interrupt a transaction if an error occurs during parsing. Instead, they will set the variables `REQBODY_PROCESSOR_ERROR` and `REQBODY_PROCESSOR_ERROR_MSG`. These variables should be inspected in the `REQUEST_BODY` phase and an appropriate action taken.

The `forceRequestBodyVariable` option allows you to configure the `REQUEST_BODY` variable to be set when there is no request body processor configured. This allows for inspection of request bodies of unknown types.

deny

Stops rule processing and intercepts transaction.

```
SecRule REQUEST_HEADERS:User-Agent "nikto" \
    "phase:1,log,deny,msg:'Nikto Scanners Identified'"
```

deprecatevar

Decrements numerical value over time, which makes sense only applied to the variables stored in persistent storage.

The following example will decrement the counter by 60 every 300 seconds.

```
SecAction phase:5,nolog,pass,deprecatevar:SESSION.score=60/300
```

Counter values are always positive, meaning that the value will never go below zero. Unlike `expirevar`, the `deprecate` action must be executed on every request.

drop

Initiates an immediate close of the TCP connection by sending a FIN packet.

```
SecRule ARGS attack "phase:2,drop,msg:'TCP connection dropped'"
```

This action is currently not available on Windows-based builds. This action is extremely useful when responding to both brute force and denial of service attacks, when you want to minimize both the network bandwidth and the data returned to the client. This action causes the following error message to appear in the Apache log: `(9)Bad file descriptor: core_output_filter: writing data to the network`.

exec

Executes the external program specified in the parameter. As of version 2.5.0, if the parameter supplied to exec is a Lua script (detected by the `.lua` extension), the script will be processed internally. This means that you will get direct access to the internal request context from the script. Please read the `SecRuleScript` documentation for more details on how to write Lua scripts.

```
# Run external program on rule match
SecRule REQUEST_URI "^/cgi-bin/script\.pl" \
    "phase:2,t:none,t:lowercase,t:normalizePath,block,\
    exec:/usr/local/apache/bin/test.sh"
```

```
# Run Lua script on rule match
SecRule ARGS:p attack \
    "phase:2,block,exec:/usr/local/apache/conf/exec.lua"
```

The exec action is executed independently from any disruptive actions specified. External scripts will always be called with no parameters. Some transaction information will be placed in environment variables. All the usual CGI environment variables will be there. You should be aware that forking a threaded process results in all threads being replicated in the new process. Forking can therefore incur larger overhead in a multithreaded deployment. The script you execute must write something (anything) to stdout; if it doesn't, ModSecurity will assume that the script failed, and will record the failure.

expirevar

Configures a collection variable to expire after the given time period (in seconds).

```
SecRule REQUEST_COOKIES:JSESSIONID "!^$" nolog,phase:1,pass,chain
SecAction setsid:%{REQUEST_COOKIES:JSESSIONID}
SecRule REQUEST_URI "^/cgi-bin/script\.pl" \
    "phase:2,t:none,t:lowercase,t:normalizePath,log,allow,\
    setvar:session.suspicious=1,expirevar:session.suspicious=3600,phase:1"
```

You should use the `expirevar` actions at the same time that you use `setvar` actions in order to keep the indented expiration time. If they are used on their own (perhaps in a SecAction directive), the expire time will be reset.

id

Assigns a unique ID to the rule or chain in which it appears.

```
SecRule &REQUEST_HEADERS:Host "@eq 0" \
    "phase:2,id:60008,severity:2,msg:'Request Missing a Host Header'"
```

These are the reserved ID ranges:

- 1–99,999: reserved for local (internal) use. Use as you see fit, but do not use this range for rules that are distributed to others
- 100,000–199,999: reserved for internal use of the engine, to assign to rules that do not have explicit IDs
- 200,000–299,999: reserved for rules published at modsecurity.org
- 300,000–399,999: reserved for rules published at gotroot.com
- 400,000–419,999: unused (available for reservation)
- 420,000–429,999: reserved for ScallyWhack [http://projects.otaku42.de/wiki/Scally-Whack]
- 430,000–699,999: unused (available for reservation)
- 700,000–799,999: reserved for Ivan Ristic
- 900,000–999,999: reserved for the Core Rules [http://www.modsecurity.org/projects/rules/] project
- 1,000,000 and above: unused (available for reservation)

initcol

Initializes a named persistent collection, either by loading data from storage or by creating a new collection in memory.

The following example initiates IP address tracking, which is best done in phase 1:

```
SecAction phase:1,nolog,pass,initcol:ip=%{REMOTE_ADDR}
```

Collections are loaded into memory on-demand, when the initcol action is executed. A collection will be persisted only if a change was made to it in the course of transaction processing.

log

Indicates that a successful match of the rule needs to be logged.

```
SecAction phase:1,initcol:ip=%{REMOTE_ADDR},log,pass
```

This action will log matches to the Apache error log file and the ModSecurity audit log.

logdata

Logs a fragment of data as part of the alert message.

```
SecRule ARGS:p "@rx <script>" "phase:2,log,pass,logdata:%{MATCHED_VAR}"
```

The logdata information appears in the error and/or audit log files. Macro expansion is pre-formed, so you may use variable names such as %{TX.0}, and so on. The information is properly escaped for use with logging binary data.

msg

Assigns a custom message to the rule or chain in which it appears. The message will be logged along with every alert.

```
SecRule &REQUEST_HEADERS:Host "@eq 0" \
    "phase:1,id:60008,severity:2,msg:'Request Missing a Host Header'"
```

multiMatch

If enabled, ModSecurity will perform multiple operator invocations for every target, before and after every anti-evasion transformation is performed.

```
SecRule ARGS "attack" \
    phase1,log,deny,t:removeNulls,t:lowercase,multiMatch
```

Normally, variables are inspected only once per rule, and only after all transformation functions have been completed. With multiMatch, variables are checked against the operator before and after every transformation function that changes the input.

noauditlog

Indicates that a successful match of the rule should not be used as criteria to determine whether the transaction should be logged to the audit log.

```
SecRule REQUEST_HEADERS:User-Agent "Test" \
    "allow,noauditlog"
```

If the SecAuditEngine is set to On, all of the transactions will be logged. If it is set to RelevantOnly, then you can control the logging with the noauditlog action.

The noauditlog action affects only the current rule. If you prevent audit logging in one rule only, a match in another rule will still cause audit logging to take place. If you want to prevent audit logging from taking place, regardless of whether any rule matches, use ctl:auditEngine=Off.

nolog

Prevents rule matches from appearing in both the error and audit logs.

```
SecRule REQUEST_HEADERS:User-Agent "Test" \
    "allow,nolog"
```

Although nolog implies noauditlog, you can override the former by using nolog,auditlog.

pass

Continues processing with the next rule in spite of a successful match.

```
SecRule REQUEST_HEADERS:User-Agent "Test" \
    "log,pass"
```

When using pass with a SecRule with multiple targets, all variables will be inspected and all non-disruptive actions trigger for every match. In the following example, the TX.test variable will be incremented once for every request parameter:

```
# Set TX.test to zero
SecAction "phase:2,nolog,pass,setvar:TX.test=0"

# Increment TX.test for every request parameter
SecRule ARGS "test" "phase:2,log,pass,setvar:TX.test=+1"
```

pause

Pauses transaction processing for the specified number of milliseconds.

```
SecRule REQUEST_HEADERS:User-Agent "Test" \
    "log,deny,status:403,pause:5000"
```

> **Warning**
>
> This feature can be of limited benefit for slowing down brute force authentication attacks, but use with care. If you are under a denial of service attack, the pause feature may make matters worse, as it will cause an entire Apache worker (process or thread, depending on the deployment mode) to sit idle until the pause is completed.

phase

Places the rule or chain into one of five available processing phases. It can also be used in SecDefaultAction to establish the rule defaults.

```
# Initialize IP address tracking in phase 1
```

```
SecAction phase:1,nolog,pass,initcol:IP=%{REMOTE_ADDR}
```

Keep in mind that if you specify the incorrect phase, the variable used in the rule may not yet be available. This could lead to a false negative situation where your variable and operator may be correct, but it misses malicious data because you specified the wrong phase.

prepend

Prepends the text given as parameter to response body. Content injection must be enabled (using the SecContentInjection directive). No content type checks are made, which means that before using any of the content injection actions, you must check whether the content type of the response is adequate for injection.

```
SecRule RESPONSE_CONTENT_TYPE ^text/html \
    "phase:3,nolog,pass,prepend:'Header<br>'"
```

> **Note**
>
> Although macro expansion is allowed in the injected content, you are strongly cautioned against inserting user defined data fields int output. Doing so would create a cross-site scripting vulnerability.

proxy

Intercepts the current transaction by forwarding the request to another web server using the proxy backend. The forwarding is carried out transparently to the HTTP client (i.e., there's no external redirection taking place).

```
SecRule REQUEST_HEADERS:User-Agent "Test" \
    "phase:1,log,proxy:http://www.example.com"/
```

For this action to work, mod_proxy must also be installed. This action is useful if you would like to proxy matching requests onto a honeypot web server, and especially in combination with IP address or session tracking.

redirect

Intercepts transaction by issuing an external (client-visible) redirection to the given location.

```
SecRule REQUEST_HEADERS:User-Agent "Test" \
    "phase:1,log,redirect:http://www.example.com/failed.html"
```

If the status action is present on the same rule, and its value can be used for a redirection (i.e., is one of the following: 301, 302, 303, or 307), the value will be used for the redirection status code. Otherwise, status code 302 will be used.

rev

Specifies rule revision. It is useful in combination with the `id` action to provide an indication that a rule has been changed.

```
SecRule REQUEST_METHOD "^PUT$" \
    "phase:1,id:340002,rev:1,severity:2,msg:'Restricted HTTP function'"
```

sanitiseArg

Prevents sensitive request parameter data from being logged to audit log. Each byte of the named parameter(s) is replaced with an asterisk.

```
# Never log passwords
SecAction "nolog,phase:2,sanitiseArg:password,\
    sanitiseArg:newPassword,sanitiseArg:oldPassword"
```

The sanitize actions affect only the data as it is logged to audit log. High-level debug logs may contain sensitive data. Apache access log may contain sensitive data placed in the request URI.

sanitiseMatched

Prevents the matched variable (request argument, request header, or response header) from being logged to audit log. Each byte of the named parameter(s) is replaced with an asterisk.

```
# Do not log any parameter that contains "password" in name
SecRule ARGS_NAMES password "nolog,pass,sanitiseMatched"
```

sanitiseRequestHeader

Prevents a named request header from being logged to audit log. Each byte of the named request header is replaced with an asterisk.

```
SecAction "phase:1,nolog,pass,sanitiseRequestHeader:Authorization"
```

sanitiseResponseHeader

Prevents a named response header from being logged to audit log. Each byte of the named response header is replaced with an asterisk.

```
SecAction "phase:3,nolog,pass,sanitiseResponseHeader:Set-Cookie"
```

severity

Assigns severity to the rule in which it is used.

```
SecRule REQUEST_METHOD "^PUT$" \
    "id:340002,rev:1,severity:CRITICAL,msg:'Restricted HTTP function'"
```

Severity values in ModSecurity follow those of syslog, as shown in Table 18.1, "Severity values".

Table 18.1. Severity values

Severity	Name
0	EMERGENCY
1	ALERT
2	CRITICAL
3	ERROR
4	WARNING
5	NOTICE
6	INFO
7	DEBUG

It is possible to specify severity levels using either the numerical values or the text values, but you should always specify severity levels using the text values, because it is difficult to remember what a number stands for. The use of the numerical values is deprecated as of version 2.5.0 and may be removed in one of the subsequent major updates.

setuid

Special-purpose action that initializes the USER collection using the username provided as parameter.

```
SecAction "phase:1,nolog,pass,setuid:%{REMOTE_USER}"
```

After initialization takes place, the variable USERID will be available for use in the subsequent rules. This action understands application namespaces (configured using SecWebAppId), and will use one if it is configured.

setsid

Special-purpose action that initializes the SESSION collection using the session token provided as parameter.

```
# Initialise session variables using the session cookie value
SecRule REQUEST_COOKIES:PHPSESSID "!^$" \
    "phase:2,chain,nolog,pass\
```

```
setsid:%{REQUEST_COOKIES.PHPSESSID}"
```

After the initialization takes place, the variable SESSIONID will be available for use in the sub-sequent rules. This action understands application namespaces (configured using SecWebAppId), and will use one if it is configured.

setenv

Creates, removes, and updates environment variables.

To create a new variable and set its value to 1 (usually used for setting flags), use:

```
setenv:name
```

To create a variable and choose its value, use:

```
setenv:name=value
```

To remove a variable, use:

```
setenv:!name
```

setvar

Creates, removes, or updates a variable. Variable names are case-insensitive.

To create a variable and set its value to 1 (usually used for setting flags), use:

```
setvar:TX.score
```

To create a variable and initialize it at the same time, use:

```
setvar:TX.score=10
```

To remove a variable prefix the name with exclamation mark, use:

```
setvar:!TX.score
```

To increase or decrease variable value, use + and - characters in front of a numerical value:

```
setvar:TX.score=+5
```

skip

Skips one or more rules (or chains) on a successful match.

Example:

```
# Require Accept header, but not from access from the localhost
SecRule REMOTE_ADDR "^127\.0\.0\.1$" "phase:1,skip:1"
# This rule will be skipped over when REMOTE_ADDR is 127.0.0.1
SecRule &REQUEST_HEADERS:Accept "@eq 0" \
    "phase:1,deny,msg:'Request Missing an Accept Header'"
```

The skip action works only within the current processing phase and not necessarily in the order in which the rules appear in the configuration file. If you place a phase 2 rule after a phase 1 rule that uses skip, it will not skip over the phase 2 rule. It will skip over the next phase 1 rule that follows it in the phase.

skipAfter

Skips one or more rules (or chains) on a successful match, resuming rule execution with the first rule that follows the rule (or marker created by SecMarker) with the provided ID.

The following rules implement the same logic as the skip example, but using skipAfter:

```
# Require Accept header, but not from access from the localhost
SecRule REMOTE_ADDR "^127\.0\.0\.1$" "phase:1,skipAfter:IGNORE_LOCALHOST"
# This rule will be skipped over when REMOTE_ADDR is 127.0.0.1
SecRule &REQUEST_HEADERS:Accept "@eq 0" \
    "phase:1,deny,msg:'Request Missing an Accept Header'"
SecMarker IGNORE_LOCALHOST
```

The skipAfter action works only within the current processing phase and not necessarily the order in which the rules appear in the configuration file. If you place a phase 2 rule after a phase 1 rule that uses skip, it will not skip over the phase 2 rule. It will skip over the next phase 1 rule that follows it in the phase.

status

Specifies the response status code to use with the actions deny and redirect.

```
# Deny with status 403
SecDefaultAction "phase:1,log,deny,status:403"
```

t

This action is used to specify the transformation pipeline to use to transform the value of each variable used in the rule before matching.

```
SecRule ARGS "(asfunction|javascript|vbscript|data|mocha|livescript):" \
    "t:none,t:htmlEntityDecode,t:lowercase,t:removeNulls,t:removeWhitespace"
```

Any transformation functions that you specify in a SecRule will be added to the previous ones specified in SecDefaultAction. It is recommended that you always use t:none in your rules, which prevents them depending on the default configuration.

tag

Assigns a tag (category) to a rule or a chain.

```
SecRule REQUEST_FILENAME "\b(?:n(?:map|et|c)|w(?:guest|sh)|cmd(?:32)?|telnet|rcmd|↩
ftp)\.exe\b" \
    "t:none,t:lowercase,deny,msg:'System Command Access',id:'950002',\
    tag:'WEB_ATTACK/FILE_INJECTION',tag:'OWASP/A2',severity:'2'"
```

The tag information appears along with other rule metadata. The purpose of the tagging mechanism to allow easy automated categorization of events. Multiple tags can be specified on the same rule. Use forward slashes to create a hierarchy of categories (as in the example).

xmlns

Configures an XML namespace, which will be used in the execution of XPath expressions.

```
SecRule XML:/soap:Envelope/soap:Body/q1:getInput/id() "123" \
    "phase:2,deny,xmlns:xsd=http://www.w3.org/2001/XMLSchema"
```

19 Operators

This section documents the operators currently available in ModSecurity.

beginsWith

Returns true if the parameter string is found at the beginning of the input. Macro expansion is performed on the parameter string before comparison.

```
# Detect request line that does not begin with "GET"
SecRule REQUEST_LINE "!@beginsWith GET"
```

contains

Returns true if the parameter string is found anywhere in the input. Macro expansion is performed on the parameter string before comparison.

```
# Detect ".php" anywhere in the request line
SecRule REQUEST_LINE "!@contains .php" \
```

endsWith

Returns true if the parameter string is found at the end of the input. Macro expansion is performed on the parameter string before comparison.

```
# Detect request line that does not end with "HTTP/1.1"
SecRule REQUEST_LINE "!@endsWith HTTP/1.1"
```

eq

Performs numerical comparison and returns true if the input value is *equal* to the provided parameter. Macro expansion is performed on the parameter string before comparison.

```
# Detect exactly 15 request headers
SecRule &REQUEST_HEADERS_NAMES "@eq 15"
```

ge

Performs numerical comparison and returns true if the input value is *greater than or equal* to the provided parameter. Macro expansion is performed on the parameter string before comparison.

```
# Detect 15 or more request headers
SecRule &REQUEST_HEADERS_NAMES "@ge 15"
```

geoLookup

Performs a geolocation lookup using the IP address in input against the geolocation database previously configured using SecGeoLookupDb. If the lookup is successful, the obtained information is captured in the GEO collection.

The geoLookup operator matches on success and is thus best used in combination with nolog,pass. If you wish to block on a failed lookup (which may be over the top, depending on how accurate the geolocation database is), the following example demonstrates how best to do it:

```
# Configure geolocation database
SecGeoLookupDb /path/to/GeoLiteCity.dat
...
# Lookup IP address
SecRule REMOTE_ADDR "@geoLookup" "phase:1,nolog,pass"

# Block IP address for which geolocation failed
SecRule &GEO "@eq 0" "phase:1,deny,msg:'Failed to lookup IP'"
```

See the GEO variable for more information on the various fields available.

gt

Performs numerical comparison and returns true if the input value is *greater than* the operator parameter. Macro expansion is performed on the parameter string before comparison.

```
# Detect more than 15 headers in a request
SecRule &REQUEST_HEADERS_NAMES "@gt 15"
```

inspectFile

Executes the external program given as a parameter to the operator against every file extracted from the request. As of version 2.5.0, if the supplied filename is not absolute, it is treated as relative to the directory in which the configuration file resides. Also as of version 2.5.0, if the filename is determined to be a Lua script (based on its .lua extension), the script will be processed by the internal Lua engine. Internally processed scripts have an advantage, because they will run faster and because they have full access to transaction information.

Example of using an external program:

```
# Execute external program to validate uploaded files
SecRule FILES_TMPNAMES "@inspectFile /path/to/inspect_file.pl"
```

Example of using Lua script (placed in the same directory as the configuration file):

```
SecRule FILES_TMPNANMES "@inspectFile inspect.lua"
```

The contents of inspect.lua:

```
function main(filename)
    -- Do something to the file to verify it. In this example, we
    -- read up to 10 characters from the beginning of the file.
    local f = io.open(filename, "rb");
    local d = f:read(10);
    f:close();

    -- Return null if there is no reason to believe there is anything
    -- wrong with the file (no match). Returning any text will be taken
    -- to mean a match should be trigered.
    return null;
end
```

le

Performs numerical comparison and returns true if the input value is *less than or equal* to the operator parameter. Macro expansion is performed on the parameter string before comparison.

```
# Detect 15 or fewer headers in a request
SecRule &REQUEST_HEADERS_NAMES "@le 15"
```

lt

Performs numerical comparison and returns true if the input value is *less than* to the operator parameter. Macro expansion is performed on the parameter string before comparison.

```
# Detect fewer than 15 headers in a request
SecRule &REQUEST_HEADERS_NAMES "@lt 15"
```

pm

Performs a case-insensitive match of the provided phrases against the desired input value. The operator uses a set-based matching algorithm (Aho-Corasick), which means that it will match any number of keywords in parallel. When matching of a large number of keywords is needed, this operator performs much better than a regular expression.

```
# Detect suspicious client by looking at the user agent identification
SecRule REQUEST_HEADERS:User-Agent "@pm WebZIP WebCopier Webster WebStripper ↵
SiteSnagger ProWebWalker CheeseBot"
```

pmFromFile

Performs a case-insensitive match of the provided phrases against the desired input value. The operator uses a set-based matching algorithm (Aho-Corasick), which means that it will match any number of keywords in parallel. When matching of a large number of keywords is needed, this operator performs much better than a regular expression.

This operator is the same as @pm, except that it takes a list of files as arguments. It will match any one of the phrases listed in the file(s) anywhere in the target value.

```
# Detect suspicious user agents using the keywords in
# the files /path/to/blacklist1 and blacklist2 (the latter
# must be placed in the same folder as the configuration file)
SecRule REQUEST_HEADERS:User-Agent "@pm /path/to/blacklist1 blacklist2"
```

Notes:

1. Files must contain exactly one phrase per line. End of line markers (both LF and CRLF) will be stripped from each phrase and any whitespace trimmed from both the beginning and the end. Empty lines and comment lines (those beginning with the # character) will be ignored.

2. To allow easier inclusion of phrase files with rule sets, relative paths may be used to the phrase files. In this case, the path of the file containing the rule is prepended to the phrase file path.

3. The @pm operator phrases do not support metacharacters.

4. Because this operator does not check for boundaries when matching, false positives are possible in some cases. For example, if you want to use @pm for IP address matching, the phrase 1.2.3.4 will potentially match more than one IP address (e.g., it will also match 1.2.3.40 or 1.2.3.41). To avoid the false positives, you can use your own boundaries in phrases. For example, use /1.2.3.4/ instead of just 1.2.3.4. Then, in your rules, also add the boundaries where appropriate. You will find a complete example in the example.

```
# Prepare custom REMOTE_ADDR variable
SecAction "phase:1,nolog,pass,setvar:tx.REMOTE_ADDR=/%{REMOTE_ADDR}/"

# Check if REMOTE_ADDR is blacklisted
```

```
SecRule TX:REMOTE_ADDR "@pmFromFile blacklist.txt" \
    "phase:1,deny,msg:'Blacklisted IP address'"
```

The file blacklist.txt may contain:

```
# ip-blacklist.txt contents:
# NOTE: All IPs must be prefixed/suffixed with "/" as the rules
#       will add in this character as a boundary to ensure
#       the entire IP is matched.
# SecAction "phase:1,pass,nolog,setvar:tx.remote_addr='/%{REMOTE_ADDR}/'"
/1.2.3.4/
/5.6.7.8/
```

> **Warning**
>
> Before ModSecurity 2.5.12, the @pmFromFile operator understood only the LF line endings and did not trim the whitespace from phrases. If you are using an older version of ModSecurity, you should take care when editing the phrase files to avoid using the undesired characters in patterns.

rbl

Looks up the input value in the RBL (real-time block list) given as parameter. The parameter can be an IPv4 address or a hostname.

```
SecRule REMOTE_ADDR "@rbl sc.surbl.org"
```

rx

Performs a regular expression match of the pattern provided as parameter. This is the default operator; the rules that do not explicitly specify an operator default to @rx.

```
# Detect Nikto
SecRule REQUEST_HEADERS:User-Agent "@rx nikto" phase:1,t:lowercase

# Detect Nikto with a case-insensitive pattern
SecRule REQUEST_HEADERS:User-Agent "@rx (?i)nikto" phase:1,t:none

# Detect Nikto with a case-insensitive pattern
SecRule REQUEST_HEADERS:User-Agent "(?i)nikto"
```

Regular expressions are handled by the PCRE library [http://www.pcre.org]. ModSecurity compiles its regular expressions with the following settings:

1. The entire input is treated as a single line, even when there are newline characters present.

2. All matches are case-sensitive. If you wish to perform case-insensitive matching, you can either use the `lowercase` transformation function or force case-insensitive matching by prefixing the regular expression pattern with the `(?i)` modifier (a PCRE feature; you will find many similar features in the PCRE documentation).

3. The `PCRE_DOTALL` and `PCRE_DOLLAR_ENDONLY` flags are set during compilation, meaning that a single dot will match any character, including the newlines, and a $ end anchor will not match a trailing newline character.

Regular expressions are a very powerful tool. You are strongly advised to read the PCRE documentation to get acquainted with its features.

streq

Performs a string comparison and returns true if the parameter string is identical to the input string. Macro expansion is performed on the parameter string before comparison.

```
# Detect request parameters "foo" that do not
# contain "bar", exactly.
SecRule ARGS:foo "!@streq bar"
```

validateByteRange

Validates that the byte values used in input fall into the range specified by the operator parameter. This operator matches on an input value that contains bytes that are not in the specified range.

```
# Enforce very strict byte range for request parameters (only
# works for the applications that do not use the languages other
# than English).
SecRule ARGS "@validateByteRange 10, 13, 32-126"
```

The validateByteRange is most useful when used to detect the presence of NUL bytes, which don't have a legitimate use, but which are often used as an evasion technique.

```
# Do not allow NUL bytes
SecRule ARGS "@validateByteRange 1-255"
```

validateDTD

Validates the XML DOM tree against the supplied DTD. The DOM tree must have been built previously using the XML request body processor. This operator matches when the validation fails.

```
# Parse the request bodies that contain XML
```

```
SecRule REQUEST_HEADERS:Content-Type ^text/xml$ \
    "phase:1,nolog,pass,t:lowercase,\
    ctl:requestBodyProcessor=XML"

# Validate XML payload against DTD
SecRule XML "@validateDTD /path/to/xml.dtd" \
    "phase:2,deny,msg:'Failed DTD validation'"
```

validateSchema

Validates the XML DOM tree against the supplied XML Schema. The DOM tree must have been built previously using the XML request body processor. This operator matches when the validation fails.

```
# Parse the request bodies that contain XML
SecRule REQUEST_HEADERS:Content-Type ^text/xml$ \
    "phase:1,nolog,pass,t:lowercase,\
    ctl:requestBodyProcessor=XML"

# Validate XML payload against DTD
SecRule XML "@validateSchema /path/to/xml.xsd" \
    "phase:2,deny,msg:'Failed DTD validation'"
```

validateUrlEncoding

Validates the URL-encoded characters in the provided input string.

```
# Validate URL-encoded characters in the request URI
SecRule REQUEST_URI_RAW "@validateUrlEncoding"
```

ModSecurity will automatically decode the URL-encoded characters in request parameters, which means that there is little sense in applying the @validateUrlEncoding operator to them —that is, unless you know that some of the request parameters were URL-encoded more than once. Use this operator against raw input, or against the input that you know is URL-encoded. For example, some applications will URL-encode cookies, although that's not in the standard. Because it is not in the standard, ModSecurity will neither validate nor decode such encodings.

validateUtf8Encoding

Check whether the input is a valid UTF-8 string.

```
# Make sure all request parameters contain only valid UTF-8
SecRule ARGS "@validateUtf8Encoding"
```

The @validateUtf8Encoding operator detects the following problems:

Not enough bytes

UTF-8 supports two-, three-, four-, five-, and six-byte encodings. ModSecurity will locate cases when one or more bytes is/are missing from a character.

Invalid characters

The two most significant bits in most characters should be fixed to 0x80. Some attack techniques use different values as an evasion technique.

Overlong characters

ASCII characters are mapped directly into UTF-8, which means that an ASCII character is one UTF-8 character at the same time. However, in UTF-8 many ASCII characters can also be encoded with two, three, four, five, and six bytes. This is no longer legal in the newer versions of Unicode, but many older implementations still support it. The use of overlong UTF-8 characters is common for evasion.

Notes:

- Most, but not all applications use UTF-8. If you are dealing with an application that does, validating that all request parameters are valid UTF-8 strings is a great way to prevent a number of evasion techniques that use the assorted UTF-8 weaknesses. False positives are likely if you use this operator in an application that does not use UTF-8.

- Many web servers will also allow UTF-8 in request URIs. If yours does, you can verify the request URI using @validateUtf8Encoding.

verifyCC

Detects credit card numbers in input. This operator will first use the supplied regular expression to perform an initial match, following up with the Luhn algorithm calculation to minimize false positives.

```
# Detect credit card numbers in parameters and
# prevent them from being logged to audit log
SecRule ARGS "@verifyCC \d{13,16}" \
    "phase:2,nolog,pass,msg:'Potential credit card number',\
    sanitiseMatched"
```

within

Returns true if the input value is found anywhere within the parameter value (the opposite of @contains). Macro expansion is performed on the parameter string before comparison.

```
# Detect request methods other than GET, POST and HEAD
SecRule REQUEST_METHOD "!@within GET,POST,HEAD"
```

20 Data Formats

The purpose of this document is to describe the formats of the ModSecurity alert messages, transaction logs, and communication protocols, which would allow for not only a better understanding of what ModSecurity does, but also an easy integration with third-party tools and products.

Alerts

ModSecurity alerts are either *warnings* (non-fatal problems) or *errors* (fatal problems, usually leading to the interception of the transaction in question). Here is an example of a single ModSecurity alert entry:

```
Access denied with code 505 (phase 1). Match of "rx ↵
^HTTP/(0\\\\.9|1\\\\.[01])$" against "REQUEST_PROTOCOL" required. ↵
[id "960034"] [msg "HTTP protocol version is not allowed by policy"] ↵
[severity "CRITICAL"] [uri "/"] [unique_id "PQaTTVBEUOkAAFwKXrYAAAAM"]
```

Each alert entry begins with the engine message, which describes what ModSecurity did and why. For example:

```
Access denied with code 505 (phase 1). Match of "rx ↵
^HTTP/(0\\\\.9|1\\\\.[01])$" against "REQUEST_PROTOCOL" required.
```

Alert Action Description

The first part of the engine message tells you whether ModSecurity acted to interrupt transaction or rule processing:

1. If the alert is only a warning, the first sentence will simply say *Warning*.

2. If the transaction was intercepted, the first sentence will begin with *Access denied*. What follows is the list of possible messages related to transaction interception:

   - *Access denied with code %0*: a response with status code %0 was sent.
   - *Access denied with connection close*: connection was abruptly closed.

- *Access denied with redirection to %0 using status %1*: a redirection to URI %0 was issued using status %1.

3. There is also a special message that ModSecurity emits when an allow action is executed. There are three variations of this type of message:

- *Access allowed*: rule engine stopped processing rules (transaction was unaffected).

- *Access to phase allowed*: rule engine stopped processing rules in the current phase only. Subsequent phases will be processed normally. Transaction was not affected by this rule but it may be affected by any of the rules in the subsequent phase.

- *Access to request allowed*: rule engine stopped processing rules in the current phase. Phases prior to request execution in the backend (currently phases 1 and 2) will not be processed. The response phases (currently phases 3 and 4) and others (currently phase 5) will be processed as normal. Transaction was not affected by this rule but it may be affected by any of the rules in the subsequent phase.

Alert Justification Description

The second part of the engine message explains *why* the alert was generated. Because it is automatically generated from the rules, it will be very technical in nature, talking about operators and their parameters, and giving you insight into what the rule looked like. But this message cannot give you insight into the reasoning behind the rule. A well-written rule will always specify a human-readable message (using the msg action) to provide further information.

The format of the second part of the engine message depends on whether it was generated by the operator (which happens on a match) or by the rule processor (which happens where there is not a match, but the negation was used):

- @beginsWith: *String match %0 at %1.*

- @contains: *String match %0 at %1.*

- @containsWord: *String match %0 at %1.*

- @endsWith: *String match %0 at %1.*

- @eq: *Operator EQ matched %0 at %1.*

- @ge: *Operator GE matched %0 at %1.*

- @geoLookup: *Geo lookup for %0 succeeded at %1.*

- @inspectFile: *File %0 rejected by the approver script %1: %2*

- @le: *Operator LE matched %0 at %1.*

- @lt: *Operator LT matched %0 at %1.*

- @rbl: *RBL lookup of %0 succeeded at %1.*

- @rx: *Pattern match %0 at %1.*

- @streq: *String match %0 at %1.*

- @validateByteRange: *Found %0 byte(s) in %1 outside range: %2.*

- @validateDTD: *XML: DTD validation failed.*

- @validateSchema: *XML: Schema validation failed.*

- @validateUrlEncoding

  - *Invalid URL Encoding: Non-hexadecimal digits used at %0.*

  - *Invalid URL Encoding: Not enough characters at the end of input at %0.*

- @validateUtf8Encoding

  - *Invalid UTF-8 encoding: not enough bytes in character at %0.*

  - *Invalid UTF-8 encoding: invalid byte value in character at %0.*

  - *Invalid UTF-8 encoding: overlong character detected at %0.*

  - *Invalid UTF-8 encoding: use of restricted character at %0.*

  - *Invalid UTF-8 encoding: decoding error at %0.*

- @verifyCC: *CC# match %0 at %1.*

Messages not related to operators:

- When SecAction directive is processed: *Unconditional match in SecAction.*

- When SecRule does not match but negation is used: *Match of %0 against %1 required.*

> **Note**
>
> The parameters to the operators @rx and @pm (regular expression and text pattern matching, respectively) will be truncated to 252 bytes if they are longer than this limit. In this case, the parameter in the alert message will be terminated with three dots.

Metadata

The metadata fields are always placed at the end of the alert entry. Each metadata field is a text fragment that consists of an open bracket followed by the metadata field name, followed by the value and the closing bracket. What follows is the text fragment that makes up the id metadata field.

```
[id "960034"]
```

The following metadata fields are currently used:

1. offset: The byte offset where a match occurred within the target data. This is not always available.

2. id: Unique rule ID, as specified by the id action.

3. rev: Rule revision, as specified by the rev action.

4. msg: Human-readable message, as specified by the msg action.

5. severity: Event severity as text, as specified by the severity action. The possible values (with their corresponding numerical values in brackets) are EMERGENCY (0), ALERT (1), CRITICAL (2), ERROR (3), WARNING (4), NOTICE (5), INFO (6), and DEBUG (7).

6. unique_id: Unique event ID, generated automatically.

7. uri: Request URI.

8. data: Contains transaction data fragment, as specified by the logdata action.

Escaping

ModSecurity alerts will always contain text fragments that were taken from the configuration or the transaction. Such text fragments are escaped before they are used in messages, in order to sanitize potentially dangerous characters. They are also sometimes surrounded using double quotes. The escaping algorithm is as follows:

1. Characters 0x08 (BACKSPACE), 0x0a (NEWLINE), 0x10 (CARRIAGE RETURN), 0x09 (HORIZONTAL TAB), and 0x0b (VERTICAL TAB) will be represented as \b, \n, \r, \t, and \v, respectively.

2. Bytes from the ranges 0-0x1f and 0x7f-0xff (inclusive) will be represented as \xHH, where HH is the hexadecimal value of the byte.

3. Backslash characters (\) will be represented as \\.

4. Each double-quote character will be represented as \", but only if the entire fragment is surrounded with double quotes.

Alerts in the Apache Error Log

Every ModSecurity alert conforms to the following format when it appears in the Apache error log:

```
[Sun Jun 24 10:19:58 2007] [error] [client 192.168.0.1] ⏎
ModSecurity: ALERT_MESSAGE
```

This example shows a standard Apache error log format. The ModSecurity: prefix is specific to ModSecurity. It is used to allow quick identification of ModSecurity alert messages when they appear in the same file next to other Apache messages.

The actual message (ALERT_MESSAGE in the example) is in the same format as described in the *Alerts* section.

> **Note**
>
> Apache further escapes ModSecurity alert messages before writing them to the error log. This means that all backslash characters will be doubled in the error log. In practice, because ModSecurity will already represent a single backslash within an untrusted text fragment as two backslashes, the end result in the Apache error log will be *four* backslashes. Thus, if you need to interpret a ModSecurity message from the error log, you should decode the message part after the `ModSecurity:` prefix first. This step will peel back the first encoding layer.

Alerts in Audit Logs

Alerts are transported in the H section of the ModSecurity Audit Log. Alerts will appear each on a separate line and in the order they were generated by ModSecurity. Each line will be in the following format:

```
Message: ALERT_MESSAGE
```

Here is an example of an H section that contains two alert messages:

```
--c7036611-H--
Message: Warning. Match of "rx ^apache.*perl" against ⏎
"REQUEST_HEADERS:User-Agent" required. [id "990011"] [msg "Request ⏎
Indicates an automated program explored the site"] [severity "NOTICE"]
Message: Warning. Pattern match "(?:\\b(?:(?:s(?:elect\\b(?:.{1,100}?)\\b⏎
(?:(?:length|count|top)\\b.{1,100}?)\\bfrom|from\\b.{1,100}?)\\bwhere)⏎
|.*?\\b(?:d(?:ump\\b.*\\bfrom|ata_type)|(?:to_(?:numbe|cha)|inst)r))|p_⏎
(?:(?:addextendedpro|sqlexe)c|(?:oacreat|prepar)e|execute(?:sql)?|⏎
makewebt ..." at ARGS:c. [id "950001"] [msg "SQL Injection Attack. ⏎
Matched signature: union select"] [severity "CRITICAL"]
Stopwatch: 1199881676978327 2514 (396 2224 -)
Producer: ModSecurity v2.x.x (Apache 2.x)
Server: Apache/2.x.x

--c7036611-Z--
```

Audit Log

ModSecurity records one transaction in what is essentially a single file. Below is an example:

```
--c7036611-A--
[09/Jan/2008:12:27:56 +0000] OSD4l1BEUOkAAHZ8Y3QAAAAH 209.90.77.54 64995
   80.68.80.233 80
--c7036611-B--
GET //EvilBoard_0.1a/index.php?c='/**/union/**/select/**/1,concat(username,⏎
char(77),password,char(77),email_address,char(77),info,char(77),user_level,⏎
char(77))/**/from/**/eb_members/**/where/**/userid=1/*http://kamloopstutor.⏎
```

```
com/images/banners/on.txt? HTTP/1.1
TE: deflate,gzip;q=0.3
Connection: TE, cslose
Host: www.example.com
User-Agent: libwww-perl/5.808

--c7036611-F--
HTTP/1.1 404 Not Found
Content-Length: 223
Connection: close
Content-Type: text/html; charset=iso-8859-1

--c7036611-H--
Message: Warning. Match of "rx ^apache.*perl" against ←
"REQUEST_HEADERS:User-Agent" required. [id "990011"] [msg "Request ←
Indicates an automated program explored the site"] [severity "NOTICE"]
Message: Warning. Pattern match "(?:\\b(?:(?:s(?:elect\\b(?:.{1,100}?\\b←
(?:(?:length|count|top))\\b.{1,100}?\\bfrom|from\\b.{1,100}?\\bwhere)←
|.*?\\b(?:d(?:ump\\b.*\\bfrom|ata_type)|(?:to_(?:numbe|cha)|inst)r))|p_←
(?:(?:addextendedpro|sqlexe)c|(?:oacreat|prepar)e|execute(?:sql)?|←
makewebt ..." at ARGS:c. [id "950001"] [msg "SQL Injection Attack. ←
Matched signature: union select"] [severity "CRITICAL"]
Stopwatch: 1199881676978327 2514 (396 2224 -)
Producer: ModSecurity v2.x.x (Apache 2.x)
Server: Apache/2.x.x

--c7036611-Z--
```

The file consist of multiple sections, each in different format. Separators are used to define sections:

```
--c7036611-A--
```

A separator always begins on a new line and conforms to the following format:

1. Two dashes

2. Unique boundary, which consists of several hexadecimal characters

3. One dash character

4. Section identifier, currently a single uppercase letter

5. Two trailing dashes

Refer to the documentation for SecAuditLogParts for the explanation of each part.

Parts

This section documents the audit log parts available in ModSecurity 2.x. They are:

Chapter 20: Data Formats

- A: audit log header
- B: request headers
- C: request body
- D: intended response headers (*not implemented*)
- E: intended response body
- F: response headers
- G: response body (*not implemented*)
- H: audit log trailer
- I: reduced multipart request body
- J: multipart files information (*not implemented*)
- K: matched rules information
- Z: audit log footer

Audit Log Header (A)

ModSecurity 2.x audit log entries always begin with the header part. For example:

```
--c7036611-A--
[09/Jan/2008:12:27:56 +0000] OSD4l1BEUOkAAHZ8Y3QAAAAH 209.90.77.54 64995 ↵
80.68.80.233 80
```

The header contains only one line, with the following information on it:

1. Timestamp
2. Unique transaction ID
3. Source IP address (IPv4 or IPv6)
4. Source port
5. Destination IP address (IPv4 or IPv6)
6. Destination port

Request Headers (B)

The request headers part contains the request line and the request headers. The information present in this part will not be identical to that sent by the client responsible for the transaction. ModSecurity 2.x for Apache does not have access to the raw data; it sees what Apache itself sees. Although the end result may be identical to the raw request, differences are possible in some areas:

1. If any of the fields are `NUL`-terminated, Apache will see only the content prior to the NUL.

2. Headers that span multiple lines (a feature known as header folding) will be collapsed into a single line.

3. Multiple headers with the same name will be combined into a single header (as allowed by the HTTP RFC).

Request Body (C)

This part contains the request body of the transaction, after dechunking and decompression (if applicable).

Intended Response Headers (D)

This part contains the status line and the request headers that would have been delivered to the client had ModSecurity not intervened. Thus this part makes sense only for transactions in which ModSecurity altered the data flow. By differentiating between the intended and the final response headers, we are able to record what was internally ready for sending, but also what was actually sent.

> **Note**
>
> This part is reserved for future use. It is not implemented in ModSecurity 2.5.x.

Intended Response Body (E)

This part contains the transaction response body (before compression and chunking, where used) that was either sent or would have been sent had ModSecurity not intervened. You can find whether interception took place by looking at the `Action` header of the part H. If that header is present, and the interception took place in phase 3 or 4, then the E part contains the intended response body. Otherwise, it contains the actual response body.

> **Note**
>
> Once the G (actual response body) part is implemented, part E will be present only in audit logs that contain a transaction that was intercepted, and there will be no need for further analysis.

Response Headers (F)

This part contains the actual response headers sent to the client. Because ModSecurity 2.x for Apache does not access the raw connection data, it constructs part F out of the internal Apache data structures that hold the response headers.

Some headers (the Date and Server response headers) are generated just before they are sent, and ModSecurity is not able to record those. You should note than ModSecurity is working as part of a reverse proxy, the backend web server will have generated these two servers, and in that case they will be recorded.

Response Body (G)

When implemented, this part will contain the actual response body before compression and chunking.

> **Note**
>
> This part is reserved for future use. It is not implemented in ModSecurity 2.x.

Audit Log Trailer (H)

Part H contains additional transaction metadata that was obtained from the web server or from ModSecurity itself. The part contains a number of trailer headers, which are similar to HTTP headers (without support for header folding):

1. Action
2. Apache-Error
3. Message
4. Producer
5. Response-Body-Transformed
6. Sanitised-Args
7. Sanitised-Request-Headers
8. Sanitised-Response-Headers
9. Server
10. Stopwatch
11. Stopwatch2
12. WebApp-Info

Action

The Action header is present only for the transactions that were intercepted:

```
Action: Intercepted (phase 2)
```

The phase information documents the phase in which the decision to intercept took place.

Apache-Error

The Apache-Error header contains Apache error log messages observed by ModSecurity, excluding those sent by ModSecurity itself. For example:

```
Apache-Error: [file "/tmp/buildd/apache2-2.0.54/build-tree/apache2/server/↩
core.c"] [line 3505] [level 3] File does not exist: /var/www/www.↩
modsecurity.org/fst/documentation/modsecurity-apache/2.5.0-dev2
```

Message

Zero or more Message headers can be present in any trailer, and each such header will represent a single ModSecurity warning or error, displayed in the order they were raised.

The following example was broken into multiple lines to make it fit this page:

```
Message: Access denied with code 400 (phase 2). Pattern match "^\w+:/" at ↩
REQUEST_URI_RAW. [file "/etc/apache2/rules-1.6.1/modsecurity_crs_20_↩
protocol_violations.conf"] [line "74"] [id "960014"] [msg "Proxy access ↩
attempt"] [severity "CRITICAL"] [tag "PROTOCOL_VIOLATION/PROXY_ACCESS"]
```

Producer

The Producer header identifies the product that generated the audit log. For example:

```
Producer: ModSecurity for Apache/2.5.5 (http://www.modsecurity.org/).
```

ModSecurity allows rule sets to add their own signatures to the Producer information (this is done using the SecComponentSignature directive). Following is an example of the Producer header with the signature of one component (all one line):

```
Producer: ModSecurity for Apache/2.5.5 (http://www.modsecurity.org/); ↩
MyComponent/1.0.0 (Beta).
```

Response-Body-Transformed

This header will appear in every audit log that contains a response body:

```
Response-Body-Transformed: Dechunked
```

The contents of the header is constant at present, so the header is useful only as a reminder that the recorded response body is not identical to the one sent to the client. The actual content is the same, except that Apache may further compress the body and deliver it in chunks.

Sanitised-Args

The Sanitised-Args header contains a list of arguments that were sanitised (each byte of their content replaced with an asterisk) before logging. For example:

```
Sanitised-Args: "old_password", "new_password", "new_password_repeat".
```

Sanitised-Request-Headers

The Sanitised-Request-Headers header contains a list of request headers that were sanitized before logging. For example:

```
Sanitised-Request-Headers: "Authentication".
```

Sanitised-Response-Headers

The Sanitised-Response-Headers header contains a list of response headers that were sanitized before logging. For example:

```
Sanitised-Response-Headers: "My-Custom-Header".
```

Server

The Server header identifies the web server. For example:

```
Server: Apache/2.0.54 (Debian GNU/Linux) mod_ssl/2.0.54 OpenSSL/0.9.7e
```

This information may sometimes be present in any of the parts that contain response headers, but there are a few cases when it isn't:

1. None of the response headers were recorded.
2. The information in the response headers is not accurate because server signature masking was used.

Stopwatch

The Stopwatch header provides certain diagnostic information that allows you to determine the performance of the web server and of ModSecurity itself. It will typically look like this:

```
Stopwatch: 1222945098201902 2118976 (770* 4400 -)
```

Each line can contain up to five different values. Some values can be absent; each absent value will be replaced with a dash.

The meanings of the values are as follows (all values are in microseconds):

1. Transaction timestamp in microseconds since January 1, 1970.
2. Transaction duration.
3. The time between the moment Apache started processing the request and until phase 2 of ModSecurity began. If an asterisk is present, that means the time includes the time it took ModSecurity to read the request body from the client (typically slow). This val-

ue can be used to provide a rough estimate of the client speed, but only with larger request bodies (the smaller request bodies may arrive in a single TCP/IP packet).

4. The time between the start of processing and until phase 2 was completed. If you subtract the previous value from this value, you will get the exact duration of phase 2 (which is the main rule processing phase).

5. The time between the start of request processing and the point at which we began sending a fully-buffered response body to the client. If you subtract this value from the total transaction duration and divide with the response body size, you may get a rough estimate of the client speed, but only for larger response bodies.

> **Note**
>
> The Stopwatch header has been replaced with Stopwatch2 in the trunk (see following sections for more information). Some limited information may still be provided in Stopwatch for backward compatibility.

Stopwatch2

Currently available only in the trunk, the Stopwatch2 header provides improved performance statistics. For example:

```
Stopwatch2: 1264256494438648 5131; combined=3917, p1=11, p2=3653, p3=3, p4=29, ↵
p5=221, sr=0, sw=0, l=0, gc=0
```

The first two values are the same as in the Stopwatch header: the first is the transaction timestamp in microseconds since January 1, 1970; the second is the transaction duration, also in microseconds.

The performance metrics follow after the semicolon:

- combined: combined processing time
- p1–p5: time spent in each of the rule phases
- sr and sw: time spent reading from and writing to persistent storage, respectively
- l: time spent on audit logging
- gc: time spent on garbage collection

All the values are given in microseconds.

WebApp-Info

The WebApp-Info header contains information on the application to which the recorded transaction belongs. This information will appear only if it is known, which will happen if SecWebAppId was set, or setsid or setuid executed in the transaction.

The header uses the following format:

```
WebApp-Info: "WEBAPPID" "SESSIONID" "USERID"
```

Each unknown value is replaced with a dash.

Reduced Multipart Request Body (I)

Transactions that deal with file uploads tend to be large, yet the file contents is not always relevant from the security point of view. The I part was designed to avoid recording raw `multipart/form-data` request bodies, replacing them with a simulated `application/x-www-form-urlencoded` body that contains the same key-value parameters.

The reduced multipart request body will not contain any file information. The J part (currently not implemented) is intended to carry the file metadata.

Multipart Files Information (J)

The purpose of part J is to record the information on the files contained in a `multipart/form-data` request body. This is handy in the cases when the original request body was not recorded, or when only a reduced version was recorded (e.g., when part I was used instead of part C).

> **Note**
>
> This part is reserved for future use. It is not implemented in ModSecurity 2.x.

Matched Rules (K)

The matched rules part contains a record of all ModSecurity rules that matched during transaction processing. When a rule which is a part of a chain matches, it will not cause the rest of the chain to be included, meaning that only partial chains may be logged. A future version of ModSecurity may log entire chains using a syntax that makes it clear what matched and what didn't.

This part is available starting with ModSecurity 2.5.x.

Audit Log Footer (Z)

Part Z is a special part that only has a boundary but no content. Its only purpose is to signal the end of an audit log.

Storage Formats

ModSecurity supports two audit log storage formats:

1. *Serial* audit log format: multiple audit log files stored in the same file.

2. *Concurrent* audit log format: one file is used for every audit log.

Serial Audit Log Format

The serial audit log format stores multiple audit log entries within the same file (one after another). This is often very convenient (audit log entries are easy to find), but this format is suitable for only light logging in the current ModSecurity implementation, because writing to the file is serialized: only one audit log entry can be written at any one time.

Concurrent Audit Log Format

The concurrent audit log format uses one file per audit log entry, and allows many transactions to be recorded at once. A hierarchical directory structure is used to ensure that the number of files created in any one directory remains relatively small. For example:

```
$LOGGING-HOME/20081128/20081128-1414/20081128-141417-↵
egDKy38AAAEAAAyMHXsAAAAA
```

The current time is used to work out the directory structure. The file name is constructed using the current time and the transaction ID.

The creation of every audit log in concurrent format is recorded with an entry in the concurrent audit log *index file*. The format of each line resembles the common web server access log format. For example:

```
192.168.0.111 192.168.0.1 - - [28/Nov/2008:15:06:32 +0000] ↵
"GET /?p=\\ HTTP/1.1" 200 69 "-" "-" NOfRx38AAAEAAAzcCU4AAAAA ↵
"-" /20081128/20081128-1506/20081128-150632-NOfRx38AAAEAAAzcCU4AAAAA ↵
0 1183 md5:ffee2d414cd43c2f8ae151652910ed96
```

The tokens on the line are as follows:

1. Hostname (or IP address, if the hostname is not known)

2. Source IP address

3. Remote user (from HTTP Authentication)

4. Local user (from identd)

5. Timestamp

6. Request line

7. Response status

8. Bytes sent (in the response body)

9. Referrer information

---

10. User-Agent information

11. Transaction ID

12. Session ID

13. Audit log file name (relative to the audit logging home, as configured using the SecAuditLogStorageDir directive)

14. Audit log offset

15. Audit log size

16. Audit log hash (the has begins with the name of the algorithm used, followed by a colon, followed by the hexadecimal representation of the hash itself); this hash can be used to verify that the transaction was correctly recorded and that it hasn't been modified since.

> **Note**
>
> Lines in the index file will be up to 3980 bytes long, and the information logged will be reduced to fit where necessary. Reduction will occur within the individual fields, but the overall format will remain the same. The character L will appear as the last character on a reduced line. A space will be the last character on a line that was not reduced to stay within the limit.

Remote Logging Protocol

Audit logs generated in multi-sensor deployments are of little use if left on the sensors. More commonly, they will be transported to a central logging server using the transport protocol described in this section:

1. The transport protocol is based on the HTTP protocol.

2. The server end is an SSL-enabled web server with HTTP Basic Authentication configured.

3. Clients will open a connection to the centralization web server and authenticate (given the end-point URI, the username and the password).

4. Clients will use a single PUT transaction to submit an entry, placing the file in the body of the request and additional information in the request headers (see the following entry for details).

5. Server will process each submission and respond with an appropriate status code:

   a. 200 (OK): the submission was processed; the client can delete the corresponding audit log entry if it so desires. The same audit log entry must not be submitted again.

b. 409 (Conflict): the submission is in invalid format and cannot be processed. The client should attempt to fix the problem with the submission and attempt delivery again at a later time. This error is generally going to occur due to a programming error in the protocol implementation, and not because of the content of the audit log entry that is being transported.

c. 500 (Internal Server Error): the server was unable to correctly process the submission, due to its own fault. The client should reattempt delivery at a later time. A client that starts receiving 500 responses to all its submission should suspend its operations for a period of time before continuing.

Note

Server implementations are advised to accept all submissions that correctly implement the protocol. Clients are unlikely to be able to overcome problems within audit log entries, so such problems are best resolved on the server side.

Note

When en error occurs, the server may place an explanation of the problem in the text part of the response line.

Request Headers Information

Each audit log entry submission must contain additional information in the request headers:

1. The X-Content-Hash header must contain the audit log entry hash. Clients should expect the audit log entries to be validated against the hash by the server.

2. The X-ForensicLog-Summary header must contain the entire concurrent format index line.

3. The Content-Lenght header must be present and contain the length of the audit log entry.

Index

A

Action part H header, 325
actions
    overview, 79
    reference documentation, 293
    tutorial, 88
Aho-Corasick algorithm, 196
alerts
    messages, 317
    periodic alerting, 131
allow action, 293
    (see also whitelisting)
anti-virus (see ClamAV)
Apache-Error part H header, 326
Apache Portable Runtime (APR), 225
append action, 294
    (see also content injection)
APR (see Apache Portable Runtime)
ARGS_COMBINED_SIZE variable, 267
ARGS_GET_NAMES variable, 268
ARGS_GET variable, 267
ARGS_NAMES variable, 267
ARGS_POST_NAMES variable, 268
ARGS_POST variable, 268
ARGS collection, 267
audit log, 52
    auditlog action, 294
    concurrent format, 55
    configuration, 43
    controlling from rules, 95
    dynamically controlling, 67
    format specification, 321
    noauditlog action, 300
    parts, 322
    remote logging, 56
    remote logging protocol, 331
    removing sensitive data from, 67
    selective logging, 68
auditlog action, 294
AUTH_TYPE variable, 268

B

Barnett, Ryan C., 201
base64Decode function, 288
base64Encode function, 288
beginsWith operator, 309
blacklisting, 157
block action, 294
blocking, 92
    advanced, 164
    delayed, 169
    external, 168
    immediate, 164
    in detection-only mode, 38
    IP address, 158
    real-time block lists, 160
    score-based, 169
    sessions, 140
    user-friendly, 166
Bockermann, Christian, 21
Boyer-Moore-Horspool algorithm, 231
brute force attack detection, 135

C

capture action, 96, 295
CentOS, 30
chain action, 295
ClamAV, 64
collections, 77
    (see also persistent storage)
    built-in variables, 125
    variables (see variables)
compressWhitespace function, 288
concurrent audit log format, 330
conditional logging, 162
configuration, 33

file inspection, 63
    ClamAV, 64
    inspectFile operator, 310
FILES_COMBINED_SIZE variable, 269
FILES_NAMES collection, 269
FILES_SIZES collection, 269
FILES_TMPNAMES collection, 269
FILES collection, 269
functions (see transformation functions)

G

GEO collection, 269
geolocation, 159
geoLookup operator, 310
ge operator, 310
Gotroot rules, 178
gt operator, 310

H

header manipulation, 163
hexDecode function, 288
hexEncode function, 288
HIGHEST_SEVERITY variable, 270
honeypot, diversion to, 168
htmlEntityDecode function, 288

I

id action, 299
if-then-else, 95
impedance mismatch, 155
inactivity timeout mechanism, 123
initcol action, 299
inspectFile operator, 310
installation, 23
    from binaries, 30
        CentOS, 30
        Debian, 31
        Fedora Core, 30
        Red Hat Enterprise Linux, 30

        Ubuntu, 31
        Windows, 31
    from development repository, 25
    from source, 24
integration with other apache modules, 161
IP address
    blocking, 157
    reputation, 157
    tracking, 120
IP collection, 120

J

jsDecode function, 289
jwall.org, 21

L

length function, 289
le operator, 311
libxml2, 27, 211
load testing, 185
local reputation management, 160
Location directive (Apache), 108
log action, 299
logdata action, 300
logging, 49
    advanced configuration, 66
    audit log, 52
    concurrent, 55
    conditional, 162
    configuration, 43
    controlling from rules, 95
    debug log, 49
    file upload interception, 62
    remote, 56
    transaction, 10
lowercase function, 289
lt operator, 311
Lua, 205
    (see also SecRuleScript directive)

controlling longevity, 122
creating, 120
deleting, 123
initializing, 122
limits, 130
retrieving, 127
persistent storage, 119
brute force attack detection, 135
denial of service attack detection, 133
implementation details, 127
namespaces, 121
periodic alerting, 131
session management, 138
user management, 145
phase action, 301
phases (see transaction lifecycle)
PHPIDS, 178
pmFromFile operator, 312
pm operator, 311
prepend action, 302, 302
(see also content injection)
processing errors
flags, 76
handling, 45
Producer part H header, 326
proxy action, 168, 302
(see also honeypot, diversion to)

Q
QUERY_STRING variable, 274

R
rbl operator, 313
real-time block lists, 160
recording data in alerts, 99
records (see persistent records)
Red Hat Enterprise Linux, 30
redirect action, 302
RegexBuddy, 174
Regex Coach, 174

regular expressions, 171
(see also rx operator)
combining for performance, 194
denial of service (ReDoS), 173
making most of, 171
optimizing for performance, 195
Regular Expressions Cookbook, 174
related projects (to ModSecurity), 21
REMO (Rule Editor for ModSecurity), 21
REMOTE_ADDR variable, 274
REMOTE_HOST variable, 274
REMOTE_PORT variable, 274
REMOTE_USER variable, 274
remote logging, 56
remote logging protocol, 331
removeNulls function, 290
removeWhitespace function, 290
replaceComments function, 290
replaceNulls function, 291
REQBODY_PROCESSOR_ERROR_MSG variable, 275
REQBODY_PROCESSOR_ERROR variable, 275
REQBODY_PROCESSOR variable, 275
REQUEST_BASENAME variable, 275
REQUEST_BODY_LENGTH variable, 276
REQUEST_BODY variable, 276
REQUEST_COOKIES_NAMES collection, 276
REQUEST_COOKIES collection, 276
REQUEST_FILENAME variable, 276
REQUEST_HEADERS_NAMES collection, 277
REQUEST_HEADERS collection, 277
REQUEST_LINE variable, 277
REQUEST_METHOD variable, 277
REQUEST_PROTOCOL variable, 277
REQUEST_URI_RAW variable, 278
REQUEST_URI variable, 277
request body handling, 38
resources
for ModSecurity, 18
for regular expressions, 174

CPSIA information can be obtained at www.ICGtesting.com
Printed in the USA
LVOW131228110312

272548LV00002B/90/P